YOLA

FORGIVE AND REMEMBER NAZI RULE

BY

YOLANDA ENTZ

xulon
PRESS

To my wonderful grandchildren
Katherine, Jacob, Andrew, Alex, Nathan,
That your future may be rooted in our past

Introduction

What does that title 'YOLA' mean? I am asked often. Ever since I can remember I was the only one called by my name. My father, who had always a penchant for the extraordinary, the unique, decided to name his one and only child by the unusual name of Yolanthe. Please don't laugh, for that is what made me change my name. At first, people just stopped for a bit with lifted eyebrows when they heard it, but when I was about eight years old, they broke out in raucous laughter. The reason was, that everybody had become acquainted with a popular play, called "Dispute about Yolanthe." It was as popular as "My fair Lady" with Audrey Hepburn. But instead of a pretty girl by that name, the main character was a blue-ribboned priced – sow! I dreaded the question, "What is your name, little girl?" Because I could foretell what would be the result: Convulsive laughter with comments like: "O, no, Yolanthe – the pig!" So I decided to part with half of my name, and since that time I have traveled unencumbered around the world. Till I arrived in the U.S., that is. How can you pronounce a name with a 'the' at the end? Try it and see your face convulse. Especially for a German, who is not on the best of terms with any word needing a 'th' in the first place. So to appease my new fellow countrymen I had my name changed legally to 'Yolanda', but to my friends I am still 'Yola'.

Many years later, when thinking about relating some of my adventurous and exciting life experiences, I was debating in my mind how to go about it. At that time a visit brought the answer.

Before us on the coffee table is a folder with pictures of a master photographer. I sift through the many photos while he watches me, sitting across on the couch. One picture holds my special attention. It is a scene at a railroad station. It is dark and a single passenger sits on the station platform bench, waiting for a train. He observes my interest and bends forward.

"Do you like this picture?" His eyes search mine.

"It expresses a certain mood in its simplicity with which I can identify," I answer.

"You have a good eye," he says and adds matter-of-factly, "This picture won a first prize."

I look at it more closely. On the right a clock shows the nightly hour. In the background a blurred train speeds by. Next to the solitary traveler on the bench on the station platform rests a folded newspaper.

"How were you able to convey this mood of darkness and loneliness?" I ask.

"I worked here without a flash, no artificial lighting, no sharp outlines, authenticity, without added light." He leans back and explains. "If you use a flash, it could also have a different meaning. Flashy means to exhibit obtrusive superficiality. My pictures try to express the substance, the core of things. That is why I often work without a flash, in order not to sacrifice the genuine for the eye pleasing." He looks at me and says emphatically: "Life wants to be shown as it is. Then it reaches the heart of the viewer."

I ponder his words. Can you really show life as it is? Does not the observer make a subjective choice, like a photographer who focuses on the subject from a certain angle, enlarging or scaling down according to his desire and perspective? I think of the possibilities of expression by writing. Words also mirror life and paint inner pictures. What did he say? "Authenticity without added artificial light." Without knowing it, he has given me my direction. I will resurrect pictures from my memory – authentic photographs. Photographs without a flash.

1

⚜

"What is the worst thing that you cannot stand?"
"Injustice!" I don't need to think about the answer. "And cruelty," I add. "I could never stand cruelty against animals. I remember when I was very young, some neighbor's kids tormented a cat, and I tore it away from them and let it run."

"But what about cruelty to people?" Erika turns around and a spray of water from her paddle hits my face. I consider it briefly.

"That would be just as bad."

"Not worse?" Erika is not satisfied with my answer.

"No, I believe that people can defend themselves. But animals, I mean domestic animals, can do nothing but bite, scratch or kick."

"I don't know if people can always defend themselves."

Well, that is true also. I remember cold shivers going up my spine, when I saw the torture chambers in some old German castles and heard the guard explain, how they used the ingenious instruments for inflicting unbearable pain on their hapless victims, pulling them apart on a stretcher till they acknowledged anything, just so the pain would subside. Or the Iron Virgin in the Nuremberg castle, in the shape of a large woman's body with iron spikes on the inside. When some suspected witch was pushed inside and the doors closed, those spikes would penetrate her body from all sides. The thought makes me shudder.

"You are right", I answer, "people can be awfully cruel against a defenseless victim."

The rhythm of paddles hitting the dark waters of the river Havel is the accompaniment to our conversation. On their downward push they leave expanding circles on the surface of the water. Ever so often a cold spray hits me. The first sailboats are out. Although the sun is shining, the clear April air still has not warmed up much. Yet the white sails against the dark green pine forests along the hilly shoreline are evidence that spring has arrived at last.

"And what about you?" I return the question to Erika. Her back seems so bare without the hazel brown orderly braids, which used to dance on it. Now her hair is cut in a fashionable bob and it gives her the appearance of a young lady. I have to get used to the new look. Yet with fifteen years one cannot forever wear braids. My hair had always been cut short. Erika had begged her parents for a long time, till they finally gave in. She proudly showed me her cut off braids, which she kept as a remnant of her childhood.

"What I can't stand is exclusion or rejection or even just being ignored."

I nod. I know this feeling too well. Painful memories shoot through my head. Erika also had these awful experiences, yet she suppresses them by changing the direction of the game.

"And the next question is: What are you most looking forward to?"

It is a question to awaken expectations and dreams, with which our young lives are filled to overflowing. I ponder it, glancing across the windswept glistening waves. On our right side I see another boat with a young couple sitting behind each other. They have laid down their paddles and are drifting, facing the sun. The girl in front suddenly laughs and turns her head around to the boy sitting behind her. He stretches forward and reaches out with his hand, catching her hair, only briefly. An exchange of happy companionship. No, of love! I cannot take my eyes off them.

"Shall we head towards Schildhorn?"

Erika's question brings me back to reality.

"If you want to."

"What takes you so long to answer?" She turns her head and I see her profile, the little upturned nose with a sprinkling of freckles, the forget-me-not blue eyes, which in their innocent clarity could see to the bottom of your soul or spot immediately any lost button on your blouse; the upturned corners of her mouth that had never seen lipstick, the curved line of her slender neck, edged by her naturally curly light brown hair.

"I have to think about it."

How could I tell her, that I wish for nothing more than a boyfriend, like I just saw in the boat that we had passed. Somebody that shows as much affection as this young man did to his girlfriend. But this is only wishful thinking, something that will never come true. Probably. All around there are boats with boys and their girls, but I am always just together with another girl, though she is my best friend. Not that I don't appreciate having a best friend, but there is something unfulfilled even in our close friendship.

"I wish most of all, that we will soon again be united with my father."

It is a harmless wish and Erika accepts it. At least she cannot read my thoughts.

"How about you? What would you like most of all?" I question her, but I know the answer already before I hear it.

"I want to become a great violinist. Perhaps play with a well-known orchestra, travel the world, get to know a lot of people and places."

"Nice wishful thinking," I murmur.

"What did you say?" She turns around.

"I knew what you would say."

"You know me well enough."

Yes, we do know each other well, even as best friends do; although our friendship had started rather strangely. We were sitting on the back of a bench at our new school, which had no courtyard to run or walk during recess, munching a sandwich, when Erika suddenly turned to me with the question:

"Would you want to be my friend?"

Startled by this direct question, I fumbled around a bit.

"Well, yes, of course," thinking, how strange it was, that some-body would ask such a funny question. Up to that time my friends had never asked me. We just knew we were friends and that without words. Playing together or talking and observing was enough to feel close to another, with whom one shared similar tastes and feelings and who would laugh at the same jokes. Friendships just grew out of becoming familiar and liking and trusting each other. It was like two budding plants, reaching out with growing branches, their tentacles meeting in the air and becoming intertwined like one single plant.

Yet it seemed that friendships grew more complicated with age. My first friend lived in the house across the street and when we were outside we played together, like hopscotch on the sidewalk or running and hiding games. On rainy days we played in the house and even spent a weekend together, when the parents had to leave for some reason. This friendship ended abruptly when we moved away when I was in first grade. In the new school Ulli became my best friend, because we shared the same walk to school, and after school I spent my afternoons as a third daughter in her family. But suddenly complications arose as we graduated into secondary school and Ellen appeared. Everybody liked her. She had a pretty face and was the best athlete in our class. Slowly Ulli divided her attention, partly with me and partly with Ellen. Finally it was all Ellen and I had to seek a new best friend.

I found it in Lucy, who had been more of a fifth wheel in our clique, that shared the same bus ride to school. She was not as smart but a real buddy. She had naturally fuzzy ash blond hair that resisted any effort at taming it, and she looked at you with dreamy, half lidded golden eyes. I helped her with her spelling, but she continued to make many orthographical errors. Yet Lucy loved sports and was always ready for some crazy idea that hit me on the spur of the moment, like emptying our piggy bank and riding the elevator up to the highest tower, the Funkturm, from which one had a great view over the city of Berlin and surroundings. Or collecting samples of fur coats. We each had an empty matchbox in our pockets. When riding home on the bus, we sneaked up behind women in fur coats and cautiously, with innocent face, pulled out some of the hair for our matchbox collection. We could hardly contain the laughter that welled up as relief from the tension of possibly getting caught in the act.

Yet all of these friends had now left and here I was in a new school with few kids and Erika putting the question to me of wanting to become her friend. She needed to have things clarified and open. So I agreed and from that time on we shared everything, our daily ride to school, our homework, our music, our fun times. Recently we had gotten into stage acting. The cause was an actor both of us liked. No, adored - no, loved with an intense passion. His name was Horst Caspar, and he played the youthful hero at the Schiller Theater in Berlin. He was the dream of girls our age, and perhaps of many older ones who crowded the theater to see him on stage. He was tall, dark and handsome with burning eyes and a passionate voice that reverberated and stirred our emotional teenage hearts. Only girls of that age are capable of this rapturous adoration. Older women smile knowingly when they watch outbursts of screaming love behind barriers erected to keep the star from being mobbed by his idolizing fans, while men shake their heads and mumble something derogatory about hysterical females.

We had attended each one of his plays, giving him a standing ovation at the end and clapping till our hands were red and the iron curtain, separating the stage from the theater, had fallen. Then we rushed to the stage exit, hoping to catch a glimpse of our hero. Endless waiting and exciting anticipation each time the door opened. Yet he must have escaped his wild fans by taking another exit. Disappointed because we never saw him, we finally took the bus home, sharing the best scenes as we recalled each detail. Yet there were the compensating nightly dreams, where I lie in his arms and he whispers in my ear, "I only play for you, for you are the one I love!"

The passion for acting has taken hold of us. With the script booklet of Schiller's "Mary Stewart" we endlessly recite the drama of the two queens battling for the crown. I am Elizabeth and Erika the disadvantaged queen of Scots. Some of the passages I can recite by memory and give it that much more dramatic emphasis. I would love to become a stage actress! Another one of these hopeless dreams.

"Let's paddle faster." Erika brings me back to reality. Mechanically I follow her rhythm. Our boat dances over the waves like a happy colt.

"Have you seen that?" Erika laughs.

"Seen what?"

"Over there, that sailboat."

"Why? What about it?"

"They were caught in a sudden swell and it looked like the boat would tip over. But then I saw on the bottom the painted word: "Denkste!" (Berlin dialect for 'That's what you think!)

"They have a sense of humor," I say and follow the boat with my eyes. There again! Now I can see it too. Slowly the boat straightens and is coming in our direction. They must have done that on purpose! I guess they are trying to impress us. As they circle around our boat I see three young men. They wave and call over to us.

"What do they want from us?" Erika asks.

"I didn't understand," I answer, though I understood quite well. Again they steer the boat in a circle around us. The young man sitting at the helm turns the boat into the wind. The sails flutter and make a cracking noise.

"Would you like to go sailing?" he calls across.

"What shall we say?" Erika leaves fast decisions to me. She needs more time.

"Would you like to?" I return the question.

"But we don't even know these guys." Erika is cautious, she has her doubts. I push mine aside.

"They look like nice guys."

I call across, "But what about our boat?"

"We will tie it to ours and pull it. Come along starboard and we will give you a hand."

"Do you have any idea where starboard is?" Erika asks.

"I guess where the tall one is standing. He looks like he wants to help us into the boat."

The lust for adventure has gripped me.

"Come on, let's go!"

Everything happens fast and without problems. We sit on leather pillows while one of them ties our empty boat to the back. Then the one at the helm turns the fluttering sails windward and the sleek boat bends and begins to skip across the water.

Our hosts introduce themselves. The one at the helm is Gerhard. He is the shortest with reddish blond hair and light eye lashes. When he laughs, his eyes crinkle and a dimple appears in his right cheek. He must have been the one with the idea of 'Denkste!' Then there is one who seems to be older. His name is Reinhold. He is somewhat reserved and more serious, yet helpful and courteous. The name of the third one is Eric and he makes us laugh to ease the momentary tension. After an initial time of shyness, we soon feel part of the group. The relaxed tone makes us feel good. We get a quick introduction to the most important sailing words and concepts, and we are taught to pull in our heads and change sides when tacking.

The feeling of the wind in the sails and the swaying of the boat is an exhilarating experience. One time I see Erika high in the air and I am close to the water. I have to hold my hand into the water to feel the speed at which we travel. The next time I sit high above the water like on a swing, and bend my body back over the side of the boat. It is fun to glide so effortlessly across the water, to see how the boat obediently follows the course the rudder directs, and to feel the wind playing with the sails, pushing it down or lifting it up again.

"I never knew that sailing could be so much fun!" I call over to Gerhard, "now we won't enjoy paddling our kayak anymore."

"Would you like to hold the foresail?" Gerhard asks and puts the rope into my hand. It takes me only a short time to control the tug made by the shifting winds. Sometimes the tension has to be released a bit, another time it has to be pulled in. I get so involved in the changing moods of the wind that I forget everything around me. This is my element!

The water has always been my favorite place. My grandparents and the whole family vacationed each year in the "bathtub of Berlin", the East Sea and in particular the tourist town of Heringsdorf. All of my cousins were there, I being the youngest. My first memories were of the sound of waves, rolling rhythmically on the shell studded beaches, feeling the hot sand between my toes, and helping with the building of sand forts, which we decorated with colorful shells.

When I grew older, my mother taught me to swim in one of the many lakes surrounding Berlin. She put a wide brown leather belt around my waist, holding me up, telling me to make frog like movements with my legs and arms at the same time, till water comes into my nose and I swallow a mouthful, snorting and gasping for air. But finally mother's patience wins and I can swim a few hasty strokes by myself. Later I go swimming with my school mates in a real public bath, Halensee, where people are taught to swim on contraptions looking like large fishing rods, on which some big human fish are hanging and wiggling for dear life. Water has always had a special attraction for me, but only now I know, I have found my very own elements, namely water, wind, and sailing.

It means more to me than just a nice sport or a hobby to pass away time. It is the answer to an inner longing for freedom from the ballast of fears of the future. Like a caged bird which has had the door opened to soar into an unknown yet beckoning world of sunshine and open skies, I treasure this wonderful feeling of unrestrained liberty which sailing imparts. The freedom I have lost and am desperately looking for in a world that is closed to me, comes within reach by the experience of the wind tugging at my hair, the rope pulling in my hand and the water spraying in my face - I know I just have to go sailing again!

The "Golden Hill" takes course to our boat barracks at the end of the afternoon. Before we part, the boys extend an invitation to go sailing with them again next Saturday.

"Then you just leave your boat in the barracks and come over to where our boat's slip is near Stoessensee Bridge," Gerhard explains. "We go sailing no matter what the weather is like, unless it rains hard."

We stand on the shore and wave after them.

"Did you enjoy that?" I ask Erika.

"Yes, a lot. But don't tell my parents about it."

"No, and you won't tell my mother." Erika nods with a serious expression on her face. But then she smiles.

"They were really nice! Eric was so funny I had to laugh so much."

I am glad that she had not said Gerhard.

2

∽❧⊱

"You don't concentrate today. You play like you did not practice at all." The soft voice of my piano teacher sounds reproachful. I hasten to repeat the difficult passage. Again I get caught at the same notes. She is right, while playing my thoughts are on other things.

"Move over and let me play it for you," she says and obediently I make room for her. While she is playing on the black grand piano the Andante by Mozart with a soft touch and much emotion, my eyes wander about her delicate fingers to her even profile, her gray hair caught up high in a bun, her white starched lace collar, surrounding a slender neck and the art nouveau brooch which appears as the only jewelry on every outfit. Outside the noise of the Underground train, which is elevated at this stretch near Nollendorf Platz, tries to drown the lilting music. The high ceilings of this aged house, decorated with intricate stuccoed work, must endure this regular noise and the false notes of aspiring pianists, who are the source of income for the old spinster.

This is the way Berlin must have looked a hundred years ago, I muse. These thick wine red velvet curtains, which hardly allow enough light into the room. The heavy dark brown oak furniture, the stiff backed plush sofa and the table in front of it with a crème colored hand crocheted lace tablecloth. But the most curious things are the gas lamps. How can you have gas lamps when all of Berlin has been supplied with electricity long ago?

"Now this is the way I expect you to play next time! No more mistakes please." The old lady looks over to the grandfather clock whose pendulum seems to be the only living thing beside the two of us. When its chimes fill the room at the whole hour and make conversation impossible, it is better to interrupt your playing and wait for the end.

"We will stop for today," she says. The clock shows two minutes to four o'clock.

I pick up my sheet music hastily and push it into my satchel. I try to hide my impatience and walk slowly to the door. I turn and curtsy while shaking hands. Really I don't need to curtsy any more at my age, but the old lady still smiles when I honor her this way in parting. So I continue to give her this little pleasure.

After the door is closed behind me, I skip down the circular staircase in which one can look from the third floor to the bottom. Sliding down the handrail is fun, but here I am afraid. Looking down one feels a strong pull. So I run down the steps, taking two at a time. Outside I run up to the U Bahn station and wait impatiently for the train to Wittenberg Platz. There I transfer to my streetcar number 75. Everything seems so slow today. So many stops till one leaves behind the crowded city. Finally the conductor calls out "Stoessensee Bridge", and I jump off. The path down to the boat barracks is bordered by blooming wild rose bushes. When I arrive, there is nobody there beside me. No surprise, it is the middle of the week. I walk over to the slip where the Golden Hill is moored. I jump into the boat and wait.

Will he come today? I wonder. He only said that sometimes he goes sailing after work. He would go by himself. This is the only chance I have after piano lesson to come here secretly in the middle of the week. It is five o'clock now. At seven thirty Mother comes home and I have to be back before that time. She must not know about this sailing acquaintance. On Saturdays we go kayaking as usual, I tell her, so she won't worry.

The minutes seem to crawl. Restlessness makes me jump up. I cannot just sit here and look up a hundred times, hoping to see a reddish head of hair coming down the path. I walk up to the tram stop. Then I can greet him right away.

"Oh, I just had some time and I thought, perhaps you'll go sailing today."

How would he react? Would he be astonished or happy? I have no idea, although we have been together often. Comradeship amongst friends seems to be the unwritten rule by which this sailing group is run. No separating in twosomes. Theirs is a close friendship. Together they had worked to repair the old rundown boat, which all three had bought with the savings from their small apprentice and journeyman wages. You would be accepted into their fellowship by abiding by the rules. If you brought along some food or drink, or better still some fast records to be played on the hand-cranked phonograph, you belonged. Some flirting was allowed, too, how could one deny that at that age? But nothing above that, please!

Anyway, as a girl you were not allowed to show your feelings openly, those feelings which seemed to explode inside of me. This impatience, hurting like an open wound. This longing, which cannot be repressed any more. These thoughts, that constantly circle around that one person. What is the matter with me?

Another streetcar arrives. Again he is not on it. Slowly I walk down the path and sit down again. I wonder how one recognizes that one means something to the other person, that he feels drawn to you also? Can I see little indicators encouraging me, or am I fooling myself? This game is all new to me and I am lost in the whirlpool of my emotions, not being able to distance myself from these feelings that control me.

Two weeks ago he told me, that he wanted to be a painter. It made me curious and I said,

"Why don't you show me some of your drawings?" and the next time he brought his sketchbook along. As I leafed through the pictures I could immediately see a special talent. In school one of my favorite classes was art and drawing. I had an A in it, but when I tried to draw some ones' face it looked good, but had not the natural resemblance I desired. But Gerhard's portrait of Adolf Hitler was perfect. I quickly turned the page, hoping that Erika had not seen it.

He asked me if he could draw my face.

"O my goodness," I said, "I hate sitting for a portrait." My cousin Irene, five years older than I, was an accomplished artist. When we met for family occasions at Aunt Hanna's house, she would often tell me,

"Please just stay as you are, don't move till I tell you!" How could a small child stick to this command! But she demanded it and started drawing.

Once she left the room for a bit and when she returned she was horrified to see, that I had erased all shadings in my face while she was gone. She berated me, but I answered,

"I never have such a dirty face!"

Gerhard had sketched me then, while we were stopped in a small cove. The others went on land to play ball. I watched out of the corner of my eye how he looked at my face. But it was the look of the artist, who saw contours, shadows, and light, nothing more. When he finally was finished he showed it to me. It was a good resemblance and I liked it. Why is it that people always want to look their best on pictures? Whenever somebody shows a bunch of photographs of a group of people, the one looking at it always looks for his likeness first. Do I look good or does this picture make me look ugly? Lucky are the ones who can call themselves 'photogenic'. They never look bad, no matter in what position or light they are caught. I was pleased with my picture. He wanted to give it to me, but I refused. I was afraid that Mother would find it. I have to be careful there.

Oh no! Mother! I look at my watch. I must take the next tram to be home before she arrives. Now he will not come anymore, anyway. It is too late. I must wait till Saturday. It seems like an eternity. And then he will not be alone again.

3

⊶⊷

The pink wild roses are in full bloom as I walk expectantly down the path to the boat barracks. Gerhard is there. He is alone. He greets me with a big smile and then looks up anxiously at the thick grey rain clouds.

"All day long I had hoped that it would clear towards evening but then I didn't even know if you would come," he says, "but should we try it anyway?"

"We would not have to sail very far, so we could turn around if it begins to rain," I answer. I have longed for this evening all day.

"All right then, let's risk it!"

He begins to take off the tarpaulin that covers the back part of the boat. I help him on my side. I have learned a lot about sailing during these last six weekends. I was allowed to steer the boat alone, to handle the main sail and tack. When I told him that I had been there last week after my piano lesson, I saw something like regret in his eyes.

"Could you come next week?" he asked, "then I will see to it that I will be there."

"But I can only sail for one hour."

"That is all right. Come anyway."

We don't talk about this private arrangement with the others. Even Erika does not know. Best friends should have no secrets! But if she would know, she might want to come along – and I want to be alone with him!

"Can you push us off?" I stand at the bow with a long hook and push the Golden Hill slowly out of its berth. It would be easy to lose your balance and fall into the water. Gerhard draws up the sails and the wind immediately catches them. Everything has to go fast now. I jump into the boat, hold the rope of the foresail tightly in my hand and off we go! Gerhard steers the helm with his left hand. With his right he holds the rope of the main sail. We gather speed on this windy evening.

There is much we have to tell each other. During the past weeks we have discovered many common interests. We love art, specially painting. Aunt Hanna had introduced me to great art early in childhood. She was a second mother to me. My mother spent her days in our store. When I was sick for instance, like the time I had whooping cough when I was five years old, I spent six weeks at her house, till she had nursed me to health again. Instead of just looking at children's books, many of which I could recite by heart, she opened her heavy large art books with colored prints of paintings and sculptures of world famous artists. I learned early to stand in awe of some of these masterpieces, for she never allowed me to turn the pages of her books which instilled a sense of their worth and grandeur in my childish heart. Then she told me about the lives of some of those great artists.

When I grew older I started collecting art postcards of the High Renaissance period. They fill two albums already. Gerhard's aim is to attend an art academy to study painting. Even now he uses every free minute to sketch and draw. Often we just share our daily happenings. We talk about everything of interest to teenagers. Sometimes we observe nature together. The joy of discovering mutual interests and convictions strengthens the common bond between us and the feeling grows that here is someone who understands me and whom I understand.

"Look over there, the dragon fly!"

"Where?"

"There, in front on the leather pillow."

"How delicate, the metallic blue of the body and the glassy see-through wings. Not easy to paint."

"I have seen Dutch paintings that were so realistic that the glass sparkled and you could see some ones image in it. They seemed to be more realistic than reality itself."

"I don't think I would like to paint reality. That would be monotonous after awhile. I want to convey feelings, or my view of reality, which does not have to be real at all. I think some of those painters which are thrown out today as degenerate art, really had a concept of life that I can identify with. But they won't teach this in the academy."

He looks at the distant horizon and I feel sadness. To live at a time when government decides the value of art and sets standards, which are shackles to the creative talent, is an added burden to an already insecure future. To change the subject I point to the sky.

"See the bird up there? Is it an eagle?"

"No, looks more like a black kite."

"How do you know?"

"By the shape of its wings."

"I once had a bird. It was a goldfinch. He could not get used to the cage or to me. He fluttered around fearfully whenever I came close and hopped from one perch to another, always looking up to find an exit from his cage. One day I could not stand it anymore, so I took the cage and the bird outside and opened the door. He flew away and I followed it with my eyes and I had a feeling of happiness in my heart, for I had returned the bird to his element, the freedom of the sunlit skies."

"I can understand that. Everybody, whether human or animal, needs his freedom. We are born for freedom!"

"Vive liberte', egalite', fraternite'! Freedom! Equality! Brotherhood!"

"You can speak French?"

"Only un peu. We had it in school as our first foreign language."

"I would have loved to go to secondary school, too. But I was not allowed to."

"The important things in life you can also learn on your own. But you know practical things which many students never learn."

"Thanks, but I'd rather been going to school instead of working at Siemens factory. My mother wanted me to learn a practical profession."

"And your father?"

He looks away and then answers haltingly.

"I have never known my father." Then he adds quietly so that I can hardly understand him,

"I am an illegitimate child."

"That does not mean anything to me," I hasten to reply. "It does not matter where you come from or what you possess. I am interested in character. What I like about you is that you are open and I can talk to you about everything and you have a heart for animals and people."

"But not for all people."

"I don't mean that. I know some too that I absolutely cannot stand, our math teacher for instance. But I like most of the people." Especially you, I would have liked to add. But a well-bred girl does not say things like that. Does he even have any idea what these few moments together with him mean to me? How I feverishly wait a whole week to be together with him for just one hour?

"Did you feel it, raindrops?"

"Oh no, now it really starts to rain. What are we going to do?"

"I don't want the sails to get wet. Can you hold the helm for me and turn into the wind, while I let the sails down?"

I let go of the foresail and jump to the helm while Gerhard lets down the sails and tucks them onto the beam. Then he throws out a little anchor. The rain is increasing in intensity. I help him throw the tarpaulin over the back of the boat.

"Come down here quickly or else you get all wet."

We sit on our leather pillows on the bottom of the boat and hear the drum beat of the rain over our heads. Gerhard lifts one side of the tarpaulin with the hook to get some air and light into our dark chamber. Outside the hard raindrops form bubbles and jump up from the surface before uniting with the river water. The reeds near the shore are blown to and fro by the wind and endure it with bent heads. Silently we sit next to each other listening to the staccato concert around us. My heart beats faster. Am I imagining it or did his shoulder just touch mine? I do not move. I feel paralyzed. The minutes pass. Slowly and cautiously he lifts his right arm and lays it around my shoulder. Then he waits as if fearful of my reaction. A long time nothing else happens, no word, no movement. I hardly dare breathe. The longing to let myself fall completely into his arms is overpowering, but I remain sitting there, stiffly and outwardly detached. Will he become discouraged and take his arm back? My heart beats wildly.

Now he drops the hook on the bottom, which he held the whole time in his left hand. Darkness closes in on us. I can hardly see his face coming closer to mine. I respond by leaning against him. I feel his breath on my cheeks. We sit like that for a long time, motionless, while the monotonous sound of splashing rain continues. Has he lost his courage? Almost imperceptibly I turn my face so I can see the outline of his profile in the darkness. He turns his face in response. Suddenly I can feel his cheek on mine. We sit there cheek to cheek, waiting, feeling the breath of the other, the warmth. Is he going to kiss me or is he afraid? I feel a soft pressure and turn my face toward him. Like in slow motion his lips draw nearer and I feel a short, but burning kiss. Instinctively I withdraw my head. He has kissed me! He also pulls back, as if surprised by his own courage. But then we fly into each other's arms and our lips meet over and over again.

A new wave of tenderness enfolds me, a never before experienced feeling of complete happiness fills my heart. Only the same words are dancing around in my head like a merry-go-round, repeating themselves over and over again, 'He loves me, he whom I love, loves me!' Never will I forget this hour, never lose this feeling. Time and space have stopped to exist. Only this moment counts, I want to savor it, feel it, experience it to the fullest, everything else is of no importance. The only thing that counts is this ecstasy of feeling.

We do not notice that the rain has stopped long ago. During a pause, while we sit tightly hugging each other and enjoying our new happiness, Gerhard says,

"Don't you think you have to leave soon?"

O Romeo, it is not even the song of the lark that brings us back to reality. How can we end this unique experience with concepts like time, hours and minutes?

"But I don't want to go home," I sigh with burning cheeks, "I want to stay with you, for ever and ever. I love you!"

"I love you, too," he answers. "I have dreamed of kissing you for weeks. But I never found the courage. You are the first girl that I kissed."

"And you the first boy! I have loved you from the beginning and I hoped that you would like me too. But now everything is wonderful. I love you so much!" and again we fly into each other's arms.

"But now we have to go or else you get in trouble with your mother."

He lifts the tarpaulin. The evening sun shines out of the grey clouds. The first thing I see is a restaurant ship by the shore near our anchor place. Its name glistens in the evening sun. 'Alte Liebe' (Old Love). The German proverb comes to mind, Old love never rusts. Our love is new, fresh, untouched – and untried.

On the way to the tram we walk with our arms around each other up the path. "Wait a minute," Gerhard says and takes his arm away. While he picks a perfect wild rose, shakes off the rain drops and puts it in my hair, I think," Never in my life will I forget this day. It is May 21, 1941." He waits with me till my tram arrives. He has to ride in the opposite direction. Through the windows we throw each other kisses and I see how his lips form the words, 'I love you!' I mouth the same words back to him. My heart sings!

4

~~~

The pot with the precooked food is still warm as I put it in the packed bag. Only one more thing, a flashlight and then I will be ready to go. Hopefully mother will call soon; it is 9:30p.m. almost my bedtime. There! The telephone rings. Mother's voice sounds far away and I have to speak louder. Through her words I feel her concern and I try to calm her fears. "Don't worry, everything is going fine. I was in the store all day. One customer has bought towels, linens, and bedding for 150 Marks from me. And tomorrow is Sunday and you will be back in the evening. Yes, I have cooked something for myself. Yes, surely. You sleep well, too."

I put down the phone and take the bag and leash. Dolly, my wire-haired terrier, runs expectantly to the door. I open the door and listen. The hall and staircase is quiet.

"Let us go for a walk," I say and lock the door behind me. We walk through the dark streets till we get to the tram stop Heerstrasse. I put Dolly on the leash. Obediently she jumps up the steps of the streetcar. Inside I remain standing, the bag between my legs. Only a few people are sitting in the car. I feel them eyeing me and the dog. We are the only passengers to get off at Scholzplatz. There is not a person in sight as we cross the square. I head for the road leading down to the river Havel. Dolly pulls, but I do not take her off the leash. The July night is warm and very dark. I fight against fear gripping my heart of some threatening danger. The leash in my hand imparts a feeling of security, though it is only a small dog with short uplifted tail and attentive ears, taking in sounds and smells that evade me.

When we come to the next curve there must be the hill on the left, where Lucy and I went skiing. How much fun we had together with our home-built ski jump! I can still hear our laughter, interrupting the stillness of the Grunewald forest. Oh Lucy, where are you now? Although Erika has taken your place now, I still miss you very much. How can I ever forget our parting, when I came to your empty house to say good bye and you walked with me to the end of the street, only to have both of us turn around again. At the second try we parted in tears, knowing, that we might never see each other again. To part from your best friend is such a hard experience!

We must have walked over fifteen minutes already and still the road leads downward. The bag gets heavier on my arm. I had no idea it would be this far. After twenty minutes I finally see the end of the road. What a relief! The worst is behind me. Dolly pulls on the leash and barks. Through the darkness I see Gerhard coming towards us.

"Stop barking, Dolly, good watchdog, it's all right, "I try to calm her. "It's a friend, quiet, stop it!" Gerhard holds out his hand and she sniffs. Then he pets her and takes my bag.

"I have been waiting quite some time already," he says.

"I could not get away. Mother called so late. Where is the boat?"

"Next to the 'Old Love'."

We enter the boat and Dolly jumps in after us. The sail is set but there is hardly a breeze. Slowly almost imperceptibly the boat moves away from the wooden bridge. Everything is so different at night. I cannot see where we are going and the stillness surrounds us like a thick blanket. I sit on my pillow on the bottom of the boat, lay my head on the seat and look up into the night sky. There are no lights around and millions of stars are visible with some sparkling brighter than others. We are like a little nutshell drifting alone through the universe.

"Can you see at all where we are going?" My voice sounds strange in this peaceful quietness.

"I am aiming in the direction of Schildhorn," he answers. "Soon the moon will come up."

I try to find familiar constellations.

"I can see the Milky Way. And there is the Big Dipper, and over there Orion. We are all alone in this universe, you and I. We are drifting between the stars. They are around and under and above us. Our boat has wings and we fly weightlessly through the galaxies. I wonder what we are going to discover?"

"That we forgot to bring a bottle opener."

"Oh, Gerhard, must you disturb my romantic fantasies?"

For an answer he bends down and kisses me. Dolly at my feet lifts up her head and watches us interestedly.

"I don't like it when you kiss me while the dog watches."

"Aha! You have a bad conscience, because you spend the night with me behind your mother's back!" he teases me.

"But that was your idea, you invited me!"

"And you said, yes!" he laughs.

"She is not going to find out about it. And anyway, what's wrong with wanting to be together? Perhaps there will not be many more opportunities." Why these sad thoughts which try to disturb the magic of the moment? "Let us just use the time that we have together to the fullest."

He pulls me close and silently we observe the secretive world around us. There, over the dark pinewoods we see the almost full moon rising. It is almost orange and one can see the face of the Man in the Moon clearly. As it rises from the horizon, darkness turns into silvery light that is being mirrored on the calm surface of the water. How close the moon seems to be, though it is far away, a secret planet, whose magnetic force influences the female cycle and makes the mighty oceans and other waters rise and fall.

After a long period of silence Gerhard asks, "Are you getting tired?"

"No. Are you?"

"Well, it was quite a long day and must be way after midnight."

"Why don't you find a spot where we can stop for the night?"

"I have picked one already, and we are almost there."

It is a landing bridge built over the water, a place where fishermen usually put their rods out, surrounded by high rushes. Gerhard ties down the boat and Dolly and I jump on land. The grass feels wet under my bare feet. Suddenly a frog leaps out of my way and scares me. Dolly is exploring the area. After a while I whistle for her and together we return to the safety of the boat.

Gerhard has made a bed in the meantime. Two blankets are laid down on either side of the rectangular box in the center, into which the keel is drawn, when the boat is pulled up on land.

"I hope you don't mind that it is a bit hard."

It certainly is. I stretch out on the right side with the leather pillow under my head. Gerhard takes the left side. Our bodies are separated by the box. Only head and shoulders are next to each other.

"Good night," I say and lift my head to look in his direction.

"Don't you want to give me a good night kiss after all I have done for you?"

"All right, here is one for making the bed – and here is another for sailing at night. Good night, Gerhard."

"I want another one!" After a while we stop counting.

A battle is raging within me. There is the desire to give myself to him whom I love with a deep, all-inclusive love, whom I want to make happy. But there is also fear. The words of my mother echo in my ears:

"Don't you ever come home being pregnant!" In my general ignorance about sex, (one simply does not talk about it or mention words that have a sexual connotation,) I believe that petting belongs to the dangerous category. The only thing allowed is kissing. The tenderness expressed in a kiss, the words of love whispered in the ear bring feelings of great happiness. Those other feelings, that rise and become more intense, must be repressed. They just must wait.

I cannot sleep but I lie quietly on my back with my eyes closed. I notice that Gerhard cannot sleep either. He would never take advantage of this situation, he also honors the code of conduct with which we grew up. He felt my reluctance at other times and he would not do anything against my will.

Slowly the sky begins to lighten. My back aches and I get up to sit on the edge of the boat and watch the beginning of a new day. After a short while a sleepy-eyed Gerhard joins me. He stretches out on the seats and puts his head on my lap.

I let my fingers run through his hair while watching the eastern sky change colors from purple to slightly pink, orange, and gold.

Gerhard is breathing long and deeply and I see that finally sleep has overcome him. Now I have a chance to study his face, to engrave every detail in my mind and memory. Yet how fleeting are these impressions! Time has a way to erase features of loved ones. Only by looking at old pictures does one discover again those forgotten lines, which combine to make up a beloved face. He looks so peaceful and relaxed, like a little boy, encircled by a rosy glimmer that magically transforms our whole surroundings and reflects on the water. I do not dare to move. Only my eyes wander from his face to the now rising sun, which heralds this new morning. Looking down upon my beloved I feel like a mother holding her child in her arms.

Over and over again my eyes take in the details of his youthful face. I see the blond eye lashes, the straight nose with a sprinkling of freckles, his 17 year old chin which already has manly lines, the downy beard on his cheeks, and the reddish blond hair. If I could only preserve these moments of pure, undisturbed happiness! I want to shield him from all evil. I want to protect our love against the dark powers threatening to destroy it. Tenderly I kiss his forehead. He opens his eyes sleepily and smiles at me.

We spend the day sailing, swimming, and eating. In the afternoon it is still hot. We stop in a small cove, almost hidden by high rushes. Gerhard pulls the tarpaulin over the beam to give us some shade. To passing boats we are invisible. Again we are in each other's arms. Time is getting short. I must be home before Mother returns from her trip. Gerhard is strangely quiet. My attempts to cheer him up are unsuccessful. Something is troubling him. Finally after continuous questioning on my part, he bursts out:

"Reinhold is being drafted."

Silently we sit next to each other. He holds his head in his hands.

"I am afraid," he whispers.

"Why, you, Gerhard?"

"I am afraid for Reinhold. He is my best friend. Although he is older, we have known each other and played together since we were kids. I just realized that I might never see him again. He could easily get killed in this war."

"But Gerhard," I try to comfort him, "he also has a chance to survive. Not all soldiers get killed."

"Perhaps not, but then they come home, crippled in body or soul. Even if they survive, their lives will never be the same. They will be haunted by what they were forced to do or what they saw others doing. How could you ever kill another human being and not be marred for life? I hate war!" He speaks passionately. "I do not want to go to war and be taught how to kill, even if they say it is for a good cause. War can never be a good cause! But what can you do against those in power? There is no other way; I will also have to go. Resistance would mean immediate death. I want to have the chance to live, to have a family, to teach my children. I want to learn to become a great painter – to create beautiful art. I do not want to destroy or make cripples of others or shoot to kill them. War is hell!"

Words of comfort are stuck in my throat. Fear creeps into our peaceful safe little nest. Ice-cold fingers clutch our sun-heated bodies, will not let go, chilling us to the bone.

Gerhard hides his face in his hands. What is this? Between his fingers I can see a tear running down his cheek. I put my arm around his shoulders and feel his suppressed sobbing. Boys don't cry, even if they have bloody knees. But these tears cannot be suppressed. Are they for Reinhold – or for himself?

"Please do not cry," I beg helplessly, "everything is going to be all right." How empty my words sound! I pull his fingers from his face and kiss a tear from his wet cheek. It tastes salty.

"I know nothing will happen to you. I love you too much! We will be happy together!"

Slowly he regains his composure.

"I am sorry, it just came over me."

I lean my head against his shoulder.

"We will never really be separated," I whisper, "even if we cannot be together for a time. Remember, I will always love you!"

5

❧

"**W**here were you last night?" In a split second I realize by the angry expression on Mothers' face that she knows the truth.

"I tried to call you again because I had forgotten to tell you something, but you were not there. Even when I called later there was no answer."

"But Mom, let me tell you about this boy…"

"You were together with a boy?" Her eyes narrow to exasperated slits.

"Yes, but it is not what you think! Please, please, listen to me! Erika and I were on the water and we met these friends there. They were nice guys and they invited us to go sailing with them."

"And so you just went with them? I cannot believe it!"

"But it was so much fun! Why do you begrudge us having some fun?" I try to appease her. "I am sorry I did not tell you the truth, but you would have never allowed me to go."

"But who is the boy you were with last night?"

"Please don't be so angry, I will tell you everything."

I paint a picture of Gerhard, a positive, attractive, and favorable picture, but I try not to divulge my feelings, not to give away too much but enough to calm her fears.

"Is it really such a terrible thing for me wanting to meet a boy? After all I am going to be sixteen next January."

"Not a terrible thing?" I see by her hands, pushing her hair back nervously, how upset she really is.

"What is his name?" she demands.

"Gerhard Hoffmann."

"And where does he live?"

"Somewhere in Spandau."

"I want to have his address. You must have his address."

"Yes," I answer hesitantly, "I have written it down."

"Get your address book."

"But Mom, what do you want to do with his address?"

"Do what I tell you! Give me the address!"

"Not before you tell me what you need it for." I am no longer the little girl that you can give orders to and that has to obey blindly. But why is she so terribly angry?

"I will tell you! Don't you see in what dangerous situation you put this boy?"

I feel like my neck is being squeezed shut. The words come out under pressure.

"I am sure if he would know, it would not matter to him."

"Perhaps not to him, but to his parents."

"He has only his mother."

"Then she must know about it."

"Know what?"

"That her son goes out sailing with a Jewish girl!"

"Oh, Mom, you make it sound so awful! How can you say such a terrible thing? I am not Jewish anymore, I am a Christian."

"It is terrible! In the eyes of the Nazis you are Jewish. You must never see him again!"

"Never see him again? You are not serious, are you?"

"I have never been more serious! And now give me the address!"

Tears rise and roll down my cheeks.

"You cannot do this to me! You have no feelings at all! You are mean and cruel! You don't know how much I love him!"

There, it is out in the open now, but what do I care. Deep sobs shake my body.

"I am going to see him again, no matter what you say!" Defiantly I rush out of the room and throw myself weeping on Father's couch. Daddy, you would comfort me, as you have done so often when I was smaller. I remember the scene.

"Daddy, I will never go to school again!"

"What happened, Yolchen?" He looks surprised at my emotional outburst.

"Don't try to change my mind; I just will not go back!"

"Now tell me what has happened."

"This terrible woman! This teacher Frau Witte, I never want to see her again!"

"But she is only a substitute when Fraeulein Seeck is sick. What has she done?"

"She stood up in front of the class and told everybody how terrible things were before the Fuehrer came to power. And then she actually said, "Die Juden sind unser Unglueck!" (Jews are our misfortune). She said it before all the kids and then she looked at us really cross and all the kids looked at us. It was terrible! Why do they hate us, Daddy?"

"Because we are Jews."

"What is so terrible about being Jews?" I sob.

"Nothing, darling," he answers and takes me into his strong arms.

I remember another incident.

"Last summer when I was on that vacation trip with the other kids from our synagogue in that small village, Hof near Kassel, I stayed with a family that had no children of their own. One morning as I was playing by myself in their back yard, suddenly some one threw a rock at me. It almost hit me and he called me "Judensau" Jewish pig. On the Sabbath all of us marched to the synagogue and the people along the way called us names as we walked by. I never dared to look up, it was terrible."

"These were evil people, little one. Don't take this to heart."

"But this now is happening in my class room, and these are my friends. I just cannot go back to school again."

"Well, let us wait then till Fraeulein Seeck is well again."

You were able to comfort me, Daddy! The tears start to flow again.

Suddenly I feel Mother's face next to mine. I did not hear her coming in.

"Yolchen", she whispers, "I am so sorry. I hope you can under-stand me. I don't want to take away your happiness – but it is too dangerous for all of us. You are not aware of the danger yet. You are young and want to have fun. But this kind of fun is too dangerous. You know that people are put in concentration camps. You don't want Gerhard to end there, do you?" I cannot answer, the thought is too painful.

"You say that you love him. Then you won't do anything to harm or hurt him."

"But what about hurting me?" the tears flow again.

"I hope you have enough of an understanding to know that I have to do this."

I know from experience that one cannot change mother's mind. If I don't hand her the address she will find other ways of getting it. What she sees as right is what she sets out to do.

All joy of the magic hours on the water has dissipated. What is left is hopelessness and despair. Resignation fills my heart. Oh Gerhard, why are you so far away when I need your comfort so badly?

6

❦

I throw my school bag into the corner. Mother is waiting already with our noon meal. We sit at the little table in the narrow passage, which doubles as kitchen and dining area and which is separated from the store by a dark green curtain.

"How was your day?" Mother inquires.

"Uh, like always. Come to think of it, not like always. Erika told me that they are forced to leave their apartment." In my mind's eye I see myself walking to Erika's house under blooming Japanese cherry trees, covering the asphalt with a soft pink blanket of fallen blossoms.

"What? That nice place? Oh, what a mean act! They are taking away one thing after another!" Mother is indignant. "Isn't it enough," she tries to keep her voice low, "that since the ninth of November 1938 they burned the synagogues and killed hundreds of Jews and hurt many hundreds more and destroyed 7000 Jewish owned stores. 30 000 men they have arrested at that time and put into concentration camps. And after all of these injustices they have the nerve to make the Jews pay one billion marks as collective special tax – to the destroyer! Then they banished the children from their schools, made a curfew, forbade them to attend theaters and movie houses or use beaches or night trains. Then they forced them to add to their signatures the names Israel or Sarah. Isn't it enough that on their ID card they printed a big J, just like you have?"

Mother's stirred up voice gets louder. I put my finger on my lips. In the store Clarissa is selling a nightgown to a customer. I am glad that Dad did not have to go through all of this. He is safely in America.

No, I will never forget the 9ᵗʰ of November, either. The experiences of that day have engraved themselves indelibly on my memory. Like a movie I recall the events of that terrible day.

"Hello, Anne," Ulli and I greet the girl from our class who gets on at the next bus stop. All of us are on our way to our private secondary school, Toni Lessler School at Roseneck in the Grunewald district. Anne's usually smiling face is distraught. "Haven't you heard what happened last night?" she asks."

"No, what happened?"

"The Nazis laid fire in the synagogues and they are burning! Shop windows of Jewish owned stores were smashed, the stores looted, people attacked and beaten, many arrested and killed!"

The three of us are standing on the open platform of the bus like on an ice floe, drifting through dangerous waters. Fingers are clenched till knuckles are white and nails dig into palms. Eyes stare into space without seeing. A crazy thought enters my head, swirling around, till I cannot think of anything else. It engraves itself like on copper plates.

"This is the most terrible day of my 12 year old life. I will never forget it. I will tell my grandchildren about it!"

Flames lick wooden beams, black smoke rises into the gray November sky. Creaking and groaning like in agony the dome of the synagogue breaks down. My temple at Fasanenstrasse, my house of God, to which I walked by myself each Friday evening, is dying. Never again will I hear the melodic voice of the cantor singing the age old texts, the Hebrew prayers, the voice, which had often sounded like wailing, resounding the pain and suffering of his people toward heaven. Never again will I hear from the choir loft the lilting voices of the sopranos and the full voices of the alto singers, whose musical fervor made an impression on my childish heart. Never again will I see the Rabbi as he kisses the velvet and gold embroidered roll of the Torah with the lions on it before depositing it in its special shrine. All of these objects and the holidays that connected my childhood with the almighty God, the hours in which my heart was touched by him – everything is taken away and gone.

Why does God allow this to happen? Why doesn't he destroy these evildoers on the spot?

When we arrive at our school, the iron gates are closed.

"Go home again as fast as possible," the caretaker admonishes each little group of students as they arrive and then obediently turn around. We huddle together like fearful sheep, suddenly surrounded by a world of wolf-like enemies. Mother is home before me. Our store windows have been smashed also, but the iron diamond shaped roll-down shutter has prevented looting. The department store of N. Israel, neighbor to the red city hall and a few stores away from us, has been completely devastated and looted, with people throwing things on the street just for fun. Mother is disturbed, takes me into her arms and tries to comfort me.

"Why?" I repeat over and over again, sobbing. But there is no answer.

I wake up from my gloomy thoughts when mother puts a bowl of applesauce in front of me and sits down again.

"There was another thing at school today. I told you that Rita Deutschkron was taken out of our school and was deported. Today our teacher read a postcard from her. It came from a camp in Poland."

"There are rumors that these so called work camps are in reality concentration camps. What did she write?"

"She only quoted a few Bible verses, in fact she only wrote down the number of the verses."

"What did it say?"

"Our teacher read us from the Bible. One was from the 91st Psalm Verse 7, "A thousand may fall at your side, ten thousand at your right hand; but it will not come near you.'"

"Oh how terrible! Can you imagine what is going on there?"

"No. The other verse was from the Gospel of John chapter 21 verse 5: "'Children, have you anything to eat?'"

"This is awful! They are starving them now! Can't we do anything about it?" Mother puts down her spoon as if the food is getting stuck in her throat.

"O yes! Our teacher prayed for Rita and the others and then told us to send food packages. Perhaps they will reach her."

"You could do that right after you decorate the shop windows."

Mechanically I eat my applesauce. My thoughts circle around Erika. When she moves, I will have to ride to school alone. I feel something like guilt. Why can we stay in our apartment, only because my mother belongs to the Arian race and Erika's parents are both Jews? How we had hoped that they would take into account that her father had fought and been wounded in the First World War and had received the Iron Cross. But now even this vague hope had been dashed like a soap bubble.

Our school in Oranienburger Strasse was slowly being diminished. Even one of the teachers had been hauled off and deported Rumors circulated that soon the Gestapo would close it altogether. Courageous Pastor Grueber, whose Apostle church Erika and her parents attended and who had confirmed Erika, was the only one in Berlin, who had opened an office to help Jews and Jewish 'Mischlinge '(children from mixed marriages of Jews and Christians, like myself) who belonged to the Christian faith. For these special children he had opened a small private school leading to 10th grade.

How I had longed to attend school after our Jewish school had been forced to close. I still see myself standing before mother and telling her emphatically,

"I cannot stay home forever since all Jewish schools were closed. I want to learn and study! Why don't you try to get me in at the girls' high school? You could talk to the director and tell her that you are Arian!" We passed the school, a red brick building, every time we walked to the S-Bahn station Heerstrasse to take the train to our store in the center of town. Every day I pestered mother more with my wish. Finally she gave in against her better knowledge.

We walk along the familiar road, shaded by large plane trees. I wear my best Sunday dress and hold under my arm a folder with my report cards. Surely, if she sees my grades she will accept me. We enter the director's room. She gets up behind her desk and reaches out to shake our hands with a friendly smile, then bids us to sit down. My hopes grow. Politely I make a deep curtsy before I sit down on the edge of a leather chair, clutching my folder. I am ready to hand it to her when she asks for it. While mother speaks a few words, explaining our situation, I see the friendly smile disappear from the director's face and instead hear her words becoming more crisp and brusque. Suddenly she pushes her chair back and gets up – a signal for us to leave.

"You may be Arian" she says to mother, "but your daughter is a Jewish Mischling according to the Nuremberg race laws and therefore is a Jew in our eyes." She turns her back on me.

"This school is for Arian children only!"

With my unopened report card folder under my arm, I slink next to the walls through the long halls of the school. In passing I hear girl's voices singing the well known folk song, adapted from Goethe's poem: 'The little rose, about to be picked, says, "I prick you so you will always think of me, for I don't want to suffer"...' I bear no thorns and still must suffer.

Enough thoughts of the past! While I decorate the shop windows, my thoughts are with Gerhard. What will he say when he hears that Erika can no longer go sailing with us, since she has to move far away to the north-eastern part of the city.

My mother and Gerhard's mother had gotten together and I had insisted on going along. After a long and heated discussion they had agreed to a compromise. We were allowed to see each other again, but only on the water with its anonymity and where there was less danger. That excluded all other activities. The result was, that we had endless telephone conversations. Gerhard, who had also attended the meeting, had been very convincing to Mother and she had given a restricted permission. Now she felt that she had done her duty and had warned all of the possible consequences. Peace between us had been restored.

Formerly Dad had decorated the windows. That was before he left to emigrate to America. Six months at the most were we to be separated. This was the plan my parents agreed on. Mother did not want to leave a secure means of livelihood and go into an unknown future in a foreign country with a language that she was struggling to learn. Dad should leave first and find work and a place to live. Then he would 'request' us to follow him, as the official term was called. One needed an affidavit, a sponsor in order to emigrate. The months passed and the plan was delayed. He was 52 years old and had not found work as an electrical engineer, not an easy thing at that age. He is trying his best, but who could have foreseen a war starting?

In September of 1939 Hitler had occupied Poland and gone on to Czechoslovakia and Austria and the annexation to the Reich had followed. Now German soldiers have made their way to the gates of Moscow. Father's sisters and families as well as my friends Ulli and Lucy have emigrated already. But our emigration seems out of reach. After the ninth of November 1939, the infamous 'Crystal Night', the Gestapo (Secret Political Police) ordered mother to appear at their feared headquarters at Alexander Platz, a few minutes by foot from our store. She was threatened with all kinds of terrible consequences, if she would not divorce her Jewish husband. Upon my upset reaction she let me in on a secret agreement with her lawyer. Outwardly he would begin divorce proceedings, but being that Father was across an ocean, he would constantly use delay tactics in order never to complete the process. Mother loves her husband and wants to remain faithful to him.

I also love my Dad. He was always the person I could speak to, who would listen and who would be my patient teacher, substituting for the working mother. An invitation to my birthday party was most desired by my small guests, due to him. In fact they stick out as highlights of my childhood memories. After we had sat around the festively decorated table with electric candles around the cakes and small gifts at each setting and had eaten enough sweets and drank hot chocolate, we would gather in the darkened den and watch fairy tale movies, which my father showed on his 16 mm movie projector. Of course they were silent movies, but that did not diminish the joy of the audience, who sat with mouths wide open, watching Hansel and Gretel escape from the bad witch. After these movies, Dad showed his own films, taken of me when I was two years old. I can still see myself standing by a fountain, splashing water with my pudgy hands, or making my way through a bed of daisies as tall as myself.

But the high point of the afternoon was the group picture. We all sat and stood in rows, while Dad disappeared under a cover behind the large wooden camera on a tripod. Then he would come out, hold a phosphor flash high up in the air and we held our breath, for he told us not to move. "Wooosh" it would explode and our hearts skipped a beat. But every child was glad to receive a picture later as a souvenir.

My life was a happy adventure, an endless chain of discoveries, either by own experience or vicariously through books. Being an only child of shop keeping parents, I hungrily devoured books. With each new book the world seemed to expand and become more interesting. I still remember the series of girl's books I read, till I discovered Karl May and his series of adventures, playing in the Wild West with the famous Indian, Winnetou, and his white friend Old Shatterhand. Even with twelve I could not wait to finish another book of the series, when I had an eye operation and could not read. I asked my patient roommate in the hospital to finish reading it to me. When the last page was turned, I hungrily looked for more. Books helped to overcome the lonely hours. I was just one year old when my grandmother, my fathers' mother, died who had led the store that she and her husband had built up through years of long hours of hard work. No one in the family was ready to take over the store. They all had their own sphere of work. Finally my mother, who was gifted with a keen business sense, sacrificed her own desires to stay home with her baby, her one and only, and leaving me to a nanny, she began a new career as a storeowner. She had to leave me each morning in the hands of hired help and attend to the many duties this store demanded. It sucked out her time and energy and spit her out each evening, dry and tired.

But that is where Dad stepped in. He helped Mother, but more in the background, being aware of his Jewish looks, which became a growing hindrance as the years went by. I was taken care of by a housekeeper named Emma, who called me 'Julchen'. But after we moved into another part of West Berlin and I attended first grade, Dad would come home at noon when school was out, to meet and greet me with a warm meal. We no longer had a full time house-keeper, but a woman who came twice a week to clean and do the laundry. Dad was the first one with whom I shared the joys and hurts of my school day. After we ate our noon meal together, I sat down at his large desk, with the hand carved lions' heads on the legs, and I would do my homework. He sat across from me in his easy chair, reading his newspaper, till sleep overcame him. He napped awhile and then looked up to see if I was finished. Then he took off to return to the store, while I walked around the block to see my best friend, Ulli.

My afternoons were spent with her and her family. We shared the same walk to public school, shared the same desk and whenever Ulli got a new book, I usually read it first. The banker's family had adopted me as their third daughter. Ulli's mother even had given me a new name, 'Koepfchen,' after a character in a children's book. It made me proud to be accepted like that.

The family occupied eight or nine rooms, the whole upper flat in a dignified building, overlooking a manicured park with signs forbidding to step on the grass and in which ball playing and bicycling was not allowed. One block away, they owned a garden of two acres, which became our private playground. It was a wonderful oasis, with a large grassy area in the center, perfect for sports and ball playing. It was framed by fruit trees, cherries, sweet and sour, different kinds of apples, pears and plums. There was a high fence with bushes shielding us from the street and one end was our private wilderness area, where we built our fort. At the other end of the large yard stood a garden house. Ullis' dog, Lumpie, a black and white terrier, was our protector and playmate, who ran to catch our balls or barked under the trees which we had climbed, to eat the ripe or unripe fruit. In our wilderness area we dug a large hole and covered it with wooden planks and branches to make it invisible. It was our secret meeting place, our clubhouse into which we withdrew when visitors came to see the garden. Before a cousin came along, whom Ulli did not like, we took off the planks and only left the branches, and sure enough the exploring boy fell into the hole and we laughed till our sides hurt.

The life style of this upper class family impressed me. Their unwritten requirements included a good education, a quick mind, which seemed of greatest importance, courtesy and good manners in everyday living. They carried themselves with an unobtrusive elegance that rejected all open display of wealth. In order to be accepted in this elite circle, surrounded by silent servants, one had to meet the criterion of intelligence and culture, as well as a certain respectful yet self-assured demeanor. Children were expected to be obedient, have a communicative and interested attitude, yet exercise self-control and discipline and show polite and well- mannered behavior.

At first I felt a bit insecure when I was invited to sleep over and to participate in the meal times of the family. We sat in the dining room around a large oval table, covered with a white damask tablecloth with gleaming silverware and tall-stemmed crystal glasses. Overhead hung a crystal chandelier. The banker-father, a tall, good-looking man about 50 with slightly graying hair, sat at the head of the table. On his left sat his dark eyed wife, whose nervous hands mirrored her quickly changing emotional states. At the other end of the table sat the white haired, perfectly coiffed little grandma, wearing a dark blue dress with a two strand necklace of exquisite pearls. She spoke in a distinctly Rhineland's accent, for she had lived in the city of Mainz, before coming to live with her daughter. On the other chairs sat Ulli and Anneliese, who was the two years older sister, and a guest, myself.

A servant girl in a black dress with white lacy apron and starched bonnet, moved silently between kitchen and dining room, bearing steaming tureens of delicious chicken soup or bowls full of potatoes and vegetables and silver platters of sliced meats. When she offered the platter on my right side, I was careful to use the fork and slide a slice onto my plate without spilling anything on the tablecloth. I sat erect and stiff on the hand-carved chairs, with a starched napkin spread over my lap, cut my meat carefully, took small bites, lifted my crystal glass gingerly and observed out of the corner of my eye what the others were doing. I tried to remember all the table manners my parents had taught me.

When the napkins were rolled up again and slid into the sterling silver rings with the family initials, I felt a certain pride about my promotion from playmate in the children's room to dinner guest at the family table.

But my pride changed to pure horror, when I woke the next morning in the pretty guest bedroom and felt my sheets. I had wet the bed! This had not happened in a long time. The 'girl', as the female servants were called, did not make a fuss or tell anybody about my mishap, not to humiliate me publicly. I was eternally grateful to her.

Servants in general were rather reserved, appeared only when a bell was rung. In between meals they cleaned, polished silver, and opened doors. They wore a slight smile, served quietly and politely. They lived in narrow rooms close to the back entrance, to which a private staircase led to their own world, which was foreign to me.

During these years Ulli and I never spent Sundays together. This was our family day, the only one the three of us shared. They were the special times that I remember, when we took the double deck bus to Kladow by the Havel River or to some other of the lakes surrounding Berlin. It was always the high point of the week for me, and I enjoyed the harmony and love of my parents, and the security of being equally loved by both, which surrounded me like a warm cloak. It had been a wonderful and happy time – till father had to leave. I relive the scene.

The railroad station is crowded with people. Our small group stands huddled together in the February cold. Father looks like a wealthy man in his new suit and coat and the new luggage. I hold my new doll, Sonja, in my arms. She is only three weeks old.

"Do you know what I wish for my birthday?" I had started the conversation with Mother, expecting resistance from the start. She never bought anything for me, for which I had not begged or fought for a long time. Her great fear was to raise a spoiled brat by doting on its every wish.

"Now what would you like to have?"

"I saw a doll in the window with blond hair and brown eyes. She is beautiful. I want to name her Sonja and take her with me on the boat to America."

"You – and dolls? You have never really played with them. The ones you have are just sitting in a corner."

"But this one is different. You said yourself, that I could not take many toys along and I just want to take her along." This time I did not have to beg forever.

It is the 22nd of February 1938, my Daddy's fare-well. He had explained to me, that he would leave first, find work and a place to live and then, at the latest six months from now, we would follow him. He bends down and gives me last minute instructions.

"Continue your private English lessons, so you will be able to go to an American school. I expect you to have good report cards there also."

His hand caresses my hair.

"Yes, I will do that, Daddy." I grab his soft, warm hand full of anticipation. Finally Father would return to the country he had told me stories about all of my life. He had crossed the Atlantic as a young engineer as representative of Bing Brothers of Nuremberg. They were one of the first to produce electric toy trains, which they exported to the United States. We had looked together at the pictures he had taken of his ocean crossings, with high waves crashing down on the ship. To my delight he had enacted, how the passengers got seasick one after another, and we had laughed at his acting out the scene. My Dad was the hero, who never got seasick.

When I had asked how Mother and he had met, he told me, that he had been on a business trip from America to his firm in Nuremberg. He had a ticket to return to America on a new ship, which made its maiden voyage. But before it could leave Germany, the First World War broke out and this undid his plans. He had to remain in Nuremberg and later was drafted into the German Army. While strolling about the main street, Koenigstrasse, he saw Mother, a beautiful 18 year old girl with a natural sort of elegance, which was one of her traits till the end. He followed her, and although he was ten years her senior, they fell in love.

"Koenigstrasse!" I had exclaimed, "That is where our store is located here in Berlin!"

"Yes, both streets have a special meaning to us. When I got drafted into the army of Kaiser Wilhelm, I was very unhappy. You know what I think of the military. I never had to shoot a human being. Instead I got Rheumatic fever and ended up in a wheel chair."

"Oh Daddy, did that hurt?" I asked with compassion.

"Yes, it did at the time. But I got well again – and today my conscience does not hurt."

"Now you be a good girl and take care of Mother!" Father bends down to me and gives me a parting kiss. Then my parents fall into each other's arms for a long, final kiss. With an effort he tears himself away, turns around, takes his suitcases and enters the waiting train. I see him again as he pushes down a window. Suddenly I realize, my Daddy is going away!

I had never been separated from him before, only during vacation. His face mirrors conflicting emotions. As he looks down at me he smiles. "See you soon!" He tries to keep his voice even. The whistle of the conductor cuts through the air and the train starts moving. I run beside it waving, till I no longer see his white handkerchief. I hold on to mother's hand. She is crying.

"Please don't cry, Mommy," I try to console her, "we will soon be together again."

7

❧

Through our shop windows I can see what is going on in the busy Koenigstrasse. I stand in the large display window to decorate it. This is what I like to do best, next to selling. I enjoy draping silky nightgowns in pleasing lines and displaying other pretty lingerie to make a nice picture, or stack linens and towels in the other two windows. Finally I put the hand-printed price signs next to it and went outside to view my creation from the view of a passer-by. The store has always been the center of our lives. I grew up in this shop. Often, when my nanny and I came to visit and my naptime arrived, Mother would pull out one of the large light green wooden drawers in which linens were stored. She put a blanket down and I would crawl into it and she would push the drawer halfway shut, leaving a space for fresh air. While customers came and went, I slept in my comfortable little nest.

As I grew tall enough to look over the counter, I started helping to sell. I fetched things for Mother and the two sales girls. The imposing metal cash register held a special attraction to me. I used an unattended moment to push down as many of the buttons that I could reach, which resulted in deadlocking the mechanism. Other comic incidents were told to me later, like the time when during the Christmas rush, no one was watching me. Mother had to change some money across the street in the main Post Office building. As she returned, she saw a group of people flocking around our large window. She looked over their heads to see me, stretched out like a diva among the lingerie, watching the smiling people watching me, and obviously enjoying their attention.

Koenigstrasse was the main thoroughfare in the center of Berlin. It ran from the king's castle to Alexanderplatz, one of the busiest squares of the city. It was filled with double deck busses, streetcars, taxis, horse drawn wagons, trucks, cars, and bicycles. Traffic passed the red brick city hall with its eighty-seven meters high square tower and its widely visible tower clock, one of the landmarks of Berlin. The building, trying to achieve a certain lightness of Italian renaissance style, could not deny its massive red brick construction. It consisted of three rows of windows on either side, symmetrically arranged around a large center entrance. City hall wanted to be an expression of a young and growing world-open city, a center of high culture. Yet it could not hide its Prussian earnestness and strictness, even in this presumptuous architecture. Built to impress, it looked solid and sturdy, an expression of its citizens, who embraced it with a certain pride and a kind of familiarity that is characteristic of Berliners, who are known for their dry humor. They gave strange nicknames to some public buildings, like 'Pregnant Oyster' to a congress hall, which was built after the war. From far off the eyes now had a goal, a center of attraction, giving order and direction to the avenues and roads, two seemingly important elementary requirements for a city dweller.

Soon I will be done decorating. I must get a few more price signs. I jump into the store. The door opens and a stooped old man enters and remains standing there without a word. I know what I have to do. I go to the cash register, take out some change and hand it to the beggar with a friendly smile. He bows gratefully and leaves again. I have learned this from Mother. No beggar is ever sent away empty. Mother's motto is: If you give, do not let your right hand know what the left hand is doing. Do not be calculating when you give or deal with a needy person. This is her general attitude when she deals with people. She has an open heart for everyone and an unconditional love, that believes everything, bears everything, gives everything.

Sometimes, I get upset with her and say,

"Don't you see that these people just use you? They steal your time with their sob stories and expect money from you."

But she only smiles. That is the way she is, full of love, especially for the disadvantaged. No wonder that so many of them come to her, using the purchase of a pair of stockings to pour out their heart for hours. In spite of her fighting, revolutionary spirit and next to her sound business sense, with which she enables a comfortable life for her family, she remains a person of emotions. Some of these emotions I have inherited, but even more of Dad's rational thinking. He, the great critical analyst, the dreamer and eternal inventor, who owns several patents, the pessimistic citizen of this world, whose utopian idealism rejects anything unjust, inadequate, or contemptible, has left his imprint on my life. He knows everything that is happening in the world. His political interest gets nourished by foreign newspapers he read daily during his coffee break at Café Wien at Kurfuerstendamm.

He recognized early in what direction Germany was heading. But Mother knows about his inability to pragmatic thought and action. He lives in his dreams, often ignoring reality. That is one of the reasons she hesitated to leave a secure home and business, and to come to a new country whose language she does not speak well. Her beloved husband should prove himself, after that we would follow. He had really tried to get into his profession but his age was against him. What she had feared had become reality – and we are still waiting. It has been three years now.

The absence of my father had created a great gap in our little harmonious family, but the bond between Mother and me has grown stronger. We cling to each other and provide comfort and support to each other. The past years have seen a change in her and this change had its far reaching consequences even in my life. When she returns at night from a day at the store, she is exhausted and soon goes to bed. She sits propped up with a book in her hands with strange sounding titles. One that she studies slowly and underlines in pencil has the name 'Meditation". The other has the title 'The Great Initiates'. They are books by Rudolf Steiner, the founder of the Anthroposophical Society. Little Aunt Martha had invited her to lectures, and soon Mother joined by becoming a member of the Anthroposophical Church, Christengemeinschaft.

One evening in December of 1938 she takes me after work to the study of a tall, serious man, who holds out his hand in greeting like a defensive weapon. He reminds me of a drawing by Albrecht Duerer and is a priest in Mother's church. On the way there, Mother had explained to me, that she bore the sole responsibility for raising me now, and since the synagogues had been destroyed and I no longer had a place to worship and she had found a way back to her faith, she wanted me to accompany her on Sundays. I was at the age to start confirmation classes and the prerequisite was that I would have to be baptized.

When she sees doubts mirrored in my face, she tells me how she had come to embrace the Jewish faith. When the two lovers wanted to get married, Dad's parents did not consent because she was a Christian. They were not practicing Jews. Dad never went to the synagogue except on Holy Days. Yet it was generally not acceptable to marry outside the faith. That forced my parents to live for many years in a so-called 'wild marriage', a concubinage. Finally, when they saw that they could not prevail, the family relented, under the condition, that Mother would convert to Judaism. It had never been a heart decision on her part, and now she had returned to her roots. I still have my doubts, but to a twelve-year old girl, Mother's advice seems to be right.

It is a small group that assembles to witness my Anthroposophical baptism. There is the priest, still more remote in his flowing robe and multicolored surplice, reminding me of a being from another world. Then there are my two godmothers, the little and the big Aunt Martha, who from now on would be responsible for my souls' well being. With words that I do not understand, he puts water, ash and salt on my forehead and prays over me. I go through the whole procedure with some curiosity and interest, but no inner participation. Following the ceremony there is a short celebration and my godmother takes a picture of me with my box camera. I wear a white satin dress, which I had designed and made a sketch of, something that I have done since I was seven and which Mother's friend has sewn according to my wishes with material from our store.

Little Aunt Martha I have known since childhood. Her deceased husband had been Dad's friend and former colleague. She has a distinctive way of speaking, more like a singsong voice and has a waddling walk due to a hip ailment. Big Aunt Martha has a strong personality. She is a fearless, active woman, a spinster, sales representative, whom Mother had met through her work. It was her courageous resistance that saved our store from being looted after 'Crystal Night', although the windows had been smashed. She sees in me the fatherless child that needs her protection. She is a member of the Christian Science church in Berlin and supplies me with youth books from her church..

Not much has changed for me through this act. But there has been a change in the attitude of my friends. I first notice it as I play ball one afternoon with some girls. One of them throws the ball to me with the question:

"I have heard that you are no longer a Jew. What are you then?"

Confused I stand there with the ball in my hands and answer somewhat defensively,

"I still believe in God as always." But this answer does not satisfy her.

"But don't you believe in Jesus, too?" she presses on. I seek for words to give a right answer, but I muddle my way through, yet find no convincing explanation. I feel an invisible wall rising, behind which my Jewish friends withdraw with unspoken accusations in their eyes. Although they know as much as nothing about the Christian religion, only that Jesus falsely claimed to be the Messiah, according to their Rabbis, they believe that to turn from Judaism is the same as treason committed against one's country. They still play with me, but I have become an outsider, I no longer belong to them.

Yes, I believe in God. As far as I can remember he has always been there. Mother has taught me to pray upon awakening and before going to sleep at night.

"We don't know the word fear", she had said when I begged her to leave the light on. "God is always with you to protect you, so there is no need to fear." I know that he accompanies me to my school and I can ask him to help me with an unexpected math test or in gymnastic class. Once, when we had to jump from the wall bars,

I fell on my back and buttocks and had the wind taken out of me. It hurt terribly. The teacher called,

"Try again!"

"Please, dear God, help me!" I shot a prayer towards heaven, and he gave me courage to jump again in spite of the pain. But God is also able to punish you. Some times after I had been naughty or said something bad or lied, I fell and skinned my knee or got a bruise somewhere. At least I know, that God can read my thoughts and can see into my heart.

In my early years Aunt Hanna, the oldest of Dad's three sisters and the only practicing Jewess, took an active part in my religious education. She was the wife of a medical doctor, who had died young and had left her a young widow with two small children. She owned a tall and spacious apartment building with front and back entrances in Passauer Strasse, close to the famous KDW department store. Aunt Hanna was the center of the family.

As a doctor's wife she could tell many horrible stories of what had happened to little girls, who had climbed on chairs near a window or who had played with sharp scissors. Terrible things happened to careless and disobedient children. My visits were accompanied by commands like

"Don't climb on that chair or lean over the balcony rail! Do not run or else you will fall down the stairs and break a leg! Hold on to my hand when we walk outside on the side walk," and many more such commands. Outwardly I was the good child, well mannered and obedient, but inwardly I laughed about her worried words and sometimes I challenged her by climbing on the leather chair near the window and looking down into the back courtyard. Under the cover of an obedient child hid often a fresh little imp, that enjoyed scaring fearful people. Mother had done her best to raise me as an independent and fear free person and now I made fun of those who, for good reasons, were fearful.

But I loved my Aunt Hanna. She showed me her large art books, she let me play on her piano, trying to find the right keys for songs that I knew, and once in a while she allowed me, under her supervision, to type on her big black typewriter. On city excursions, she took me along to museums and art galleries. Those trips ended often in a café, where I always ordered a Mohrenkopf and a cup of hot chocolate. Friday evenings we walked to her synagogue, where the women had to sit on the gallery, which I was not used to, as in my synagogue, men and women sat on either side of the ground floor. On the way home, she made an effort to explain to me in childlike words, what the Rabbi had said.

But what I anticipated most, were our visits to the famous Berlin zoo. Days beforehand I started to collect pea shells and greens, old bread and fruit peelings to take to the animals. With my bag of food in hand, we first went to the children's zoo, where one could pet the baby animals, which was a lot of fun, till one day a haughty looking llama spit in my face and I hurriedly ran to my Aunt, who wiped my face carefully with her lace handkerchief. But the absolute high light was a ride on the back of an old elephant. Children sat tied down in little seats on either side of the animal's back and swayed with every step the huge mammal took on its slow walk through a part of the spread out zoo. Down again from the dizzying height, I hurried Aunt Hanna to my favorite chimpanzee cages, where the clever animals performed tricks for the visitors, like riding little bikes or sitting on small chairs and eating at a table. I could never get enough of them, whereas I did not like the open area where the noisy baboons with their red buttocks cavorted on rocks and fought each other with shrill screams.

Animals held a special attraction to me who never had a pet. Only after Dad had left, and it seemed that we would not be able to join him in the near future, Mother allowed me to get a puppy dog, our Dolly, who became my best playmate. Sometimes Aunt Hanna visited her cousin in Treptow, in the Northern section of Berlin. After a long subway ride we walked to their house, where old Aunt Jenny and her unmarried son Max and his spinster sister Alice lived. On her nose balanced a gold-rimmed pince-nez, a pair of glasses that wiggled when she spoke. For a young child the conversation of these older people became so boring, that I still remember it. The only ray of hope at these monotonous visits was a fat brown guinea pig sitting on some hay in a box. I was not allowed to play with it, but watching it helped while the time away till we finally left again.

Most of the family gatherings, the special holidays and birthdays that I remember, took place at Aunt Hanna's house. Of the religious holidays I liked the Passover feast best. I 'helped' with the preparations for the festive evening that Aunt Hanna started days in advance. Setting the long pulled out table for the whole family for the Seder evening, I was careful to put silver ware and napkins just right in front of each chair. When all had gathered and sat around the table, I loved to follow the story of the exodus of the children of Israel from bondage in Egypt. As the youngest member of the family, it was my part during the reading of the story in Hebrew to ask the age-old question: ' Why is this night different from other nights?' Many times I had recited the few sentences in Hebrew till I knew the 'Mane stanu' by heart. I had Hebrew lessons in school, when the other children had their Christian religion classes.

My new Haggada, the book of the story of the exodus, was on the table before me, while the men read and sang the old Hebrew texts. My new book had pictures that could be pulled and moved. According to the story, I moved the persons concerned by pulling down and thus bringing them to life. I ate some of the bitter herbs, the sharp horse-reddish that bit into my nose, to remember the hardships of being slaves. This was followed by a glass bowl of shredded apples, raisins and honey. On other plates were symbols of bondage, an egg, a dry bone. Then the first of three layers of matzos, the unleavened bread, was uncovered of its white napkin and passed around. I broke off a piece and ate the tasteless bread, crackling between my teeth. When the dramatic part came, where Pharao and his troops disappeared in the water of the Red Sea, I pulled like mad on my pictures with a gloating joy of drowning horse and rider, who were trying to force the Israelites back into servitude.

After the happy melodies of the Psalms had subsided, which all joined in singing, and before the wonderful dinner, which Aunt Hanna had prepared, was carried in from the kitchen, the most exciting moment of the evening came. My uncle stood up and opened the door of the dining room. I looked at the empty plate setting at the table, which was reserved for the prophet Elijah. Perhaps this year he would show up! I held my breath – but no one entered the room and my uncle sat down again. Disappointed I turned to the soup on my plate.

"The prophet Elijah," Aunt Hanna had explained to me, "will come before the Messiah arrives. God has promised in the Torah, that he would send the Messiah and we are still waiting for him. When he comes, he will bring peace to the world." Well, perhaps next year. With this greeting one took leave of each other. "Next year in Jerusalem."

8

All of this seems so far away now. Only once in a while I am reminded of it. It is Saturday afternoon. I am home alone. Mother told me to do chores, vacuum, dust, clean the floor in the kitchen. I hate to do that, for one can see every spot on the linoleum.

"Then you can bake a cake, for Big Aunt Martha is coming over Sunday afternoon." I like baking cakes. As I stir butter, sugar and eggs, my thoughts wander back to the Saturday afternoon, six months ago.

My chores are the same. While I dust and vacuum, the big radio of Dad's is playing music. Suddenly I hear the soprano voice of the famous singer, Erna Sack. She sings coloratura arias and her cadences rise effortless to high C. I turn off the vacuum cleaner to listen. As her voice climbs in unheard heights, I remember having seen a poster announcing a concert by her in Berlin.

Would not Mother be happy if I surprised her with two tickets? The thought will not go away. If I leave right now I could take the train to Zoo station and be back in time for the cake to be baked. Quickly I leave the house. Impatiently I stand in line for tickets. Precious time passes. Then I see that the person at the head of the queue turns around and the people standing in line disperse. Sold out! All for nothing! Annoyed by the waste of time I take the train back. Now I will have to rush, if I want to be ready before Mother comes home. Hurriedly I walk the ten minutes from the station to our house. It had not been such a good idea, after all. I won't tell Mother about it.

I open our door. Behind me I hear the neighbor's door open. I turn around. She looks at me like she has seen a ghost.

"Where have you been?" she gasps with eyes wide open.

"I? I just was in town for an errand. Why?"

"They left just five minutes ago!"

"Who left?"

"A truck stopped, then two SS-men came to the house. They rang your bell and when no one opened they rang mine. They asked me if I knew where you were. I said I did not know. They wanted to pick you up and take you some place, I don't know."

I knew the place, the concentration camp! When I closed the door behind me, I began to tremble and shake. At first one is numb, as if a leg had just been severed, but one does not feel anything or is aware of the loss till the body's own anesthesia wears off and one realizes, how close to death one is.

The shock did not wear off till Mother arrived from the store. Only when I tell her what had taken place, the dam breaks and crying I flee into Mother's arms.

"Yolchen," she says stroking my hair, "God has had his hand on you. He has protected you in the moment of greatest danger by taking you out of the house and bringing you back, when the danger was past. Now let us thank him for it." She presses me close to her. Somehow, I feel reassured. God had his hand on me this time. Would he do it again?

Beginning with this day everything changes. In spite of Mother's efforts, fear has come into our lives. Yet deep inside I have a conviction, which cannot be expressed in words. Whatsoever might happen to me, I stand under God's protection.

When you are fifteen and for the first time in love, one is transformed into a fairytale princess. Every thought turns around the prince. How can I look more beautiful to please him more? I am going to try a new hairdo, instead of the old boring bob. In the bathroom is the curling iron, which can be heated over an open flame. When it is hot, one can change straight hair into a beautiful curly head of hair. When I was thirteen years old I almost burned the whole house down. I felt that the burner was too slow to heat the curling iron, so I poured fresh methylated spirit into the open flame. Suddenly a jet of flame shot up into the air, singeing my hair and setting on fire the nearby curtains. I raced next door to the caretaker's apartment and he came running in, took the hand shower over the bathtub and doused the spreading flames. I was truly a 'burnt child'.

Critically I observe my reflection in the mirror. I really like the curls around my face. Would Gerhard like them also? But what would Mother say when she comes home? I will set the supper table and start the water for our tea. Now, when the evenings are getting cooler, we change from cold drinks to hot tea with our sandwiches. Wistfully I think of the fleeting summer days that bring with them the inevitable end of sailing. September seems to be the last month that allows water sports. After that time it is getting too cold. That would be the end of our opportunity to see each other. Well, who knows? Why allow these sad thoughts?

Dolly runs to the door, a sign of Mother's arrival. I open the door for her, before she puts the key into the lock. Expectantly I stand in front of her with my splendid curls. But she passes me without seeing, does not even notice my new appearance. She walks into the bathroom and then comes out and sits down at the supper table without speaking one word.

"What is the matter?" I ask, feeling fear climbing up, "did something happen?"

Mother looks at me sadly.

"Yolchen," she says with an effort, "I must tell you something. Something bad, so be strong." Then she stops while my heart begins to race. She raises herself from her bent position and tries again. Then she pulls a piece of yellow material from her pocket and puts it down on the table. Between platters of sausage and cheeses lies the yellow thing. I see a Star of David, on it in Hebrew -like letters the word 'JEW'.

"What does that mean?" I cry horrified, "What has that to do with me?"

My hands are shaking, while I hear Mother's explanation through a fog of whirling thoughts.

"A new devilish idea will become law on the first of September 1941, stigmatizing all Jews in public. From now on they must wear a yellow star to be marked everywhere as Jews. And since you fall under the Nuremberg race laws, you must wear this star also."

I jump up from the table.

"Never will I wear that!" I shout with flaming eyes, "Not even you will be able to force me to do that! I will not be so humiliated!"

Mother gets up, runs after me, trying to calm me. She has expected this reaction.

"But Yolchen," she says, "There is no other way, you must submit, otherwise..."

Tears flow down my cheeks.

"No, never, never will I sew on this Jewish star!" I throw the yellow piece of material down on the floor and stomp on it. "I will not be marked like a leper! That would be an invitation for everyone to do with me whatever they please."

Mother tries to regain her composure.

"There is nothing else you can do; it is a law, another devilish way of persecuting innocent victims. But there is no use to rebel against it."

"It's easy for you to say!" I scream in her face, "You don't have to wear this thing!"

Mother bends over to pick up the star. She walks to the closet to get my overcoat. I run after her, holding back her arm.

"I hate you! I hate you!" I cry while trying to wrestle the star from her hand. "Why did you have to marry a Jew and make me suffer like that?"

Sobbing I run into Dad's room and throw myself on his couch, hiding my face in the pillows. Dad – whom I love, and whom I want to get rid of.

Mother won't be stopped. She follows me, caresses my shoulders. I push her away. Mother – whom I love but whom I fight fiercely..

Alone – left alone – at the mercy of every evil person – the feeling is unbearable. Never could I walk among people marked like that, drawing all eyes on myself, hateful, sneering, spiteful eyes rejecting me. I, who already get red in the face if somebody looks at me longer than necessary, should be the target, yes even invite people to treat me as a castaway!. My body shakes with sobs.

Mother sits down next me. She is at her wits end. Her words of comfort I will not listen to. They do not reach me. I have given myself over to pain and am snapping at her hand like a wounded animal.

"Yolchen," she tries again. I feel her face next to my tear-stained cheeks. "I have a suggestion. Your overcoat has these wide lapels. If we sew the star under the lapel, you can button it at the neck if you have to show it. But when you open the button, it disappears under the lapel and nobody sees it. Let us do it that way, shall we?" She rises to get her sewing kit. I am too exhausted to defend myself. Slowly the sobbing stops, but I remain as I am. I feel burnt out.

This awful injustice, this inhuman treatment will not be the last thing in a chain of mean measures of persecution. What else will they come up with next out of their devilish brains? What makes this whole situation even harder for me is the fact, that I have begun to feel and think like a Christian. During the years of preparation for confirmation, I have become acquainted with Jesus and what he said and did. He is no longer the nebulous figure he had been at my baptism, but in him I meet the God of the Old Testament in a personal human form. He mirrors the way God is, his being and character, and shows me by example that God loves me as a Father loves his children.. Jesus' program, announced in the Sermon on the Mount, has become the standard of living by which I judge my actions and thoughts. But now this fledgling faith is going to be put to the test. Will it pass?

9

❧

The shrill sound of the air raid siren jars me out of my dreams. The British are on another bombing mission of the city of Berlin. Sleepily I get dressed while I can see outside the long arms of floodlights searching the dark sky and the sound of anti-aircraft fire from the distance. I take my small packed suitcase and follow Mother, who is waiting already by the door. She also carries her suitcase. While we descend the stairs to the air raid shelter in the cellar of our apartment house, we hear how the gunfire gets louder. We are the last in the cellar. The other neighbors are already sitting on the hard benches along the walls of the makeshift bunker. We take two seats next to each other by the door.

Suddenly a sharp voice cuts through the silence. The man lives with his wife and two children on the third floor. He sits across from us and looks at me with piercing hateful eyes, but his words are addressed to everybody.

"I cannot sit in the same cellar with a Jewess. Either she or I will have to leave!"

His words cut into my heart and I feel naked as all eyes turn in my direction. Curious, unsympathetic eyes. What will happen next? Without a word Mother rises, takes my hand, pulls me outside. I follow her, carrying my little suitcase. The door falls shut behind us. Accompanied by the noise of exploding bombs and gunfire, we walk up the steps to our apartment. Very slowly can I breathe freely once more.

Every day, when I leave the house, I have to pass the broad side of the building. In one of the glass-enclosed balconies sits an observer, who registers every person coming and going. There is no other way to the street. The watchful eyes of the spy follow me, though I never look up. On my coat I wear the yellow star. When I have turned the corner, I put my satchel over my chest, so the star is covered. When I am in the train and see no familiar face, I unbutton my coat and hide the star under the lapel. In the anonymous big city and the rush of traffic a young girl is not as conspicuous, so I tell myself. But when I get close to my school, I hold up my satchel again. It is a dangerous compromise. My schoolmates also have to wear the star. Erika had to move to a small place with her parents, but she does not complain. But her blue eyes have lost their luster. She is not the only one. We all have to bear the same burden, to be excluded from a society that not only despises us, yet threatens to get rid of us completely.

More and more the truth spreads of what is really happening. Often one can see it with one's own eyes. The later excuses, 'we did not know what was going on' are hollow and self-protecting excuses. Mother tells me to bring some lingerie to Little Aunt Martha's store in Augsburger Strasse. Only Mother and I know, that she is hiding a Jewish seamstress, who sews for her and whom she gives shelter and food. Yet not even we know where she is hiding her. After I deliver the goods, I start my way back to our store. The button of my coat is open to hide the star. In front of an apartment house entry a group of people are gathered, looking curiously in the direction of the open door. On the street a flatbed truck is parked. My heart beats fast and I am gripped by fear, but I decide to stop.

Suddenly I hear the metallic sound of nailed boots coming down the stairs. Two men in uniform push a young family ahead of them to the waiting truck. Over the heads of the spectators I see a pale young woman with a baby in one arm, a suitcase on the other, followed by her husband, also carrying a suitcase. With the other hand he is dragging a boy of about three, who fearfully clings to his father's hand. His small legs try to keep up with the hurrying adults. The heads of the parents are bowed down, but I can see the fear in the dark eyes of the child.

"What is there to see? Keep going, don't stop!" the uniformed men command the bystanders in a rough tone of voice and slowly the people disperse, looking back over their shoulders curiously so as not to miss anything exciting. They observe how the four of them are roughly pushed onto the waiting truck and the uniformed men enter the cab next to the driver. The truck slowly starts. This is going on in broad daylight. I want to scream, "Don't you see what they are doing to these people? They are going to kill them all, even the child and the baby! Don't just stand there and gawk! Do not allow them to do this!" But silently and equally powerless, than those that have witnessed this human tragedy, I continue on my way like the others, with helpless rage against the cruelty and injustice of a regime of inhuman monsters, gorging themselves on the flesh of human sacrifices

Not only Reinhold is in the army, now Gerhard has been called for the pre-military Arbeitsdienst (Labor Service) for young men under eighteen. He calls me with the news. No longer can we see each other, it is too dangerous. Now the phone is our only means of contact. He writes letters, telling me about his work and how he is coping. Once he calls me to tell me he is passing through Berlin and wants to see me between trains.

"But Gerhard," I hesitate.

"Couldn't we see each other just for a few minutes? How would the subway stop Westend be? I just have to see you!" His voice sounds urgent.

"All right then, but only very briefly!"

"I will be there in about half an hour! I love you!"

My hands tremble as I lay down the receiver. We have not seen each other for several months now. I change clothes hurriedly and walk to the station. I am wearing another jacket with wide lapels, hiding the star as I stand there waiting in the recessed entrance of an apartment house. There, suddenly I can see him! He comes bounding up the steps, looks around and sees me. A few more steps and we are in each other's arms. I pull him back where nobody can observe us and look at him. He has changed; his face looks different, more grown up.

"Aren't you glad to see me?" he asks questioningly, looking into my eyes. "I could not wait to get here to see you. I just had to come, even if it is only for a few moments. I miss you so!"

"I miss you too!"

But something is different. I had so anticipated this unexpected meeting. But now there seems to be an invisible barrier between us, which I seemingly cannot overcome. He looks at me and I see disappointment in his eyes.

"What is the matter, you seem so reserved?"

I see how his eyes anxiously focus on my face. His reddish hair shows from under his cap. Here is my beloved Gerhard. But the uniform, the boots and the leather belt with the hated swastika on the buckle push a barrier between us.

"You look so....different....with the uniform," is all I can say, "older, more grown up. I don't know."

"Uh, forget about that. We only have these few minutes. Every night I dream of you." He pulls my face up to his and kisses me. But it is not the same thing and he can feel my inner resistance. He stops kissing me.

"Don't you love me anymore?"

"Of course I love you! I am just afraid that someone could watch us. I am always under this pressure – always fearful of people. And then the time is so short. You must leave again." I try to find believable explanations, but it is the uniform, the hated symbol of the swastika that divides us, more than space and time could ever do. His voice sounds unhappy.

"I must catch my train. Promise you will write me?" I nod.

"Remember, I love you!"

"And I love you!" He walks down the steps and turns his head. I smile. But in my heart there is anger. Anger and disappointment, growing out of the knowledge, that we stand on opposite sides, not of our own making, but because of a cruel regime, which enjoys making innocent dreams of happiness impossible. As I walk home I feel very much alone.

10

At the end of January I celebrate my sixteenth birthday. Sweet sixteen! What mockery! Mother lives in constant fear for me. Will they pick me up too? We have not heard anything from Dad for a long time. His last letter sounded hopeful. Soon he would have enough money for our affidavit and then we could leave within a few weeks. But this bubble bursts in a hurry, when the United States declares war on Germany, following the bombing of the American fleet by Japanese bombers at Pearl Harbor on December 7, 1941. Our hopes of leaving Germany are dashed.

Our little school, which had been the only place where we could be children and forget briefly the hostile world around us, does not exist any more. The Gestapo has closed this little harbor of relative safety. The courageous Pastor Grueber has been deported to a concentration camp, in part for allowing Christian Jews to attend his congregation and openly confirming children wearing the Jewish star. He also preached the truth without compromise, which was the worst you could do in the eyes of the Nazis.

Our class was cut short before reaching the end of 10th grade, which is called Mittlere Reife. Our teacher, Frau Dr. Landsberg, wanted us to have this diploma at least. So a couple of the teachers rented a flat in Kalckreuthstrasse to enable us to finish our education. We were twelve children. Every morning we came one by one to this apartment house with our satchel pressed over our chest to cover the star. Then after school we left one by one in order not to rouse suspicions. During recess we remained in the classroom. The teacher prohibited loud laughter or rough play, for no sign of our presence should reach the surrounding apartments. We have become masters in hiding and ducking.

Two of our group, the Kutscheras, a brother and sister, did not make it to the diploma. They were deported before the end of the class. By now it is common knowledge, that the so-called work camps in Poland and other places are in reality camps of destruction, in which people were tortured, starved, and killed.

The Gestapo also closed the Christengemeinschaft, the Anthroposophical society and its church. One day Mother received one of the feared orders to appear before the Gestapo at Alexanderplatz, accompanied by her daughter. This was an ominous sign that we were being watched. Often, when talking on the phone, I had heard the sound of someone tapping our conversation and listening in. Mother had observed the same man waiting at the station when she came home, and she had seen him at other places too. If we feared anybody more than the SS men, it was the Gestapo. And now we were called into the lions' den. I could not sleep the night before, imagining all kinds of terrible things that I had heard they were doing to innocent victims. But you had to follow their orders or that would be the end of you.

We are sitting on a bench in a long hallway, waiting to be admitted. I hardly dare breathe. The atmosphere is dark and threatening. My heart is in my throat. I feel like an animal led to slaughter. Finally we sit across a desk from a man, who looks at us with steely eyes, then reads something from a folder before him. While he fixes his eyes on Mother, he speaks in an emotionless staccato voice.

"If you think you can make a fool of us, you are mistaken. We know all about you and your tactics. Our patience is running out. If you do not finally divorce your husband, there will be dire consequences."

His voice is threatening as he looks over at me.

"You and your daughter will be taken to a concentration camp. Do you want that?"

I don't remember how we got out of the building. As we face the heavy traffic swirling around Alexanderplatz, I look at Mother's face. It is white, yet there is an expression of determination, a set jaw and a head held high. This fighter will not be forced into going against her faith and her convictions. Even the Gestapo threat is not able to change her mind. She is going to stay faithful to her husband, no matter what happens. What a strong person my mother is! I secretly admire her courage.

Friends and my godmothers, upon hearing the story, try to advise Mother, how to defuse this threat at least for the time being. Her lawyer will make an effort to contact Dad, but due to the war, this will not be possible. Mother is trying to gain time. In regard to my safety, she will file a petition of mercy (Gnadengesuch) a plea to have my status changed from Jewish Mischling to Arian Mischling, to save me from the threatened deportation. Listening to their plans I feel like a dog that has lost its master. Of course not a purebred dog, but a bastard, evading with pulled in tail the kicking feet of dog-hating people, straying through the streets, trying to stay ahead of the feared dogcatcher.

After some time passes, Mother sets out for a personal visit to the Ministry of the Interior. She wants to inquire about her petition. She wears her nice fur coat, but returns in her wool suit. She 'forgot' her coat and left it hanging there. Another time she returns without her diamond ring. She is buying precious time for me. The official in charge of these petitions of mercy, hoping for more valuables, assures her, that as long as the petition is pending, I would have a special status, being neither Jew nor Arian, a strange kind of legal neuter, which does not really exist according to the Nuremberg law. But what is the law to one who is greedy for bribes? It is only a word of mouth by a corrupt official, but to me it is a ray of hope, however fragile or deceptive.

With sixteen and a half my life has come to an end. After the 10th grade diploma I have reached the end of my higher education. There is no possibility to continue to study nor is there any profession which I could learn. Briefly stated I have no future. But I am young, full of dreams and hopes and I would love to study and grow. I want to discover art and music, read books, meet interesting people, love. But there remain only thwarted hopes, dashed plans and longings for love and growing impatience.

I pressure Mother to push my mercy petition to a favorable decision. But she hesitates, knowing quite well, how difficult the situation could become.

"Leave it as it is right now," she tries to curb my impatience. But with each unfulfilled day I get more tired of waiting.

"Something just has to be done", I insist. "If you don't want to do it, then just let me go there and ask." She does not stop me.

Again I sit in a long hallway and wait before an office with the sign 'Mischling affairs." It is not the same room Mother used to go to. She told me to go through the official way. I rehearse the words in my head that I am going to say, while my heart beats in my throat. The door opens and a man exits and turns down the hallway. "Next!" I hear a gruff voice. I jump up and enter the room, greeting the official behind the desk courteously. Then I start my rehearsed little speech with the necessary humility and politeness. Suddenly I see the face in front of me changing to red, the veins on the forehead become visible and through squinted eyes cascades of hateful words crash down on me like whip lashes. I am not prepared for this treatment; it is as if the floor beneath me starts shaking, taking my breath away.

"You riff-raff, you hoodlums! You all belong in the work camps, you pigs!" the man shouts.

I turn on my heels, fling the door open and run down the halls, through the marble entrance out to the street. I keep running, faster and faster while the shrill word 'work camp' resounds in my ears. Finally I turn the corner and slow down. I am out of breath and feel so degraded, as if someone had raped me. To be scum of the earth and whipping boy, that is my lot – that is my future. To finally be killed in a concentration camp will be my end. There is no use trying to fight it.

11

⌒◦⌒

"Pack your bag and take a few books along," Mother tells me as she comes home.

"You have to leave for some time. You will go to Little Aunt Martha's place."

"But why?" I ask reluctantly.

"The friendly police man, whose wife is my customer, came to the store just before I left and warned me to hide you, because a new action is planned." Action is the harmless code word for the rounding up and deportation of all Jews in one section of the city.

Aunt Martha lives in an art nouveau building in Regensburger Strasse. She has a large apartment, and because her two sons have moved out, she was forced to take in renters, who occupy several rooms and share kitchen and bath. More and more people are homeless through the bombing raids, so the others have to share their living space with them. I must not arrive before the renters have left for work. She opens the door for me and shows me into the one room behind the living room, which her son had occupied.

"I have to go to work now," she explains. "There is something to eat in the kitchen. Use the bathroom before the renters come back. Stay away from the windows, you must be completely invisible. The renters return before me. I will make you something warm to eat when I come back tonight." I hear how the entrance door is being locked. I am alone.

Carefully I explore my 'prison'. I decide to remain in the son's room, for the living room curtains cannot be completely closed. Somebody from the opposite building could perhaps see me. I must be 'invisible'. As I ponder this condition, which means that as a person I have ceased to exist, I find that it deftly describes my situation.

I take out a book from my bag and begin to read. But my thoughts cannot concentrate. They roam about like scared chickens, running in different directions. I imagine what is happening outside at this very hour. Heavy boots stomping up staircases, then loud, commanding voices and knocking: "Open the door immediately!" Frightened huddled people being herded like so many cattle down into the street and onto the waiting trucks, as I had witnessed just recently. Voices of crying children are in my ears though everything around me is quiet.

Again and again I tell myself to be grateful that I can be here, when the hours and minutes of the long days and nights crawl by, while I am just waiting, waiting, waiting.

I am lonely, deserted, in my invisible state. Only when Aunt Martha comes home in the evening do I have a companion to talk to. How terrible and cruel it must be to be in solitary confinement, deprived of any human contact. I had read of people, who had been tortured that way for long periods of time. Some had breakdowns. Humans are social by nature and need other humans, or perhaps even a pet could help me by sharing this time all by myself.

Finally, after several days of confinement the hour of liberation arrives. I remember the story by Franz Kafka, where he turns into a bug, a loathsome insect. I know that the fumigators have done their job with Prussian thoroughness. The vermin has been exterminated. But as I climb out of my crevice into the fresh air and day light, I am grateful to still be alive.

Mother is getting more depressed. Constant fears for my safety prey upon her nerves. She debates with friends whether she should allow me to get out of Germany on a children's transport, arranged by the Quakers for Jewish children to go to England. But then she decides against it. She can and will not be separated from me during this war, where nobody knows when and how it will end. Again she goes to the Ministry of Interior and returns without her gold watch, but with the happy news that the official assured her, that nothing would happen to me, until there has been a decision reached on my mercy petition. We cling to this promise made by word of mouth only.

"If I am neither Jewish nor Arian, then I don't need to wear this Jewish star any longer." I try to convince Mother and tear off the hated emblem from my jacket. But while doing it, I am stabbed by the thought of Erika and her parents. Since the end of our school time together we hardly ever see each other. She lives too far away. But I will invite her to my seventeenth birthday party.

Since the Gestapo closed down the Anthroposophical church, we attend services at the little Lutheran church in our neighborhood. The shepherd's eye of Pastor Guertler had noticed, that Sunday after Sunday this lady and her daughter attended his church, and with the first sound of the organ the lady would begin to weep silently. All the fear and desperation that had accumulated during the week, was released during the music of the old hymns. And what is my reaction? I sit next to her, waiting for her tears, and feel embarrassed. Why does she have to cry all the time? What will people think? Other people seem more important to me than the pain of my own mother. But the pastor comes up to her after the service and she pours out her heart to him. Now she has won a friend and ally. When I tell him that I love to sing and that earlier I had sung the Passion according to St. Luke together with Erika, he invites me to sing in the church choir.

I am reminded of a strange scene that takes on new meaning now. While we sing the four- part Bach chorale, I notice at one verse that Erika has stopped singing. I ask her afterwards why she did not sing that particular verse and she answers: "Because of the words 'I will sleep in my little chamber' meaning my coffin. I don't like the idea of worms eating up my body." Strange, I never gave it a thought, but perhaps Erika has a premonition.

I get to know the organist and choir director. He is like a fatherly friend to me and introduces me to the intricacies of Bach's compositions. He allows me to sit next to him on the organ bench and turn the pages for him. He points out a fugue that he plays normally at first and then mirror reversed. What a genius Bach was!

One afternoon he invites Mother and me for tea. We walk through his large rose garden with all kinds of different beautiful roses. He selects and clips one off. It is a pink rose bud. "This one is for you", he says and smiles as he gives it to me, "it reminds me of you." Then he leads us into his library filled to the ceiling on all sides with high shelves. As I look at the titles I cannot read them, they are in strange languages.

"Can you read all of these languages?" I ask in awe.

"Yes, that is my hobby to learn foreign languages. I am just starting on the 64th."

I can hardly believe what I hear.

"You mean you can read and understand and speak 64 languages?" I ask incredulously.

"Well, I don't get many opportunities to speak them, but I can read and understand them." A remarkable man!

My seventeenth birthday falls on a Sunday, the same weekday that I first saw the light of day. I was born at home on a Sunday noon, after two harrowing days and nights, as I was a breech birth. When I finally saw the light of day, all present thought I was dead, for I made no sounds. Only after the midwife had cleared my throat and lungs, did I let out my first cry to the delight of my relieved parents.. How fragile life is, depending on a few deep breaths, which make the difference between living a full life or dying a brief death. Everything that has breath, praise ye the Lord!

Although the choir does not sing today I climb up, and sit down next to my friend who is arranging the sheet music for the service. I smile at him

"Today is my birthday," I look at him, "Could you play something happy for me? I just turned seventeen today." "Congratulations," he says and takes my hand, but then he sadly shakes his head and answers quietly,

"I am sorry, I wish I could do this for you, but my heart is too heavy and sad. My son is in the embattled and enclosed Russian city of Stalingrad, fighting for his life and he might never get out alive."

I feel his pain and take his hand in mine.

"I will pray that he gets out." His eyes mirror the sad certainty that it is too late already. Slowly he concentrates on the music and begins to play the prelude.

I have invited Erika and Gerhard to my party in the afternoon. He had written me that he had a weekend pass on my birthday. I had begged Mother for a long time till she permitted Gerhard to come to our place, but without his uniform. Erika arrives first and we embrace each other after a long separation. She seems more grown up than I remember. Her slender body looks thin now. Her face with the large blue eyes is drawn. She straightens her hair with her slender fingers.

"Do you still play your violin?" I ask.

"Of course, I cannot give that up, although I had to give up my music lessons. But I practice all the time." Then she adds quietly, "as long as I can." The doorbell rings.

Gerhard arrives in a dark blue suit with white shirt and tie. He looks great and festive! I have never seen him dressed up. He hands me a blooming pink azalea. The flowers are beautiful. Erika gives me a book with which she has covered the star on the way. She turns to Gerhard.

"And how is our soldier today?" she asks.

"Most of the time I hate it, but right now I even enjoy it."

"How is this possible?" we ask almost in unison.

"I was ordered to decorate a wall of the officers' club and I am painting most of the time. This is what I really love to do."

While we eat cake, we reminisce about the lighthearted times on the water with our beloved 'Golden Hill'. How long ago it seems to us now, that we were free and easy, even happy and full of plans for the future. It was only one and a half years ago, but it seems like an eternity. How much has changed in the meantime. We inquire about our friends. Eric, the funny one, is battling the Russian winter, Reinhold, the older one, is in France fighting for the Fuehrer. Soon Gerhard will be sent to France also. Erika saddens me with the news, that another one of our former teachers has been deported. Again the dark present intrudes into our little group.

"What are you doing now by the way?" Erika looks at me, changing the topic.

"All I can do is to help Mother in the store, but I don't know how long this will be."

"Who knows that anyway?" she says. We are silent. We all know without mentioning it what kind of future is awaiting Erika and her parents. It is only a matter of time that they also will be deported. Erika had named Theresienstadt, known as a lesser of two evils because of the military background of her father.

"Can't you stay here with us?" I burst out, "we could hide you!"

"And what will happen to my parents?" It is unthinkable for her to leave them alone. "And anyway you yourself are still in a dangerous situation."

The afternoon passes too fast. It is getting dark outside.

"I must go home now," Erika gets up, "I have a long way to go."

We put on our coats while Mother makes a food package for Erika to take to her parents. She holds it up over the star, at least till she has passed the spy. I wonder what he thinks about me, going in and out now without a star? Who knows if he has not reported me?

We walk together to the Westend Subway station. The January cold cuts into our faces.

Erika walks between us. My heart gets heavier with every step. Is there no other possibility to flee from the coming destruction? How can I allow my best friend, who stands at the threshold of life, to be killed in the horrors of a concentration camp? She, whose goal in life is to make beautiful music for people to enjoy. It cannot – it must not be!

Yet I feel as helpless and paralyzed as the proverbial rabbit facing the deadly snake. It watches with fear filled eyes how the snake slithers closer and closer, but is unable to move for fright. It just waits for the deadly strike.

We have arrived at the station.

"I guess I better say good-bye now," Erika stops at the head of the stairs, "Thank you for the nice afternoon and for the food. Thank you for everything."

Gerhard holds her hand. He will not let go.

"Farewell, Erika," is all he can say, "I will think about you."

We embrace. What can I say? Words are so meaningless in a situation like this. I must not cry now to make it even harder for her.

"Thank you, Erika." I feel her hair against my cheek. We embrace once more. Then she descends quickly down the stairs and disappears. I can no longer hold back the tears.

12

⚜

Spring is my favorite time of the year. When I look out of the window I can see fresh green leaves on trees and bushes. At night I listen to the lilting tunes of a near by nightingale which reserves her beautiful song for those who would listen instead of sleep. I am staying in a small house surrounded by a garden in Finkenkrug outside of Berlin.

Our dear Pastor Guertler has found a family for me, to get me out of the city with its many actions. Almost all of the 55 000 Jews in Berlin have either left the country or been rounded up and deported. Now I live here with this family with their four little girls as an au pair. The parents know the pastor and he had told them about my status. They were willing to give me this chance to get out of the immediate danger. I sleep in a small room under the roof and help the young mother with all of her work. The garden provides extra food for the family, which lives only on the small amount of food they get on ration cards. Once a week, on Sundays when I am home with Mother, they eat meat. The special egg a week is reserved for the youngest sickly girl. The other days it is mainly potatoes and vegetables.

When I arrive for the weekend like a hungry wolf, Mother is waiting with good nourishing food. Through the store she barters food for clothing, as both are rationed, and she always has a piece of sausage for me to take along to eat at night in my little room to quiet the gnawing stomach.

This afternoon I am home alone. The family is invited to a birthday party. Finally I have some time to myself. I turn on the radio and beautiful music fills the room. As the violins play their lilting melody, I remember Erika and how she practiced after we did our homework. I waited and after she was finished, we made music together, she on her violin and I on my flute. What innocent fun times we shared!

I move close to the radio. Never have I heard this piece of music before. It touches something within me with its romantic violin theme. I follow it, standing by the window, listening to the rising melody till it reaches a high point, only to return to a minor key. I forget everything around me and just take in these violin melodies that stir something deeply inside me as no other music has ever done before.

Before things got so bad, Erika and I had often gone to concerts and enjoyed them, but this is different. This music reaches some deep buried layers of feeling. It conjures scenes of yesterday before my eyes, till a dam breaks inside of me. All the longings for harmony, for love and security, the desire to be together with Gerhard – I am inundated by these emotions, while tears roll down my cheeks and I give in to the feelings of loss and sadness.

I think of my beloved father. Where would he be now? He must be worrying about us, not being able to contact us. Where would my friend Erika and her parents be? Is Gerhard actually fighting at the Western front? I am filled with dark forebodings. When the music, which stirred me so deeply, has died down, I hear that it was the violin concerto Nr.1 in g minor by Max Bruch.

The ringing of the phone jerks me out of my dreams. It is Mother who tells me that Gerhard called. He will have a short furlough and wants to see me on the weekend.

"But only on the water!" Mother cautions me. What wonderful news! My sad mood is gone. I will ask the family if I could leave Saturday afternoon and then I could meet Gerhard at the boat barracks.

It is a beautiful day in May with little white clouds dotting the blue sky. The air is still brisk but the glittering water looks inviting. Gerhard had his 19th birthday a few weeks ago. I hand him a small box.

"What is that?" he looks surprised.

"It is my belated birthday present for you. I wanted to give it to you in person." He carefully unwraps it and opens the box.

"Oh! A ring! And with my initials!" He embraces me.

"Thank you, thank you so much!" He slides it on his finger. "It fits exactly!"

"Why don't you look inside and read what it says?" He holds it close to his eyes and reads, "May 21, 1941."

"Do you remember that date?"

"That is almost two years ago!"

"Have you forgotten our first kiss?"

"How could I? Never!"

He puts his arms around me and gives me a long kiss.

"Now I will always carry something with me to remind me of you."

The Golden Hill is hibernating in the spacious barracks, so we walk to our boat barracks to take out the neglected kayak and paddle around the river Havel. Gerhard sits behind me and shares his experiences as a soldier. "Soon I will have to go to France," he says and I am relieved that it is not Russia, where the German army is in retreat.

"And how are things with you?" he asks.

"At present relatively quiet," I answer, "in light of the fact that Berlin has been declared 'free of Jews'. Of Erika and her parents I have heard, that they have been deported and are now in Theresienstadt."

I tell him about my new role as au pair girl and about the family that was brave enough to take me in. We lay down the paddles and drift, allowing the warming afternoon sun to shine on us. I close my eyes. How wonderful to be together again! Even when we are not talking I feel so close to him.

"Do you sometimes think about dying?" Gerhard asks pensively. "I have thought about it lately what happens when a person dies."

"I believe what the Bible says about death," I answer. "When we sang those great Bach chorales, which are based on words of the Bible, something within me just knew that this was the truth."

"But I don't really know the Bible – or God. There are so many questions I have."

"I also have questions, but one thing I know for sure, God is a living reality."

"How can you be so sure about it?"

"After all the things that happened to me, for instance how he protected me when the SS came to deport me."

He ponders my answers. "I wish I could know more about him," he says.

"Why don't you come to church with us tomorrow? We could see each other once more, could walk through the Grunewald forest, at least to your train station."

Gerhard nods and I am happy for another chance to be together with him.

Sunday morning my eyes scan the worshipers in our little church till I have spied his reddish blond head. He sits on the opposite side. Our eyes meet without an outwardly visible sign of recognition. Yet my heart skips for joy. We have to be careful in public for he is wearing his uniform. After the sermon by Pastor Guertler we stay for Communion.

Only a few people remain, Gerhard among them. After the service is over, I linger till everybody has left. Mother walks home to fix our noon meal.

"Be careful!" she admonishes us. We cross the street to the other side to the edge of the forest.

Together we take a path hidden from the street, leading in the direction of the Heerstrasse station. Gerhard walks silently, lost in thought. I feel that the worship service has touched him deeply.

"Do you know that this was my first communion after my confirmation five years ago? I wish my mother would be like yours. I mean, she has taught you from your childhood on to trust and rely on God."

"That is true. I have always believed in God. I have prayed and he has answered some prayers."

"I pray too, but more with the wish to find him."

"You can find him, Gerhard. He is a personal God, not a nebulous idea"

"But don't you ever have doubts?"

"Of course I have doubts," I admit, "I am often afraid and worry about many things. And sometimes I even doubt hat God could really help me."

"That is the same with me. I really want to believe in him, but then I see all of the injustices and the sufferings in this world…"

"But who is unjust, and who must suffer because of these injustices? Can you accuse God for what people do to each other, treating each other like enemies? When people fight and kill each other because of hatred, selfishness, and greed, is that God's fault?"

"But couldn't he prevent it – this senseless war for instance, this killing and murdering of innocent victims?"

"But he has given free will to man. Everybody can choose between good and evil. So if man chooses evil, God is not responsible for his choice, don't you think?"

"Yes, but why do so many good people have to suffer?" We walk along in silence. The pine needles under our feet are like soft cushions. I often ask the same question, especially about Erika and many others. It is a question that man has struggled with from the beginning.

"I wish I would have a satisfying answer – but I don't have one. The only explanation I found is that suffering produces something in people that would not be there otherwise. You can tell when a person has gone through much suffering. They are either stronger and meeker, or bitter and closed towards God."

"But I am afraid of suffering. It's hard enough to be separated from you, not knowing if we will ever see each other again."

"But Gerhard," I take his hand, "there are so many uncertainties in life and so many questions. But in it all I know for sure, if I should die today that would not be the end. A change, perhaps, a new dimension, but I would continue to live – a life that has no end."

"How can you be so sure?"

"Because I believe the words that Jesus said."

He stops and looks at me, then holds me close.

"Thank you that you invited me to come to church with you. I have a lot to think about."

"Do you own a Bible?" I ask.

"Yes, from my confirmation."

"Why don't you take it along and begin to read in it?"

He nods and puts his arm around me. We walk slowly the last steps till we see the station.

"Please, let's make it brief and painless," I beg, "I hate saying good bye."

"Please, don't leave yet! I have to tell you something before you go. I love you!"

His arms hold me tight and he covers my face with kisses. In his eyes I see different emotions battling within. Why must the time together always be too short, the longings for each other getting ever stronger?

"I love you too, Gerhard. Come back soon!"

A last kiss, then I turn and walk across the street without looking back once.

13

⚜

"Could you please come into the living room?" The father of the family stands in the kitchen door with a serious face. I dry my hands and follow him. His wife is sitting on the sofa, her hands folded in her lap. She does not look up.

"Please sit down," he points to a chair. I obey with a weak feeling in my stomach. He picks up a card from the table.

"You know," he addresses me, "that we took you in because Pastor Guertler asked us. We are quite satisfied with you, you have been a good help to my wife these last three months and the girls like you. But today we received this card from the Department of Labor" he passes the card to me across the table, "asking us, whether we knew that we had employed a Jewish girl."

This is the end, over and gone – my deceptive security!

"Since we do not want to endanger our family, especially the children, we would like to ask you to leave right away, so we can go to the Labor Department tomorrow and tell them that we did not know it."

"We are so sorry," his wife adds with a sympathetic look at me. "I wish we could help you, but…"

I hardly hear the well-meant words for the thoughts race around in my head. Where shall I go? What am I going to do now?

"It would be good to notify your mother. No, the best thing would be to take the train home. We can gather your things later and bring them to you."

I take off my apron and climb upstairs to my room for the last time and pick up my purse.

The children watch me perplexedly as I say good-bye and leave the house. Like a sleepwalker I move along the tree-lined road and beside blooming gardens to the train station.

It is a mild June evening and the roses are giving off a sweet smell. I climb to the first floor of our house and ring the bell.

"Yolchen, what are you doing here?" the happy surprise turns to anxious alarm as Mother sees my expression. Her face turns pale as she listens to my explanation.

"You must get out of Berlin, there is no other solution," she says with determination.

"It must be done right away. Tomorrow may be too late. They might come and get you!" The coiled fear in her words jumps at me.

"But where in the world could I go?" I have no idea what the next step should be.

"I have always feared this moment and I have prepared for it. I had an ID card made for you, other than the Jewish one with the big J on it. You need it to get through the controls. This is your only chance to flee. Leave the other ID here."

"How in the world did you get this?" I ask incredulously.

"You know that there are some people in the main Post Office who know me, because our store is right across from it. I applied for a Postal ID with my picture on it and an official seal, and I brought a picture of you along and just said, "Please make one for my daughter also." They never questioned me and I got you this little card, which you must sign. But be sure to only sign your name, not Sarah."

I open the little card. A serious faced passport picture looks at me. I am wearing a coat with metallic round buttons that could easily pass for a uniform. Over the lower right corner is an official seal with a swastika.

"Do you really think this thing will get me through?"

"We will pray that it will! You will travel to my friend Anni in Pfaffenhofen in Bavaria. As soon as I have a substitute for the store, I will join you and then we will see what we can do next. Now hurry up, we have no time to waste!"

Without packing anything, with only my purse in hand, we rush out of the house.

At the railroad station Mother finds a train to Munich. She gets aboard and discovers an empty compartment and I take a seat by the window. Then she quickly gets out and I pull down the window to watch her. What else is there to be said? Her eyes mirror worry and fear. Slowly the thought creeps into my mind, that this is no ordinary parting.

From now on I will be on my own, alone, without father and mother, without relatives and friends that love me. Up to this point Mother has been my faithful companion. Her love and compassion, her fighting spirit have encouraged and comforted me when I needed it. We shared joys and sorrows and were knit closely together. She was mother and father to me, gave me her unconditional love, even when I rebelled or was unreasonable. Now the time that she feared has arrived and she must let go of me. I see the battle in her eyes, her protective instinct, wanting to hold on to her only child, to shield her from unknown dangers and a threatening future.

We grasp each other's hands for the last time as the shrill whistle of the conductor gives the sign for leaving. I try to hold on to her but her fingers slip out of my hand. With tear filled eyes I see that she walks beside the slowly moving train. She looks lonely and waves a white handkerchief, like father had waved so many years ago. Standing alone on the platform, her figure gets smaller and smaller Suddenly it hits me, our little harmonious family – now it is completely torn apart and scattered in all directions.

An elderly couple opens the door and finds seats in the compartment. I close my eyes. I don't want to see anybody. I want to be alone in my pain, live again in my mind through the events of the day that have happened in such rapid succession. This new experience of rejection, though perfectly valid and understandable, nevertheless hurt deeply. I should be used to it by now, to expect nothing from life but rejection, but there had been this foolish hope of a little haven of safety which now had been taken from me in a hurry.

My thoughts race as I try to think what would happen to me next. Surely soon the conductor would come and ask for our IDs. Would he be satisfied with this ridiculous little Postal ID? And if not – what would he do with me? Hand me over to the police? That would be the end, the inescapable road to a concentration camp. Mother would never find out. Her daughter – missing, never heard of again, leaving no trace behind. I must stop thinking these thoughts, they are eating me up. I sit up and look out the window into the twilight.

The door opens – and my heart stands still. Two SS men in their ominous black uniforms enter the compartment.

"Hey, didn't I tell you we would find a nice compartment? May I sit next to you, Fraeulein?" The first to enter sits down next to me, the other takes the opposite window seat. The hated and feared emblem at his collar pierces my eyes. Awful memories arise. I feel helpless, handed over to the enemy. I turn my head to the window. Outwardly I must remain calm but inwardly my thoughts and heart race like an out of control motor.

"Your tickets please and your ID cards or passports." The conductor and another uniformed man wait in the door. The older couple follows the order obediently. The SS men need no tickets; their uniforms are their ID. Then he takes my ticket and the little Postal ID. I hope no one notices that my hands tremble.

"We cannot use this; we need your regular identification."

"I forgot it," the words come out shaky.

"Where are you getting off?" the uniformed man asks with cold voice.

"In Munich, I am visiting my aunt in Pfaffenhofen."

"You cannot travel without a regular ID!"

"I did not know it," my words sound helpless.

"Now you know it. Next time we won't make an exception." He returns my little ID and shuts the door.

Saved! My whole body is trembling. I use every ounce of strength I have left to hide it. I must get out of this compartment or I will choke. Slowly I rise from my seat, open the door and close it behind me. I stand in the walkway, and then make my way in the direction of the toilet. I must not be outside too long, just till the trembling subsides, or else it looks suspicious. I cannot see through the windows, for with the beginning of darkness the shades are drawn to keep the light from shining outside. It is a protection against air raids. Often in nights of new moons the streets of Berlin were so dark, that in order not to bump into other people, I would wear a phosphor pin that I held under the light before going outside where it glowed for a while.

The window glass reflects my seventeen-year old image. The cheerful summer dress, light blue with little dots, does not seem to match my frightened face. I take a deep breath. I must relax, must try to act naturally. Slowly I turn and open the door to return to the lion's den.

"I heard that you are going to Munich," the SS man next to me opens the conversation, "that is where we are going also. It's too bad that they no longer brew that good strong Bavarian beer," he laughs and the man across joins in his laughter.

"In France, where we just come from," he continues, "they still have good food and wine. Frenchmen are certainly not good soldiers but they know how to cook."

Whether I want to or not I am being drawn into their conversation. There is nothing else I can do but listen. In the semi darkness of the compartment, the man takes my silence as a sign that I am interested to hear more of his experiences.

He rambles on while the others, overtaken by sleep, close their eyes. He talks about the good times he had in Paris with the fashionable Mademoiselles, while I wonder what French girl would be friendly with a man of the occupation forces. But there are opportunists everywhere, just look at Marshall Petain. While he talks, watching me out of the corner of his eye, I feel his leg getting closer to mine. I withdraw but he does not give up. As he tries to put his arm around my shoulder, I turn abruptly away from him.

He sits up straight and after a time of silence he continues to let the happenings of the last days pass before his eyes. Like a movie I am forced to see the scenes as he relives and shares them in a quiet mumble.

As he talks I see the scenes before my eyes, the SS hunting underground fighters and arresting them to be tortured, I am sure, and thrown into some dark prison cell. The next scene is where they 'fumigated' Jews out of a hole in which they were hiding. Like a hunter on safari he proudly relates every step that lead to the capture. I see frightened people before me, hands up as they crawl out of the hiding place, fearing for their lives. He continues this dark monologue as if he had forgotten my presence. The horror pictures continue.

I feel like a priest taking confession. I try to distance myself inside, try not to allow these words to penetrate my mind, not to become a witness to the human tragedies that he parades before me, but to no avail. He is still young, but war is a fast teacher of how to deaden emotions and give way to indifference to suffering. If once the borderline of killing a human being has been trespassed, the perpetrator will never feel the tender compassion with other humans again. He remains an amputated soul. That is the price a murderer has to pay, a part of his soul dies with the victim and never gets resurrected again.

A sudden rage takes hold of me. Why must I be the victim of this hardened man? What right does he have to dirty me with the filth and scum of his life? Does he get a sadistic satisfaction from making an innocent girl an accomplice to his crimes?

"Excuse me," I say quietly, "I am really very tired and would like to try to sleep a bit." I put my purse between us and close my eyes. But I cannot sleep. Will this terrible night never end?

After several stops of the train, other controllers come and again my little ID is the subject of arguments. But this time I do not tremble, instead I react almost defiantly. Towards morning I feel the head of the SS man on my shoulder. He is sound asleep. I shove him away. I must have finally fallen asleep shortly before the train reaches Munich.

14

The pigsty stinks. The two pigs grunt as they see me, but I have no time for greetings. I must clean up their manure. With a pitchfork I throw the dirty straw on a pushcart, roll it out to the big manure pile and empty it. Rolling the cart back to the stable I suddenly stand still. A thought has struck me. I look up into the grey November sky that promises snow.

"What am I doing here?" is the thought that struck me suddenly. "Will there ever be an end to this? Will I see my father again? And first of all, will I survive to see the end of this terrible war?" There is no answer but the moment engraves itself deeply on my memory, as certain times in life leave marks even long after they have passed. I pick up the cart again. My rubber boots are full of manure. The palms of my hands have thick calluses from handling so much wood for the wood-burning stove on which we cook. Under my apron I wear a wool sweater for the cold bites through the clothes. The manure pile is steaming just like my breath is in the cold air. While I breathe through my mouth to bear the smell, I spread out new straw for the pigs. Of all the many kinds of jobs I have, I hate this one most. Or may be cleaning the dirty toilets in the work shop, where the apprentices once locked me in from the outside, and even the master laughed as I begged to be freed again. The master, who seemingly has nothing against me, but who thinks it is funny to humiliate me.

Mother's friend, Anni, has found this family for me. The master carpenter, whose house and work shop is situated in a small village of twelve rather large farm houses outside of the town of Pfaffenhofen, is known as an opponent of the Nazis. They accepted me under the guise of duty year girl. The regime had decreed that all girls had to serve a year in a family or on a farm for room and board and some pocket money. The master found out the truth about me a few days after my arrival. The only person who could have told it to him was Anni. But he keeps the secret to himself and permits me to stay.

He is a tall well-built man with black hair and large dark eyes. His nose sits in his face a bit diagonally and divides the face into two asymmetrical halves. His voice is deep and he speaks slowly.

At first it is difficult for me to understand the Bavarian dialect. He laughs as I try to pronounce words he thinks of that are hard for foreigners, as I am, to pronounce. I am really a foreigner here, though I come from the same country, but Berlin belongs to the hated Prussians with whom the Bavarians had long battles throughout history. He laughs heartily as I try to bring myself to pronounce his tongue twisters.

His large hands are hardened from working with wood for many years. He is a very good craftsman who builds wonderful furniture, some with inlaid work. Everything in his house he built himself. But he is also artistic and can whittle dancing figures for a lamp over the family table or the crucifix in the corner. He repairs motorcycles, soles the shoes of the family, or builds small replicas of the machines in the carpenter shop with little motors that make the saws move as Christmas presents for their two young sons.

Sunday afternoons, my only free time, he takes out his accordion and with his callused hands plays Bavarian folk music for my enjoyment, or dances the famous Schuhplattler dance, hitting his palms on his leather breeches and the soles of his shoes, while his wife accompanies him on the zither.

He brews his own beer, because the war time beer is too weak for him, makes fruit wine with high alcohol content, grows and dries his own tobacco for his Sunday afternoon cigar, slaughters the pigs and makes tasty sausages and hams which are hung in the smoke of the chimney, shears the sheep, makes soap for the Monday wash day, tears down and rebuilds part of the house and work shop, and a thousand things more. In fact there is nothing that this man cannot do. If he has never done it before, the challenge is to learn how to do it perfectly.

Work gives them meaning and is their reason for living. They have been married for ten years and boast that they had never taken a vacation. The only times of rest are the Sunday afternoons and the evenings after supper. Bavarian men have a hard outer shell and they are rough in dealing with people. Their way of talking is not meant for sensitive ears, for they speak their mind, regardless of who listens. But in spite of these characteristics the master carpenter is a fair, hardworking man with a bent for independence and a strong will to stand up for his convictions. The reason he was still working at home instead of fighting in the war was an old motorcycle accident that had crushed his knee, making him unfit for military service.

Although he is the "Master", lord of his domain, and known by this name, his wife is my master. She is the other half of this super charged, energy driven team. With her watery blue eyes in which I read reserve, she had mustered me, the foreigner, at our first meeting from head to toe. After this inspection I was admitted into her domain, which encompassed house, courtyard, stables, field and garden. Somewhat short and a bit on the heavy side, her ash blond hair tightly drawn back into a bun, she fights a never ending and enthusiastic battle against dirt of every kind. In the morning she gives out her commands for the day, supervising and attacking even the most hidden particles under benches and especially in out-of-the-way corners. With satisfaction bordering on pride of discovery, she begins the hit and destroy mission, armed with brooms, scrub brushes, dust cloths, rags, scouring agent, and home made soft soap. If she discovers carelessness in the pursuit of her enemy, which my untrained eye had overlooked, she gets angry and reprimands me.

The clock governs the day. Exactly at 7 a.m. on the dot, at noon and at six o'clock in the evening the shrill bell, heard through house and work shop, is activated from the kitchen as sign for the workers to come and get it. The steaming hot food must be on the large wooden table when they enter.

She draws up a timetable for each task, with a time limit that must not be exceeded. From that moment on I am running from six thirty in the morning to seven thirty at night.

Her special pride and joy is the cellar with the cupboards filled with rows and rows of home-canned food. Only she carries a key to it. She inspects the rows of glass jars, accurately standing in line like soldiers at roll call. Then she decides between fruit and vegetables or she cuts off a thick slice of smoked ham, or fetches a bowl from one of the two big kegs of home made sauerkraut, which has been trodden down by the large washed feet of the master.

I try my best to meet her demands. But since I have once said when baking a cake, that the wooden stove does not brown as evenly as our electric stove, I have incurred her displeasure.

"I would never have one," she had answered annoyed. As hard as I try to please her, she always has something to nag or find fault with. She is an expert in homemaking and everything that goes with it. I am an uprooted young girl, trying to find my way in a completely new and strange world. I am being judged by how fast and accurately I can cut a bunch of chives from the garden, and my value decreases when in my race against the clock I first cut into my right thumb while peeling a huge heap of apples and then for good measure into the left thumb. She expects perfection, whether cleaning, baking, or cooking on the large wood stove, whether washing by hand the heavy linen bed clothes and the week's family laundry, or weeding the large garden, or feeding the pigs, ducks, chickens, sheep, rabbits, cats and dog, or turning the soil of the large potato field with a spade. Perfection and speed – both are needed to keep her in an even mood. At the end of the month of hard work and long hours I get 15 D Mark.

In spite of or perhaps because of this strict regimen I begin to expand like a yeast dumpling. Starved from the three months of mostly vegetarian diet, I eat everything I can get my fingers on. I lick out the pots before washing them and the fat food makes me round and heavy in a short time. We cook and bake with butter, and that in the fifth year of war! Many customers pay in natural produce. Soon I look like a typical Bavarian servant girl with round red cheeks and even my speech has mastered the dialect, causing one customer to say, "You can't fool me, you are no Prussian, you are Bavarian!" My hands have thick calluses and I can lift heavy loads.

Yet in spite of my outer wellbeing, the snake has entered paradise. I get a citation to appear before the mayor of the village.

"Watch out for that guy Niedermeyer," the master warns me, "he is a mean dog!" The community clerk had once tried to do him in because of his anti-Nazi stand. But he had been unsuccessful. Now he is an important person for he distributes the food ration cards. I enter the room in the mayor's farmhouse that serves as official bureau when he comes once a month. Niedermeyer interrogates me and I can feel his animosity before he speaks. Suddenly he points his finger at me and says,

"You are a Jew!" I pale. How does he know or is he trying to bluff? Is he looking for an opportunity to harm his archenemy, the master? I relate the story of the mercy petition and the neutral state, as we were assured I would be exempt till the result of the petition would be known.

"Do you have anything in writing or other evidence?" I have nothing, only the promise of a corrupt Nazi official who sits in far away Berlin.

The clerk looks at me with a malicious smile.

"If you think you can fool me, you are wrong. I will find out the truth about you. I will write to Berlin to the Ministry of the Interior, and when I get my answer than God have mercy on you!"

The master sees my stricken face as I relate the threat. He paces up and down like a caged lion.

"That dirty son of a bitch!" he shouts, "he knows what I think and he wants to catch me. It's not about you but me!"

"Do I have to leave now?" I ask fearfully, remembering the episode in Finkenkrug and expecting a repetition.

"He would really like that, that pig head," he shouts, followed by some special Bavarian curses. "This is my house, and you don't have to leave because of him."

"Thank you, Master!" I shake his hand gratefully. He nods and turns to return to the workshop. I am grateful for the courage of this good man, but fear has raised its ugly head again, and I cannot help but worry.

The pigs have fresh straw again and I push the cart into the shed. From far off I can spot the mailman on his bicycle. Every day I ask him for a letter from Mother. I have not heard from her for a while. Her letters are the highlights of the week. There is no one with whom I could talk about my personal problems or worries. She encourages me when I suffer under the changing moods of my taskmaster. "Hold out, Yolchen," she writes "and be grateful that you can be there!"

I agree with my mind, but my feelings rebel.

Over the radio we often hear the cuckoo call, the sign that enemy airplanes are flying toward Berlin to drop their bombs, even in broad daylight. Then follow the long uncertain days of anxious waiting, till I hold a sign of life in my hands.

The mailman pushes his bicycle against the wall and waves for me. Expectantly I rush over to him.

"Here is mail for you!" he waves a postcard. A card? Written in pencil? What does that mean? My eyes fly across the few words.

"Dear Yolchen, Our house has been completely destroyed by bombs. I am safe. The Lord has given. The Lord has taken away. Blessed be the name of the Lord. Love, Mother"

I stand there and cannot move. How can these few words have the power to completely change my life? I no longer have a home! No secure corner in the back of my mind, if everything fails, you can still go home. There is no home any more! Dazed I return to the kitchen. The shock is visible on my face.

"What is the matter?" the woman asks and I tell her haltingly.

"Oh, that is too bad, to lose everything. Your poor mother!" She stops a moment and then returns to her work. Yes, it is too bad, but it happens to thousands of people every day. It is a common fate to be bombed out. One should be thankful when no lives have been lost. Things can be replaced. That sounds so logical – and cold.

This was MY home – MY family – MY life! A huge part of me is buried under tons of debris, that part that cries for security, for belonging, and love – all nestled in that one word 'home'.

In bed at night I walk in my mind through all the rooms. I see the antique Flemish dining room with its black and white tile-like rug, with the hand carved heavy oak furniture, the bull's-eye glass windows, the many old pewter pieces and selected ceramic plates and jugs. Inside the buffet the antique Delft china set, which we used on Sundays. Dad did the dishes by himself for fear of somebody breaking or chipping a plate. The main attraction in this room was for me the beautifully detailed large-scale warship on top of a cabinet with its three masts and many sails with an array of lines just like a real ship. Out of its side small cannons were pointed to shoot at the enemy. I never was permitted to touch it, but I climbed on a chair just to look at it and played pirate's games in my imagination. Then there were the two large oil paintings on either side of the alcove bench, copies of Breughels 'Farmer's wedding' with all of the different people preparing and attending a wedding meal, beside the dining table around which my birthdays had been celebrated and many delicious meals, often cooked by my Dad, were eaten. In the living room there was the huge almost life sized picture by a Nazarene painter. The subject was "Abraham banishing Hagar and Ishmael". How often had I stood before that picture till it became a part of myself. I can resurrect it at any time, even though it is gone now, for it left an indelible impression on my childish heart. I had read the story in the Bible and wondered. How could anybody cast out a woman with her son, which also was Abraham's son into the desert, where they would meet almost certain death! I still see the eyes of the boy Ishmael, how he looks back over his shoulder at his father and younger half-brother Esau. There was deep hatred in his face, a hatred that has survived the centuries and is still alive between the unequal brothers, from which the children of Israel and the Arabs descended.

I see the many other paintings and sculptures and antiques, with which my father had made our home into an artistically stimulating and beautiful place, radiating harmony and culture with which I grew up. Then I think of the loss of my personal belongings, my collection of glass animals, my books and diaries, my hand written stories and poems, my drawings, my photo albums, my favorite dress of turquoise silk velvet, which Mother had bought me for substituting in the store, while she went on a needed vacation. Everything is gone, destroyed in the twinkling of an eye, never to be replaced. As I begin to fathom my loss, I am overcome and press my face into the pillow to stifle my sobbing.

Slowly I become aware that the bad moods of my boss, under which I have to suffer, are not caused by my inadequacy. I observe her face when she enters the kitchen in the morning. She is angry and upset before I can even say 'Good morning!' I see how she looks at her husband when he passes through the kitchen. Often there is icy silence when they sit down for a meal. Some days go by without speaking to each other. If there is an important message to be relayed or a phone call for him, she orders me to go to the workshop to tell him. Her dissatisfaction stems from a growing estrangement between her and her husband. The resulting tension is reduced by a lightening rod, in this case, me. The children are also involved, and they react rebelliously, causing more tension. I try to keep out of the power struggle and am careful not to show more sympathy for one side over the other, although I am drawn to the side of the master, whom I like more with his uncomplicated roughness than her reserved, obsessive compulsive nature.

Next to the loss of my home and the ever-present fear of Niedermeyer finding out about me and making good on his threat to have me deported, there is the constant worry about Gerhard. In his last letter from France, in which he enclosed a small book about the History of Art, he mentioned that he might soon be sent to the Russian front. I tell myself that the reason for his silence is because during a change of location there will not be time to write, but the worry and anxiety remain.

Soon I hear from Mother that Gerhard's mother called to tell her, that her son, after just a couple of weeks in Russia, had been wounded and is in a field hospital, being treated for a bullet wound in the pelvis. Mother encloses his field address.

I can hardly wait for the evening, when I can retreat into my unheated room. Sitting on the edge of my bed I write him, pouring out my heart, my anxiety about him and his injury, my desire and hope to see him soon. I tell him that I am praying for him and am waiting to hear from him and longing for a sign of life from him. Tomorrow morning I have to ride my bike to town and will mail the letter right away. My poor Gerhard, somewhere in the cold Russian prairie in a field hospital with much pain! I can hardly stand the thought of not being there in person, holding his hand and cheering him on. "Dear God'" I pray, "Please protect him and give him strength." Then I fall asleep.

15

❦

Soon Christmas will be here. My heart is heavy in the midst of all the preparation for the holidays. I have heard nothing from Gerhard. Every day I wait for mail, but in vain. Growing impatience and worry occupy my thoughts. Finally I see the mailman stomping through the snow. My hopes rise again. May be today he will have the long awaited letter. It would be my best Christmas present! He shakes off the snow from his boots and comes into the kitchen, takes out a letter from his leather pouch and hands it to me with a smile.

"You get it first today, you have waited long enough!" Filled with anticipation I run into my cold room, sit on the bed and open the envelope. It is Mother's writing.

"Dearest Yolchen," her letter begins, "I wish I could be with you today." Her words cut me to the quick. Hurriedly I fly over her next sentences.

"I want to put my arms around you instead of telling you the news in a letter. I wrote you last that Gerhard had been wounded on November 8, 1943 and was being treated in a field hospital. He was there for four weeks, fighting for his life and he was making progress. Then there was an epidemic of scarlet fever. He caught it and in his weakened condition, it was too much for his body. On December 12, 1943, God called him home."

Gerhard – my Gerhard – dead? Forever and ever, irrevocably, irretrievably, irrecoverably! Departed, without a chance to ever see him again, read his letters, hold him in my arms, kiss him, share those intimate moments, tell him how much I love him. He has not begun to live yet with his nineteen years! How can he be dead then?

It just cannot be! It is unfair! He cannot just leave me like that! We belong together!

I feel only a raw throbbing, painful wound, there, where a part of me has been torn out. I am faint and empty, as if I lost a lot of blood. Still in shock I return to the kitchen. Even my boss sees that something is very wrong.

"A friend of mine," I mumble, "has been killed in action in Russia."

I hear my own voice and cannot believe what I am saying. I want to cry out, "It is a lie! He is not dead!"

She stops for a moment and looks at me startled.

"I am sorry," she finally says, and then continues to stir the pot on the stove.

The next hours are spent in an icy wilderness, alone, surrounded by frozen emptiness. No sound penetrates the silence. It is like being under a glass bubble which isolates and shields me from others. Mechanically I do my work. Only at night in my bed I read over and over again the few sentences that have changed my life forever. Tears stream down my face and my body shakes from suppressed sobs. Night after night I cry myself to sleep. Lonely mourning is an almost unbearable burden, the feeling of loss and loneliness a nagging pain that is not to be quieted. Why is there no shoulder to cry on? Why not a comforting word, only indifference around me? I shout some accusing 'Why's' against heaven. "Why, o God, did you not prevent it, that such a hopeful and talented young life had to be sacrificed for this senseless and inhuman war? Why did you not stop Erika and her parents from being deported and perhaps killed already? Why did you not direct the bomb, which crushed our home, a few meters further into the garden? Why did you not help Dad to get us out in time? Why do I have to go through all of this pain all by myself?"

There is no answer, only desperate sorrow is my companion through these days

Christmas has come and gone. In the workshop I find a piece of white birch wood. I fashion a small white cross of it, like the crosses that dot the Russian landscape, where a German soldier found his death. I hang it over my bed. When I look at it, I see a lonesome grave in the Russian steppe, which holds my love.

A few days after Christmas, I receive a letter from Gerhard's mother. She is grieving the loss of her one and only child. She wants to share with me the last weeks before Gerhard's death. My letter, with which I wanted to comfort him, has never reached him. She encloses a letter by a Catholic priest, who cared for Gerhard in his time of suffering. He describes, how he was drawn to Gerhard because of the courage with which he bore the pain and the concern he felt for the other wounded men around him, even though he himself was fighting for his life.

"We have often prayed together," he writes, "and he has always enclosed his comrades in his prayer. Once he said to me: "I pray for them that they might find strength in God. I could not bear this all without his help." His life and death was a witness of his faith in the power of God. He died in peace and in the hope of his Lord."

Gerhard, my beloved, this knowledge that you have found him or that he found you, that you received the gift of faith before your end, which helped you in your pain and in the hour of death, that is your last and greatest gift to me!

In my drawer is a small New Testament which Mother gave me but which I had not opened. I take it in my hands. Where should I begin to read? What am I looking for, anyway? The book opens and my eyes fall on a sentence with the word 'hope'. I begin to read. "For in this hope we were saved. Now hope that is seen is not hope. For who hopes for what he sees? But if we hope for what we do not see, we wait for it with patience."

Will God tell me something through this verse from Romans 8? I continue to read.

"For we know that all things work together for good to them who love him, who are called according to his purpose." What mockery! "Work together for good!" Everything I experience seems to laugh this to scorn. My life has been anything but good. It has been depressing, destructive and discouraging. I cannot imagine how all of this suffering, all of the tears I cried could be good for me. And what about this hoping and waiting with patience? That is all I have done, waiting, to see Gerhard again and my friend Erika, for the war to end, for my family to be together again, for my life to change from servitude to freedom. But nothing ever is fulfilled, neither my wishes nor my dreams. Still this verse does not let me go. Perhaps God is throwing this lifesaver to me to hang on, even if I do not understand, so I will not drown. I underline the verse and climb into bed. It is the first time I can fall asleep without crying.

16

❧

It seems that the summer of 1944 never arrives. I count the days till the end of the duty year. The days seem to go too slow. I want to get away from the Damocles' sword hanging over me in person of the Nazi Niedermeyer. Every morning my first thought is, "Are they going to come for me today?" Often I have the desire to just run away. But my mind wins over my feelings. I will stay here to the bitter end. Work has become routine. I have developed from a clumsy teenager into an efficient housekeeper. I even cook by myself without constant supervision. But the cold, moody and nagging way of my boss pulls me down and burdens me. Mother writes that our store has been bombed and she had to open per government decree at a different location. Many people need at least a few towels and linens after they are bombed out. The place to which she had moved, has also been bombed and again she had to move.

Finally the day comes when my duty year is over. I am ready, packed and have said good-bye to every one. Optimism takes hold of me with the deceptive thought, that everything from now on won't be half as bad as what I had before.

Seeing Mother again helps me get over the first shock when returning to Berlin, bleeding out of a thousand wounds. I want to see the ruins of our house. Our street with the linden trees, bordered by stately villas surrounded by large gardens, has not changed. Only as I come near our house I see the destruction. Burst brick walls pierce their accusing fingers into the sky. Two empty holes, once our kitchen windows, stare at me like blind eyes. The rest is a confusion of broken beams and crushed bricks. Carefully I balance myself along the remainder of an outside wall and look down into the chaos as into an open grave. Between the rubble I suddenly discover the hand carved lion's head of the desk chair on which I used to sit to do my homework, while Dad took his nap. At least he does not have to witness the destruction of his lovingly put together and carefully orchestrated dreams!

While I search for a safe place to put my foot down with tears falling into the grave of my childhood, the decision stands suddenly before my inner eye like a large sign: "Do not ever hang your heart on things! It hurts too much when they are taken away from you."

I wipe off my tears and walk to the back entrance. The staircase is still there reaching up to the first floor. On the upper step I stretch as far as I can and reach through a small hole in the wall. Behind it is where my bookshelf had been standing. On tiptoes I reach inside and my fingers feel something soft. I pull it through the narrow opening. It is a small photo album with pictures I took with my first box camera. I brush off the dust and open it. There are pictures of my parents and of Ulli and me at ten years. Again I put my hand up and pull out another album. I see pictures of a magic summer on our 'Golden Hill', with Erika and Gerhard and friends sailing and smiling. What an unexpected joy! It is like a discovery of hidden treasure. What a special gift these pictures are! As I try a third time I come out with a narrow book and realize it is my first diary which I started writing with 14 years. I cannot reach anything else. But I realize, this is God's way to comfort me in the hour of pain and loss. He allows my friends and loved ones to be resurrected to save them from becoming a pale memory. I can look at them again and they talk to me through the pictures.

Back in the store at high noon the howling of the air-raid siren startles me. Mother and I walk to a makeshift air raid shelter that has been dug out in front of the building.

"Don't you have a regular shelter here? This is just a dug out." I question Mother.

"The shelters are not as secure as they seem. Many people get killed when the house is hit and collapses and they are buried underneath and cannot get out." Several people crowd together on benches along the sides. From the ceiling dangles a lantern. We don't have to wait long before a tremendous din of anti-aircraft fire begins while airplanes roar overhead. Another whining noise joins the hellish music, ending with a tremendous crash of exploding bombs. Again our ears are pressured as we hear the howling sound of another bomb coming closer. Are we the target this time? Is it going to hit now? Instinctively I hold my arms over my head.. ""Protect us, God!" is the only clear thought in my mind. Gauging by the sound of the explosion it must have hit near by.

One wave after another of attacking planes flies over the city. They drop their destructive freight over our heads, where we huddle, cowering together in our fragile mouse hole. But during a pause in the din I hear different sounds which at first I cannot explain. With eerie comprehension I realize that they come from the people around me. It is the sound of chattering teeth. Teeth trembling from deathly fear, an unforgettable accompaniment of this brief descent into the hell of real war.

It seems like an eternity till finally the wailing of the all clear sign is given and we climb out like walking dead of our almost tombs into the hot sun of this July afternoon surrounded by a burning city, belching black smoke into the cloudless blue sky.

"I have to see about our store," Mother says matter-of-factly. "What? You want to go to the store? After this harrowing experience? I feel so weak; I can hardly walk. How can you stand it?"

"You get used to it," she answers. How can you get used to being eye to eye with death every day? Is there a force inside that denies the reality of a possible sudden death, or does fear, lived through in excess, have a numbing effect that minimizes danger in retrospect? How could Gerhard and all the other soldiers, who face death in battle every day, endure these experiences? How could they keep functioning after being shot at for any length of time? I find no answer to these questions and drag myself listlessly through the rest of the day.

"We need a vacation," Mother decides and leaves the store to the sales ladies. We end up in the Bavarian Alps. For three weeks we recuperate in a village high up in the mountains, which seems like an oasis that the war had not touched. On our hikes through the beautiful scenery we talk about my future. What should we do next?

As long as we have nothing in our hands to show for the mercy petition, it is too dangerous for me to return to Berlin. After the experience of the bombing afternoon, I am not drawn back there anyway, though it is my native city.

Mother took along some addresses of friends. We visit one after another, from Garmisch to Lake Starnberg. We receive a friendly reception everywhere, but nobody offers a concrete solution to my problem. There is no place where I could fit, balancing like on a high wire between legality and illegality, as I had done last year. The address list shrinks and with it my hope.

Finally Mother says,

"I see no other possibility for you than to return to your Bavarian family."

"You can't be serious!" I exclaim incredulously. "You yourself have told me that you would have never endured it as long as I have!"

"Do you have a better solution?" Mother asks, "or another idea?"

"They won't take me back," I hold on to illusions in my desperate attempt to prevent the inevitable.

"Why don't you call them and ask?"

"I'd rather die than knuckle under that woman again!"

"Then I will call her!" Mother has made up her mind and enters the telephone booth. I don't want to listen nor even consider the possibility. Mother returns.

"She has said that they have not found anybody and that you can come back." The thought makes me cringe. Mother takes my hand and looks into my eyes.

"Yolchen, I know how you feel, but you are old enough to know that there are things in life which one has to do, although one does not want to do them."

"That's the story of my life," I wail.

"Let us hope that it won't be for long. Perhaps the war will end soon. Niedermeyer probably won't get an answer because much of Berlin has been so bombed. Hold out a little longer and be strong!" She pulls me close to her and kisses me

I return like a beaten dog, kicked out of the house with pulled in tail, cowering before its master. That is how I see myself, who just six weeks ago left the place, happy as a lark. I see the look of triumph in the cold eyes of my boss. She seems to enjoy my humiliation and my discomfort. Now I am completely under her dominion, a slave without any rights, but with lots of duties. -

A jeep stops in front of the house. Through the kitchen window I can see two American soldiers climbing out and entering the mayor's house. I get up from the bench I have been sitting on and walk towards the door. Before I get there, it is flung open from the outside and the soldiers enter, draw their guns and point them at the mayor.

"Hands up!" they command, "hurry up, up!" one shouts while the other frisks the stunned mayor for weapons. Before I can translate, the man holds up his hands and I shout into the mixed up scene, "Hold it! This is the mayor!"

The soldier lets the gun down and pointing to his black high boots, he says, "Tell him not to wear these boots." I translate for the mayor that he should not wear boots because they are associated with being a member of the SS. He sits down shakily on the bench by the kitchen table, while I converse with the soldiers in English. They tell me to relay to him that until tomorrow afternoon all weapons in the village have to be turned in to the mayor's house. If after that time any weapon should be found, the village would be burned to the ground. I translate and he nods. Then the soldiers jump into their jeep again and drive off.

The once so proud and highly exalted Gauleiter, a high Nazi official, sits at the table, bent over and his head down over his chest. His haircut and little mustache remind you of the Fuehrer, whom he had served so faithfully. I sit down again and pick up the small booklet with German-English phrases, which one of the soldiers had given me. I page through the booklet trying to learn some of the phrases, while the man sits there, staring at nothing. Strange, but I feel something like pity for this person, as he sits there like a destroyed man, shrunk into a little heap. He had called for me, as I am the only one in the village who can speak English. During the last weeks things have gone topsy-turvy. I put down my phrase book and look out of the window, reliving the happenings.

I had to suffer for nine more months under my moody dictatorial boss, till Mother arrived in Pfaffenhofen. She had caught the last overcrowded train leaving Berlin before the Russians occupied her sector of the city. Our dog Dolly and one suitcase was all she could take along. With Anni's help she had found a room in a farmhouse belonging to Resi, a busy mother of four young children, whose husband was fighting in the German army. Shortly after her arrival I could finally leave, for a young girl who worked for air force communications appeared at the door and was happy to get my job and take off her uniform. I packed my things and my bicycle and moved to Resi's small village. Finally we were together again and enjoyed a wonderful time. I helped Resi on the fields and in the house with the children, while the American front came closer each day.

The last few weeks had been very exciting. Fleeing German soldiers, artillery gunfire, white flags out of the windows as sign of capitulation, and then the waiting for the 'enemy' whose tanks we could hear from the distance, rolling day and night. A few days later a field hospital was set up just outside our village. Nothing could keep me back and I walked right up to the tents with a large Red Cross that G.I.s were setting up. One soldier was erecting a fence and I went up to him and told him excitedly in my best Oxford English,

"I am so happy to see you! You have liberated me!" No answer. Then he turned his back on me. Out of the corner of his mouth I heard a whispered word which at first I did not understand, 'Non-Fraternization'. I did not know that soldiers were not allowed to speak to enemy civilians. There was still a war going on. Then he looked around cautiously and with a hand movement to his mouth he asked,

"You got some liquor? I have chocolate. Tonight after dark I come to the village." I nodded and was disappointed. My liberator did not want to talk, just exchange chocolate for alcohol. Shortly before they had fled, the German soldiers had opened up a warehouse with thousands of bottles of liquor and the mayor had distributed it to the inhabitants of the village. Now everybody had something to barter, but there was also a lot of excitement due to drunken soldiers. When it got dark the bartering took place and after years of deprivation I slowly let a piece of heavenly tasting chocolate melt in my mouth.

When the mayor of the village called for me to interpret when American soldiers stopped at his house, I went there with mixed feelings. Why should I help an active and influential Nazi politician? But the opportunity to be able to speak to American soldiers and try out my language skills was too enticing

During my time as interpreter the fall of the Third Reich was being played out before my eyes in the person of the mayor. At first he had sat straight at the table, yet with every day his back was bending a little more and his face grew more haggard. He became more nervous with every vehicle that stopped before his house. He probably suspected the truth of what would happen to him.

Another exciting day! The American officer, who commanded that weapons be collected, is beside himself. Somebody informed him that a farmer had not turned in his weapon. I have to accompany him to the culprit's house. The angry face of the officer promises nothing good. I fear that he will fulfill the threat he made before, to burn down the village, even Resi's house. There is no use trying to change his mind. Other rules are valid in times of war. What is going to happen to us? Where could we flee? Suddenly we hear shooting in the nearby forest. The officer bellows out a command to go after the source of the shooting. They immediately leave to hunt the soldiers hiding out in the woods. They don't return. Once more we are saved by the skin of our teeth.

Two days later the mayor waits in the kitchen. He wears regular brown shoes. The experience with the boots has left a mark. He stares into space till he hears the sound of a jeep. Fear is in his eyes. I walk to the door to greet the soldier.

"May I help you?" I ask.

"Thank you, but that won't be necessary," he says in fluent German. He introduces himself and tells me that he works for the CIC, the Counter Intelligence Corps. This means nothing to me. Then he turns to the mayor,

"You have fifteen minutes to get ready and pack a small suitcase and to say good bye. Then you will come with us."

Obediently the heavy man gets up and climbs up the stairs, while another soldier guards the entrance.

While we are waiting I tell him the story of my father and how we have not heard from him in years, and that we don't even know if his address has changed. He wants to know more about me, especially how I have survived. He himself is a Jew, having been raised in Germany. That is the reason for his fluency in the language. He offers to try to find my father and I give him an address, which I have kept all through the years of separation. It is of my aunt in California; she would know where her brother lives.

Heavy steps come down the stairs. Behind the mayor I see his wife who is white in the face. He holds a suitcase in his hand, which he puts down once more to embrace his wife. Then he climbs into the jeep. With the handkerchief that she uses to wipe the tears away, she waves behind her husband till the jeep disappears in the distance.

Why do I feel sorry for these people? They are Nazis. They have supported the maniac who tried to wipe out the Jews altogether and killed six million of them. They were the ones who cried, "Heil Hitler" and "Death to Jews!" But they look so desperate. I know from experience how they feel. I say good-bye to the weeping wife. My first interpreter job is finished.

17

Finally, finally the war has come to an end! I sit in an open jeep next to my boss, Lieutenant Perry, who leads the Department for Travel Passes in the Military Government of Pfaffenhofen/Ilm. We are on our way to Munich. The Autobahn is almost empty; only once in a while an Army truck or jeep meets us. After Mother and I moved to the district town of Pfaffenhofen, I continued to take more English lessons from a private tutor. I also applied for a job at the American Military Government, which had set up residence in the town hall. I was accepted and now I am writing out travel passes which people need to go from one place to another.

After all the years of persecution and the never-ending daily fear of being deported, my life has finally become stable and happy. I am nineteen years old, work for the Americans and hope to be able to go to America soon. As employees of the Army we can get a daily hot meal at the canteen, a privilege that other Germans do not have. For the first time we put our teeth into soft white bread, spread with something we never knew, peanut butter. Mother also found work in a recreation facility for G.I.s sponsored by the Red Cross. Sometimes she brings home some wonderful round sweet baked goods, called doughnuts or the luxury of a Hershey bar. My boss is a tall blond good-looking man with friendly smiling eyes. He surprises me with little gifts some times, for instance a piece of fresh smelling soap, just when my last piece of simple German soap is coming to an end and there is no place where one can buy another one. With personal interest he had listened to my story and, without asking, took it upon himself to contact a refugee organization trying to find missing persons.

When I hear that he is driving to Munich for official business, I beg him to take me along. Not only for the drive which I enjoy, but because I heard about an office in Munich, where one can get information about survivors of concentration camps. I want to know what really happened to my friend Erika and her parents.

Every opportunity to ride in a car is a highlight of my day. Even the open hard-riding Army jeep I enjoy to the fullest, allowing the wind to play with my hair and seeing the green fields and forests fly by. Riding along once with another soldier, he wanted to show off as he watched me enjoying the ride.

"Americans drive fast, don't they?" he said stepping on the gas. Suddenly, instead of in a curve, we ended up on a bumpy potato field. He was embarrassed but I could not stop laughing as we slowly made our way back to the road. Because I would love to drive a car myself, I have begun to take driving lessons in a pre-war very old boxy black Opel in which I sit straight and erect like on a dinner chair. The commands of my heavy weight elderly driving instructor keep me on edge. "Push down the clutch! Give gas! Now shift! Let the clutch come up slowly! Gas again!" When the sheer joy of driving on the empty country roads overtakes me and I drive above his limit, which is 35kmh (about 25mph), he asks in his Bavarian dialect: "You want to be a race driver, girl?"

Lieutenant Perry whistles a happy melody.

"Do you know the musical 'Oklahoma?" he asks. Of course I have never heard of it. He tells me a little about the story and then begins to sing in a warm baritone voice, "Oh, what a beautiful morning, oh what a beautiful day." Soon I join in the refrain and the happiness of the music makes my heart put on wings. Finally I can look forward to a beautiful day without fears. Then he thinks of another song from the musical, like 'Surrey with a fringe on the top,' and singing in harmony we arrive on the outskirts of Munich. He finds the place where he drops me off and where he will pick me up again after his official business.

I climb up the stairs and find the office. In a room behind the reception desk there are several people, oblivious to anything going on around them. They are bent over tables, pouring over long lists of names. The tension in their faces and the oppressive atmosphere of the place clings to my recently so happy heart. This is no general list like a telephone book. These are death lists, I realize. I have to wait till one of them leaves and take a seat before the list that he had just inspected. My heart begins to beat rapidly. What will I find? Will they have survived? These lists are survivors' names. And if not, what then? The names before my eyes start jumping. My fingers begin to tremble. I take a deep breath to make myself calm down enough to find the W's. Dear God, let me find their names!

As I go down the alphabetically ordered names starting with W, I come to We. I go down the line. As nervous as I am I think I must have made a mistake and again begin to read from the top down. But there is no Erika Weil. Like a crushing blow I suddenly realize the truth: Erika, my best friend, and her parents are not among the survivors. They were killed, their lives deliberately murdered, starved or who knows what! What I had feared in my darkest nights of desperation has come true. The feeling of utter helplessness, that I have felt that night when Erika walked down the steps to the train, overcomes me again.

Why did I not hold her arm and run away with her to hide her? Because I knew that the bloodhounds would find us sooner or later? Or because there was still a tiny glimmer of hope of survival? Why have I been spared? Why, God, why?

In the reception room I sit down to wait for Lieutenant Perry to pick me up. My thoughts are on Erika and her fate. I cannot help but imagine what has happened to her. I had seen pictures and read about the fate of the concentration camp inmates. Erika, my friend, with the clear blue eyes, with her orderly parted hazel hair, with her open smile, her long, slender fingers that made beautiful music. With her girlish figure, just at the threshold of growing up – what must she have suffered on the way to Theresienstadt and the stay there? And what did they do to her in the gas chambers of Auschwitz? It is more than I can imagine.

How could I feel the terror, to be led like cattle to slaughter, to be pushed with other naked women into a room, called shower, in reality a gas chamber. Humiliated, naked, helpless, filled with an overwhelming fear as the waves of flowing gas stream over the masses of screaming people, gasping for air like fish on dry land. My Erika, who shuddered at the thought of lying in a clean lined coffin, now surrounded on all sides by screaming women in agony fighting for every breath and feeling how the lungs are filling with the poisonous gas. The deafening screams, the howling and praying in her sensitive ears. Every second an unbearable eternity of clinging together, stepping on each other in midst of excrements, bulging eyes, hands grasping into nothing, finally the screams becoming whimpers till the lungs give out, the last gasping sound dies – after fifteen minutes of eternal torture. Then the opening of the doors. Like manure being dragged out, the gaping mouths being searched by callous helpers for gold teeth, broken out and stored with shaved long locks of hair. Then rolled to the crematoria to be burnt like sticks of wood, black smoke with the smell of burnt human flesh rising up day and night in the tall chimneys of these efficient factories of human destruction and into the nostrils of an angry God of wrath. But why? Why must humans make other humans suffer like that?

18

It is a cool October morning. I sit in my office typing. As I look up I see Lieutenant Perry standing before me.

"I have to tell you something," he says. "You are requested to go upstairs to report to the CIC. You can leave right away." I am surprised by this summons. What does the Counter Intelligence Corps want from me? They have their offices above us in the town hall, but nobody knows what goes on behind their secretive doors. I only know that they are separate from the Military Government and that they work with secret information and do secret activities.

A uniformed young man opens the door and I am being led into the former mayor's office, an imposing room with dark paneling, overlooking the market square of the town. Behind a large heavy desk with carved ornaments an officer rises from a high backed red leather chair to greet me and asks me to sit down across from him. The officer who let me in takes a chair opposite from me.

"We want to ask you a few questions," the man behind the desk begins. It is like an interrogation and I soon realize that they know quite a bit about me.

"We have some work which we would like you to do, which is important to us. We have some secret information and you will be trusted not to take any secrets out of this room. You are not to talk about it to anybody, not to your own family, nor pass on any information to anybody. We have talked to Lieutenant. Perry already and he told us that you are trustworthy, according to your life story. He has agreed to make you available to us for this service. Are you willing to do it?"

I don't have to think it over. I nod and say yes. A thousand thoughts run through my head as they show me the office where my place of work will be. From the window I also have a view of the market-square up to the white church with the pointed steeple at the far end. One side of the room is lined with bookshelves on which I see grey documents standing in rows pressed together.

"We have discovered these documents which are the record books of pay for each SS man of the whole district, and we want you to make lists for us, so we can go after these men." Aha, go after means like interrogation and possible arrest, I muse. The officer leads me to the door.

"You can go down to your desk now," he tells me, "and after lunch you come up here and start with your work." I take leave of my colleagues and my friendly boss, who shakes my hand and wishes me good success. Every change has in it a bit of sadness for leaving familiar faces and places and some fear of charting unknown territory. But for the young the adventure of discovering new opportunities and experiencing the widening of horizons incite the urge of taking chances in life. A bit wistful, yet with butterflies in my stomach I begin my new work.

I am alone in my office this grey October day. I am typing long lists of names and addresses. There is a knock on the door and I am called out into the hall. Lieutenant Perry, my former boss, stands there with a sheet of paper in his hand. His face is beaming as he waves the piece of paper into my face.

"Here this is for you!" he says and hands it to me. A telegram! I race over the words. It is signed by my beloved Dad! Tears of joy well up in my eyes as I read his few words, words which resurrect long ago promises anew. My Dad lives! We have found each other again! I embrace the Lieutenant, for it is he that made this contact possible through a refugee organization. He shares my obvious joy and then leaves to go downstairs again.

I rush into the office of my boss with the telegram. He allows me to leave for the rest of the day, so I can bring the good news to Mother. Together we celebrate this unexpected miracle of finding each other after so many years and with so many changes of address. Now it is only a question of time before we will be together again! I

will write him right away in English and share our immense joy and
gratitude. Now a new life will begin for all of us!

19

O n this November morning I enter the office with fear and trembling. This day will be the most difficult of all the hard ones I have lived through so far. After I had finished the job to their satisfaction, I did not return to the Military Government but my status was changed to secretary/interpreter for the top boss. My desk was moved into the former mayor's office, right next to the large desk of my boss. Now my job is to interpret at interrogations, to write protocols and translate them and do the many things an office such as ours requires. I am the only secretary working for three men. I love my work and my colleagues. Through our special work, which is always different and never boring, a strong bond of comradeship has developed. As carriers of secret information we are a closely connected team. Not one day is like the other. Surprises or sudden excitements happen almost on a daily basis.

I feel an inner satisfaction to add a little part in bringing to justice those helpers of the despicable inhuman regime, who have made so many innocent people suffer or caused their death. Not even Mother knows what happens here behind closed doors. And that is better for her or else she would get too upset. I do not mind the excitement, in fact I relish it. To me it is part of the 'good cause' I am fighting for. In some inscrutable cases there are so many imponderable, confusing details, and it is a challenge to assemble them like little mosaic pieces, ending up with a complete picture. I love the tingling tension of a face-to-face interrogation that I have to translate and the satisfaction at the end to realize that your hints were right and have led to a satisfactory solution.

But what awaits me today fills me with fear. A guard brings a man from prison, takes off his shackles and sets him on our interrogation chair across from me. Then he leaves the room to wait outside. Many people have sat there before, but this time it is different. I can hardly force myself to look at this man. My boss begins the interrogation, fixing his eyes on the man as he speaks and never taking them off. His fingers drum the cover of the folder that lies before him. I can tell he is also agitated.

"Your name, age and last place of work," his voice has a metallic edge to it. I translate into German.

"My last place of work was the concentration camp Dachau." The word stabs my heart. Dachau is less than 50 kilometers from where we sit. How often did I fear to be deported there, fearing Niedermeyers' threats!

"And what was your specific work?"

"I have worked there in the medical facility."

The questions become more specific. Did he experiment on living human beings? Yes. What kinds of experiments were they? Give us details. How many people did you torture thus?

Every question and every answer passes through my mind and my mouth, gets translated, written down and becomes part of my memory. I must not think about it, although the terrible pictures, like scenes from a horror movie of a crazed man, live before my inner eye, as the monotonous voice of this man, who shows no emotion whatsoever, continues his shocking tales.

Often I am at a loss for words, something that never happens to me during other interrogations. While I am thinking of meanings to put into the right words, the details of the sadistic experiments seem to die in my throat. The atrocities that this man, sitting there before me, describes in terms of a scientific experiment are beyond my comprehension. My face is white, my voice trembles. I can hardly hold the pen as I write the protocol. I feel sick to my stomach.

"We will continue tomorrow." My boss, looking over at me, pushes his chair back and goes to the door to call the guard. He puts on the shackles and both leave the room.

"I am sorry," there is empathy in his voice, "You can take off the rest of the day," he tells me. We are both shaken by what we have heard and we need time to recuperate. Mechanically I put the cover over my typewriter. I cannot repress these terrible pictures that have been etched on my mind. They accompany me on my way home and return in my dreams as nightmares. Tomorrow we will have to continue the ordeal.

The official preparations for our emigration have dragged on for over a year already, although Dad has done everything to speed them up. It is still too close to the end of the war and nobody gets out of Germany but a small group about 12000 D.P's Displaced Persons, mostly concentration camp survivors. Through my work with the war criminals and their willing helpers, who now claim to have obeyed orders only, a wall of hatred has built up in my heart, one stone at a time. Through the grace of God I am alive and have been spared the lot of all the innocent victims. I feel not only empathy for them, but what has been done to them and their lives, has also been done to me in a way. I am under a certain obligation as a survivor to do what ever I can for those, who had to pay with their lives for the evil decisions of a maniac and his obedient companions. In my mind I give room to vengeance and use every opportunity I have to work on uncovering each criminal act and to lead the perpetrators to their just retribution. With satisfaction I hear that the man, whom former Polish forced laborers ran into and apprehended on our market-square and dragged into our office, accusing him of murdering many Poles and Jews, has committed suicide by hanging himself in his prison cell. I am upset upon hearing that some high-ranking Nazi had been freed from jail again. I cannot hide my glee when I am told that my arch- enemy, Niedermeyer, has been knocked down and beaten in the street.

My desire is that every one who took part in bringing suffering to others, would have to pay for it – without mercy. Every arrest becomes a personal triumph. My work at the CIC becomes more and more my crusade for justice, while I interpret and play my part with righteous indignation. I am fully in the grip of hatred.

Yet there are other times, when we are not so busy and my boss continues our endless debates. He is an educated man and observes this strange country to which he has been sent and tries to under-stand its citizens. He had read about Germany being the cradle of the Reformation, starting with Martin Luther, had read Kant and other philosophers, had listened to the music of Bach, Mozart, Beethoven and Schubert. How could a cultured people, once known as the country of the writers and thinkers, with musicians and painters known and admired in the civilized world, descend into such a barbaric state in such a short time and bring so much suffering and ruin to so many people? Is humanistic education and culture only a thin veneer over the aggressive cave man mentality that had governed humanity for thousands of years, which, if once let loose by some mad mans' arrogant illusion of being a superior race, cannot be contained till there is total destruction? I found no satisfactory answer, asking myself these same questions.

Our debate had started when he declared opera to be a bastard between music and theater. Of course I could not take this comment lying down. Father had told me that his father had gone to the opera regularly, and some of my father's black shellac records of the famous Italian tenor, Enrico Caruso, whose arias my father enthusiastically, if not right on pitch, accompanied with his voice, were among many opera singers with whom I was acquainted from childhood. How could he call this a bastard? I myself had gone to operas when I was not wearing the star, and had enjoyed the Flying Dutchman and the Magic Flute and others. Yet he would not withdraw from his position of either – or. It made for some interesting conversations. And it lightened the load of dealing with evil and the many who defended their actions even when confronted with atrocities and sadistic acts of inhuman treatment of helpless victims. Their standard answer, instead of 'I am sorry I did wrong' was, 'I just followed orders.' Would they have followed orders if they had concerned them and made them victims?

20

❧❦❧

Tomorrow Mother and I have to take the train to Munich to appear at the U.S. Consulate. Mother is distraught because of the possibility that the visa will be denied. During the last part of the war she finally was forced by the Gestapo into giving in, after fighting against the divorce for six years! What will the Consul General say to this situation?

After waiting a while we are admitted into the consuls' office. He offers us two chairs across from his desk and starts reading our applications. Tensely we sit there and watch his face.

"You know that there are certain problems," he takes off his glasses and lays down the applications. Mother sits erect on her chair, straining to understand each word. Her fearful eyes are glued to his face.

"I have here the divorce documents. Your Ex-husband, from whom you are divorced, can not be your sponsor." Mother looks at him aghast and then she begins to weep quietly.

"But you don't understand…" I try to explain.

"I understand perfectly, it happened under pressure."

"My mother has fought for years against the feared Gestapo. She was summoned several times and was threatened with deportation. But she did not want to get a divorce, for my parents love each other. What she has done was to try to save me from deportation. She fought all the way, but in the end there was no way of escape."

Mother takes out a handkerchief and wipes her eyes. She cannot speak.

"What she has done, she has done out of love for me! I owe her my life in more than one way. Her courageous stand saved me!" I am close to tears myself.

"I can understand all of this," the voice of the consul sounds compassionate. "Nevertheless this is an official document which I cannot ignore."

"Can't you do something for us?" I beg. "We have been separated from my father for nine years and he is waiting for us to come and join him so we will finally be reunited as a family."

The consul picks up the papers again and ponders the issue. For a while he is in deep thought. Finally he turns to Mother and says,

"I see only one possibility." We look at him expectantly.

"We will permit you to enter the United States under the condition, that you and your husband get remarried." Mother and I jump up from our seats. If the large desk had not separated us, we would have embraced the consul! The relief and joy are almost too much. We shake his hands and he addresses me,

"But I see here that in a couple of months you will turn twenty-one and we must hasten your emigration. When you are no longer a minor, your father has no legal right to call for you. We must put you in the category of Displaced Persons, for they are the only ones who get permission to emigrate. There are about 12000 of them. I will see that this is done right away and you get your D.P identification and can get into a D.P camp."

Glowing with joy we leave his office. D.P camp? We have no idea what is behind this word, but we would gladly go through Siberia in order to be reunited with Dad and to come to the land of my dreams: America!

21

It is Christmas Eve and we sit on the edge of Mother's bed at the scarred wooden table. Anni had brought us a Christmas present, a little square of real butter and a tiny bag of sugar. We spread the butter carefully on a slice of dark heavy bread and then pour a little sugar on the butter. Slowly we munch each bite. It makes us forget the wretched surroundings. Our life has drastically changed from the day in December 1946 when we packed our belongings and moved into this D.P.camp in the former Funk Kaserne (barracks) in Munich.

We live in a narrow long room with a pot-bellied stove whose pipe leads outside through a broken and cardboard patched up window. It uses wood, but the wood is still green. When the fire is finally burning, smoke pours out of the oven and we have to open the windows for fresh air, which in turn cools off the cold room some more. There are two bunk beds, one behind the other, along one wall. On the other wall is a single bed, a wardrobe and another single bed with a table beside it and two chairs.

There are six people living in this room, an elderly couple from Eastern Europe, speaking a foreign language, a mother and her seven-year old daughter and the two of us. My bed is the upper one on the right side of the door. It has a wooden bottom and I sleep on a bumpy sack filled with straw with a pillow and two Army blankets. Under me sleeps the 80-year old woman, whose racking cough shakes my bed at night, waking her grouchy husband, who bawls her out in a rough voice for disturbing him in his sleep.

We belong to the group now known as D.P.s, mostly survivors of concentration camps and homeless refugees. From the moment we set foot in this camp, sponsored by the UNRRA, the United Nations Relief and Refugee Association, we felt robbed of our human dignity in humiliating ways. We become a link in a chain of uprooted, down trodden survivors, herded together like cattle and processed from one procedure to the next. Crowded together in narrow hallways, we wait to be deloused. Men with hand held pumps spray the white powder into our clothes. After that we have to wait for the medical exams, where we have to undress and are examined, obediently following bellowed out orders. The next procedure is filling out endless forms, always waiting in long lines of shuffling feet.

Although the UNRRA supports this camp and provides food from the USA, there remain only leftovers for the refugees. Most of the food never reaches us, as corrupt officials sell it on the black market. During Christmas week, for instance, we receive for breakfast an aluminum dish filled with watery salted oatmeal and a slice of dark bread; for our midday meal, a couple of potatoes in their skins, one beet or other vegetable, and in the evening another bowl of slimy salty oatmeal and a slice of dark heavy bread.

To escape the monotony of the long days, I join a group of young people who meet in one room around a ping-pong table. We sit around talking and watching endless rounds of ping-pong being played. I discover that most of these young people are from Eastern European countries and have survived the horrors of the concentration camps, due to their youth and stamina. Many have lost close relatives and are now waiting to be shipped to some uncle or other relative in the United States.

Their youth has helped them to overcome the deprivation of food and hard labor, but all of them have scarred souls. One young man who can speak German, asks his Hungarian friend to relate a story to me that he translates. He tells me about a sadistic game which the guards plotted for their entertainment.

"He spit on the ground," the young man said, "and then he pointed at me. I had to creep on all fours on the ground and had to lick up his spit, otherwise he would have shot me dead." I can hardly believe this scene, but I can tell by his hate-filled eyes that he is telling the truth.

On this Christmas Eve the other roommates have left and Mother, Anni and I are sitting around the table and enjoy the pine branch and one candle that Anni has brought. It is the only sign of Christmas in this cheerless room. Mother begins to sing an old Christmas song and we join her. How different this Christmas is from those of the past! Celebration started days ahead of Christmas Eve. As is customary in Germany, the children do not see the deco-rated tree till the evening has arrived and the wax candles are lit. Then the door is opened and the sight takes your breath away. While the old songs are sung, the searching eyes have spied under the tree the dreamed-of toy or whatever was the greatest wish of the childish heart. The joy of running and hugging the fulfillment of the dream, jumping up and down for joy, brought smiles of happiness to the parents' faces. Yes, Christmas has been a wonderful time. Sitting here in these squalid surroundings, not much better than the stable in Bethlehem, the words of 'Joy and Peace to all men' take on new meaning, and the message of Christmas fills the shabby room with glory. Only after experiencing war, can one appreciate what it means to live in a time of peace, where one does not have to be afraid of bombs falling or the sound of gunfire interrupting our singing.

Every time when a new list of emigrants to be shipped to America appears on the bulletin board, our name is not among them. Then we find out that the people in the office expect to be bribed with some valuables. Mother separates herself from her last gold ring; she only wears her wedding ring now. And sure enough, as if by magic, on the next list our names appear. Finally we will leave the depressing Funk Kaserne in Munich to travel to the Northern city of Bremen.

The winter of 1946/47 is extremely cold. Finally we climb into freight cars, like the infamous trains crammed with people heading for extinction. The floor is covered with straw. In the center stands an iron potbellied stove, but there is no wood or coal for starting a fire. There are only small window-like openings to let some light and air in. Each of us receives a grey cardboard box, formerly a ration box for American soldiers. There are enough men and women in the car so that at night we can all lay down on the straw in a star pattern with our feet by the stove. It is going to be a long cold train ride. Once on our many stops we see an open railroad car with coal and some of the men 'organize' enough coal so at least our feet get warm. Thirty-six long ice cold hours we are cooped up in this dark freight train, a trip lasting under normal conditions about seven hours. Finally we arrive in the city of Bremen.

We are taken to a school building and it is clean and spacious. But when we come inside, it is as cold as the outside. There is no heat in the classrooms that serve as dormitories. But there are sheets on the beds, an unusual luxury, and we climb in, sitting up with coats, gloves and caps drawn over our ears. At least after a while we begin to feel a little warmth. Only for the meals we walk to the dining hall, where it is a little warmer from the heat of the kitchen. Suddenly I get shooting pains in my tooth. There is no dentist near by. With my throbbing tooth I have to walk through the icy streets to a streetcar to find the dentist. He looks into my mouth and tells me, that he will try to save my tooth by making a bridge, and if I have some gold for it. I have only a little golden ring, which I hand over to him. Then he informs me that there will be no anesthesia, since he has nothing to take away the pain of drilling and filling and that it would take several visits. I walk through endless streets in below freezing temperatures with my hurting and throbbing teeth and wonder why life can be so cruel.

My 21st birthday has come and gone and we are still in Germany. One after another of the lists appear on the bulletin board but our names are never on them. Our last valuable piece, a wristwatch, is needed to finally get us on the list. It is already the end of February 1947. Finally we are getting closer to our goal! We send a telegram to Dad that we will be arriving soon. We are taken to the port of Bremerhaven by train. When I get out and walk along the pier I can hardly believe what I am seeing. Instead of a mighty ocean liner, such as Dad has showed me as a child, there is this small boat, which I would call an apple Kahn. This should be the ship that takes us across an ocean? How can they crowd a thousand people into this little banana boat that had been used during the war as a troop transport ship. I read its name, "Marine Marlin."

We are directed to the lowest deck of the ship, the hold, below the water line, to an open room with 25 other women. There is no window and the air is stifling. The room is filled with hammocks. We are given three hammocks hanging one above the other. In the top one I make my bed with some difficulty; in the middle one Mother will sleep and in the lower one we put our meager baggage. After we stowed everything away I walk around, trying to get acquainted with our new home for the next ten days. Across the hallway is a large lavatory with long rows of sinks and shower stalls and toilets. I am amazed to see naked women washing themselves, a luxury with the warm water. These women had been deprived of any privacy for so long, that it is only natural to them to walk around naked. I run upstairs on deck to breathe the fresh North Sea air and get away from these cramped quarters.

Outside I walk to the side of the ship to look down on the pier. I want to observe the moment the ship leaves the shore. From the railing I watch the activities prior to departure. The gangway is drawn in and the workers take off the heavy ropes and throw them into the dark water. A tugboat maneuvers in position to pull the ship out of the harbor. Tomorrow it will be nine years less one day that Dad went before us the same way. Only he went on a real ocean liner with all the entertainment and luxuries. Yet I am so filled with gratitude for this cramped little hammock-filled ship that I feel like exploding for joy. How I have waited for this moment! Nine long difficult years! How I have dreamed about it, longed for it, hoped for it – and now it is finally becoming a reality! The last rope cracks the surface of the water.

This is the signal for me. It is the end of my relationship with this country, once having been my beloved homeland. But it turned into the land that denied me my birthright, pushed me out and hunted me, that persecuted me, that hated and hurt me, tried to destroy me; that land, which took away my home, my youth and my education; that land which killed my best friends, made tears my food and taught me nothing but fear. Finally the time has come to leave it! My decision stands firm: I will never set foot on German soil again! Determinedly I turn my back to the receding coastline and walk up to the bow of the ship. Deeply I breathe in the salty air. I am ready for my new life to begin!

The first day on board is an American holiday, George Washington's Birthday. The kitchen crew is American and I marvel at the speed and efficiency with which they pass out the tasty holiday food. Only a small group of us can sit down at a table in a recessed corner where waiters serve us, an unexpected pleasure. After the deprivation and humiliation of the last months one appreciates the taken-for-granted privilege of being served food in porcelain dishes on a white tablecloth. There are not too many people beside us at our table, relishing a festive meal. When did we eat food like this? It seems too long ago. When we finish our main course, a waiter comes, bringing on a tray, which he balances on his right hand, little glass bowls. They are filled with something that makes my mouth water: Real ice cream! How many years ago did I eat my last ice cream? Slowly I let the cool sweetness fill my mouth and heart, slowly savoring each spoon full and finishing up by scraping my bowl till it looks like I licked it clean. What is this? Another bowl in front of me?! The waiter has watched my enjoyment and brought me more! I look up gratefully into the smiling face of the man. Again I savor each spoon with delight and follow the same procedure. All of the other passengers have left the table, only Mother and I are still sitting there. And suddenly, like magic, there is a third bowl before me! I break out in the biggest smile and look thankfully at my donor. I love the ice cream, but more than that, I cherish the fact that there is a human being with a loving heart, who enjoys making a deprived person happy with a few spoons full of a long missed delicacy. To discover that human kindness has not been eradicated from this earth gives me new hope and encouragement. The third bowl I eat slowly in honor of the Father of my new country!

Beside the dining rooms, which are only accessible during meal times, there are no other rooms on the ship where one can sit. A thousand people are crammed into its body and there is no room left for anything else but hammocks. Either you stay in your hammock, which soon becomes boring, or you go up on deck. There are no places to sit down, so many take a blanket and find a sheltered place from the wind and let the sea breeze and the sun in turns cool and warm you. It is winter and the air is chilly, but it is better to have fresh air and sit on wooden planks than to be in the sticky crowded cabin with 25 other women, some of them seasick.

From the start I have been walking the ship from bow to stern, back and forth, catching the waves in my knees, learning to roll with the ship. Dad was proud that he never got seasick by this method. So I am determined not to get sick either, as I see that there are fewer and fewer people at our table for meal times. I enjoy the wide expanse of the ocean, the changing light and reflection of the water, the wake we leave behind, like wide tracks in snow, the invigorating sea air. I love everything about the ocean and enjoy each day as we are getting closer to our new home.

Like a tiny insignificant nutshell we ride across the wide expanse of the water, like a piece of driftwood, occupied by cowering survivors. Outwardly ragged, a band of homeless people, every one carries with him a personal story of tragedy and sorrow. But they all have the same hope, the same dream. The hope that carried them through the hell of the concentration camps, and the dream to find a place of freedom and human dignity, where they can live as equals among equals.

Now every mile takes us closer to the land of our hopes. But mixed in these musings about the future are anxious thoughts. Will the dream be realized or will it end in disappointment? Will freedom really be what I expected it to be in times of slavery? Will the deep wounds, torn by inhuman treatment ever be healed? Will it be possible to find understanding and develop trust? Can one regain a positive and healthy outlook on life, when the soul has been damaged through years of living under fear and repression? These unspoken questions are on many minds, as we search the horizon like Columbus for the appearance of the Promised Land.

Finally! After ten days we see for the first time in the distance the remarkable skyline of the city of New York, silhouetted against the pink morning sky. It is the third of March 1947. Everybody has gathered on deck and pushes against the railing. Quietly, in hushed tones, yet with rapt attention we pass the Statue of Liberty, holding up the torch of freedom in a welcoming greeting. Looking at the people around me, we are the perfect illustration for the apt poem by Emma Lazarus:

"Give me your tired, your poor,

Your huddled masses,

Yearning to breathe free,

The wretched refuse of your teeming shore.

Send them, the homeless, tempest-tossed to me,

I lift my lamp beside the golden door!"

The thrilling sights and feelings of anticipation are almost too much for Mother. Her beloved husband will soon be in her arms again! I am more caught up in the happenings of the moment, watching the tugboats pulling us closer to the pier. I can see a crowd of people awaiting our arrival, pushing against fences, trying to catch a glimpse of a relative or friend, whom they had thought dead or lost for years but with whom they would soon be united again. A woman standing in front of me holds a small pair of binoculars to her eyes. I tip her on the shoulder.

"When you're done, do you mind if I take a look?"

She hands me the glass and I wonder, where should I start to look at this large crowd. I lift the glass to my eyes – and the first person I focus on is – Dad! I recognize him immediately. I jump up and down like crazy, shouting and waving, "Daddy, Daddy!" but of course he cannot see or hear me. There are two many people and we are still too far away from the pier.

We must bridle our impatience for another two hours of formalities before we can leave the ship. Mother following me, I run straight to the place where I had seen my father waiting behind the fence. The green wooden fence posts between us we grab his hands reaching out for us, Mother taking one and I holding on to the other. In spite of eyes brimming with tears of joy, I can see that he has hardly changed. He still looks like the picture I carried around in my heart all these years. After the last examination of our papers we finally can kiss and fall into each other's arms, never to let go again.

Riding in a taxi through the impressive streets of New York, I lean closely against my beloved Dad. He looks at me again and again, as if he sees me for the first time. His little girl, whom he saw last as a kid of 12 years, running and waving beside his exiting train, has now become a young woman of 21. I share his thoughts. Will we ever be able to bridge the gap of nine lost years, those important character forming, growing up years where I would have needed his fatherly protection and advice? How can I explain to him the experiences that have molded me, and the spiritual development and conviction growing out of them that made my belief a personal possession, a faith that he did not share? Yet one thing I know as I cling to his arm: We love each other and God has made a miracle come true by bringing us finally together again! My heart is filled with so much gratitude that I could embrace the whole world!

We end up on the tenth floor of a down town hotel with a breath-taking view of tall skyscrapers. I cannot tear myself away from the window. No bombed out buildings, no ruined cities, no brick-strewn rubble lots on which children played, no more grey people carefully sidestepping bomb holes in streets leading to nowhere, no more endless queues standing in line for bread or potatoes. This here is paradise, a paradise filled with pulsating, colorful, energy-laden life!

"Let's get something to eat," Dad suggests and we walk through the streets. I stop to get a look at the top of the skyscrapers and still cannot comprehend how anyone could work way up high in these offices. How could they concentrate on their work with such a view?

"After we eat," promises Dad," we will drive to the Empire State Building, the highest in the city, and from the top you will get a good view of New York."

He opens a door and gently pushes us inside.

"What is this?" I inquire.

"This is a cafeteria. Here, take this," and he shoves a tray into my hands.

"Now look at the food and take what ever your heart desires; just follow the line, I will pay at the end."

I take a look along the counter, displaying rows upon rows of the most colorful and fantastic looking food I have ever seen. The sight is overwhelming! How can this be possible? So much wonderfully inviting food? The fairy tale comes to mind of Schlaraffia land where roasted pigeons fly into your mouth. This here is even better than a fairy tale! I look up and down undecidedly. Dad comes back for me with some dishes on his tray.

"You must make up your mind," he whispers, "there are people waiting in line behind you."

I reach for the first plate before me and move on. On a lettuce leaf and a slice of red tomato and white onion rings rests a piece of sour herring. My first unforgettable meal in America!

After the visit to the cafeteria Dad takes us to a soda fountain in a drug store, where we sit on round stools in front of a bar, watching a fast working sales clerk putting together a wonderful concoction called a hot-chocolate ice cream sundae with whipped cream topping. More delicious things are in this world than I ever dreamed of!

We pass a large department store.

"Do you need anything?" Dad asks. Do we need anything? We look like rag-a-muffins in our patched stockings and worn coats. On a display table I spy a cute looking red cap. Dad sees my longing eyes and picks it up from its stand.

"Here, try this on!" I look in a mirror and smile. What a red cap can do to a girl! It makes you forget the stockings with the darned runs in them. He buys it along with new stockings and I strut through the streets of New York like the whole world belongs to me. What an overwhelming world of riches, a land of freedom blessed with milk and honey! And it is to be my very own world!

22

I can hardly believe that the Golden State of California, of which I had read and dreamed about, will be my new home! After a long train ride, three nights and two days across the expanse of the great continent from coast to coast, we are welcomed to Los Angeles by bright sunshine and the deepest blue sky I have ever seen. As we drive through streets, filled with bungalows surrounded by lawns and overflowing gardens with bushes and flowers of every hue and color, I see my dream come true. I cannot get enough of the Pacific Ocean with its wide sandy beaches and blue water, crowned by white waves, rolling peacefully against the shore. Gently sloping hills, dotted with light colored Mediterranean-style villas, surrounded by dark green bushes and high palm trees swaying in the breeze, are a delight to the senses, that still are used to drab and depressing surroundings of a war torn country. If I were a painter, I would be constantly finding new motives of symphonies of color, like the riotous bougainvillea bushes exciting the eye. My hunger and thirst for life, for unencumbered youth, is insatiable. I want to make up for the years I have lost, want to taste all the joys I have missed and enjoy life to the fullest. This is the place to be, a city catering to a public hungry for the easy life and for entertainment.

One week after our arrival I find a job with an insurance agency in downtown L.A. Dad's widowed sister, Martha, has taken me in, for my parent's apartment, within walking distance, is too small. The first thing they did upon arriving was to get married again. Now they celebrate a second honeymoon.

Soon I discover that my aunt sees in me a substitute for her late daughter who had died in her thirties. As a child I had loved this cousin. She had been my favorite one, with her doe-like gentle eyes, her soft voice and beautiful face, while I despised her cigar smoking father, who always pinched my cheeks roughly with the question:

"And what poem are you going to recite today?" She had trained to become a physician and emigrated to Palestine as one of the early Zionists, who had a dream of Palestine becoming a homeland for the Jews. Soon after her arrival she began working in a hospital, where she contacted an aggressive strain of tuberculosis and returning to Lausanne, Switzerland, she died and was buried there. My aunt never got over her death.

Her other daughter, Ursula, who married a physician, lives in well-to-do Beverly Hills, where her husband, Fritz, has his practice. Proudly she tells me that they have Thomas Mann among their patients. She herself had helped her husband in Berlin in the X-ray room, before anyone knew that unprotected exposure to x-rays could cause infertility. Since they have no children, her manicured black poodle, Conchita, wearing a little bow on her brushed and shaped poodle locks, takes the place of a child. Whenever we come to visit, Conchita has to perform her many tricks, like rolling over or pretending to be dead or playing the piano. The crowning piece is the command, "Conchita, pray!" where the dog dutifully sits on her haunches and puts her front paws together. Every body claps and laughs and Conchita jumps around and barks hysterically!

Ursula spends most of her days going from one social event to the next or improving her golf game, where she brought home many trophies, which she proudly displays. Upon my first visit she takes me, her poor cousin, who does not own one good-looking dress, into her walk-in closet in the mansion where they live and sorts through her dresses for me. She laughingly lets me in on a secret. She buys clothes at a cheaper place, but then sews labels of famous brand names, which she saves from other pieces, into the dress or coat, so anybody picking up the piece thinks it is the real expensive thing. I guess in the social world she lives in this is enough to impress people with your worth, to have a label of Saks Fifth Avenue in a May Company coat. Her clothes fit me and I leave with an arm full of nice, a bit outdated dresses, and with shoes that are half a number too small for me and pinch my toes.

Aunt Martha lives in an apartment hotel with maid service. I occupy one of the two bedrooms with my own bath and we have breakfast together before I leave for work in the morning. When I got my first paycheck of $120 for a month of hard, very responsible work, I turn it over to my parents and Aunt Martha dishes out my weekly allowance of $2.50. I have to pay for bus transportation, stamps, stockings and other things, so there are not 10 cents left over for a candy bar at the end of the week.

It takes me a while to get accustomed to the carefree California life style. At first, while riding the bus to work, I had to reassure myself, that there was nobody on this bus, who could do me any harm. I was a free person for the first time in my life! I did not have to be afraid when somebody looked at me twice, where before my heart had cringed. I was a human being with rights and privileges. I did not have to register at the police station, nor would there ever be a knock on the door at night, nor need I be afraid of seeing a person in uniform. The longed for freedom had to be tried on like a new coat, covering the rags of my insecure and fear dominated past. My self-assurance grew slowly but steadily and with that new assurance my love for this free country grew, which had welcomed me with open arms and offered me the chance of a productive and fulfilled life. No one, who has not been living under suppression or in slavery, can understand what it means to be free! It is so overwhelming, as if the prison guard announces unexpectedly to the man on death row,

"Come on out! Your door is open! You are a free man!"

Too many people in this country take for granted the freedom that their forefathers fought for to make it the basis of a new kind of government. Even when there are still shortcomings in reality to this 'liberty for all,' it is by far the most humane of all governments. "Freedom from fear" is the greatest gift a country can offer those, who knew nothing but fear or were forced to live their lives under the constant threatening shadow of being at the mercy of evil-minded men without possibilities to defend themselves or to change existing situations. Where the foundations of freedom are assailed or eroded, the very roots of compassion and human sympathy die out and selfishness and hatred begin their destructive work.

Ursula wanted me to meet some young people and took me along to a dance in their temple in Hollywood, where I met a young man, who had emigrated from Germany before the war. He had just bought his first car, a used Chevy convertible, and he invited me to discover the beauties of California with him. Every weekend we spent exploring and sightseeing, going to the beach or driving up to the mountains. How I loved these excursions along some winding roads through canyons or to the side of a lake high up in the mountains. The air was clear and the snow-covered Mount Baldy framed acres of orange orchards with their sweet smelling white blossoms and their round-the-year fruit. What a beautiful country I was privileged to live in!

The insurance firm has trouble paying the salaries of their employees. It is tottering on the brink of bankruptcy. After three months I look for and find another job that pays twenty-five dollars more. It is a wholesale jewelry firm for fashion jewelry. The work is easy and I spend my brown bag lunchtime on the roof of the ten-story building in downtown L.A., enjoying the view and the sunshine. The weekends are spent with Henry and his Chevy. But sometimes I have a nagging feeling that something is missing in my life. I miss my little church and the faithful Pastor Guertler. On Sunday morning I attend some neighborhood churches, but their different names and ways of worship confuse me. In Germany there was only one church for Protestants, the Lutheran church.

Perhaps to join some choir would help. Singing in a choir has been a good experience in the past. As I browse through the paper I come across an ad seeking voices for a new choir in Hollywood. I audition and am accepted. We sing songs like "Stardust" or "Smoke gets in your eyes" or "Tea for Two" and other 'in' tunes. The choir director is training us to become a background choir for Hollywood movies. It is fun to sing songs by Gershwin instead of chorales by Bach.

Tonight is another choir practice. I sit in the Hollywood bus. A lanky strange looking man gets on the bus. He has fuzzy reddish hair and his eyes peer through glasses with thick lenses. He wears a blue-white striped seersucker suit. Under his arm he carries a big black Bible. Why of all places would he have to sit next to me? I look out of the window.

"Excuse me," he turns to me, "could you please tell me the time?" I look at my watch.

"It is a quarter past seven," I answer.

"Oh, I hope I won't be late," he continues with this unfettered lightness in conversation, this breaking through barriers, which Europeans have erected for centuries to hold people at arm's length and in their place, keeping them back from mingling with different classes, like aristocrats and peasants. This is so new to me that people converse without knowing each other. I like this informality yet I have difficulty to begin a little chat.

"Where are you going?" I try to practice the art of light conversation.

"I am going to a meeting of young people to hear a woman, who has just returned from Europe."

Europe? My curiosity is aroused. I have not heard of anybody traveling to Europe in July 1947.

"You should hear that woman speak! You won't regret it! She speaks each Wednesday evening. Wouldn't you like to come and hear her?"

What does this guy want from me? Is this a new way of contacting girls?

"No, thank you, I have other plans."

"But next Wednesday perhaps?" He does not give up easily.

"Perhaps." I am not going to fall for his trick. What does this funny looking man want from me anyhow?

"This woman speaks in the College Department of the First Presbyterian Church of Hollywood. I could meet you there next week!"

Did he say church? What is this inner voice whispering? 'Don't refuse this invitation!'

"Do you have anything to write?" he asks.

I look inside my purse, but all I can find is a sales slip from a drug store. Under the printed words "Thank You" he writes an address. I put the paper into my purse.

"Excuse me, I have to get off at the next stop." Politely he makes room for me.

"Thank you," I say.

"See you next week!" he answers.

What a strange person!

Two weeks later the choir practice is cancelled. I take the bus as usual and get off at the stop he wrote down. I can see the church with its square red brick tower from afar. As I come closer, there is the man in a blue white striped seersucker suit standing on the street corner. He is actually waiting for me! As he sees me, his face lights up in a smile.

"I have expected you," he says as he shakes my hand, "I knew you were coming."

How did he know? I did not even make up my mind to come until an hour ago. He leads me into a hall filled with college age people.

At the reception table I am registered as visitor and assigned to a 'Big Sister' Emmy Lou, who takes me under her wings, explains what is happening and introduces me to other people. I feel at ease already after this friendly reception.

I sit down among the young people and am curious what will happen. Their songs, which are so different from the mediaeval anthems I am used to, are easy to sing along. Then a young man, their leader, gets up and asks that every head be bowed and every eye closed. I wonder why. He begins to pray. I look up, nevertheless, to see where his prayer book is, but there is no book.

I guess he makes it up in his head. After that he asks the audience, if there is anybody who would like to share an experience with God. I cannot imagine anybody getting up. Such personal things you don't share with everybody! Yet one after another stands up, tells a story and sits down again. Sometimes the people clap. How can you clap in a service? I am flabbergasted.. What did I get myself into? What kind of group is this?

Now appears the woman whom I came to hear. The young man introduces her lovingly as 'Teacher'. Emmy Lou whispers,

"Her name is Henrietta Mears." I guess she is in her mid-fifties, of medium height with a sturdy figure. She is fashionably dressed and wears large earrings. Her gray hair is freshly coiffed and ever so often she uses a lace handkerchief to dab her near-sighted eyes sparkling vividly from behind thick glasses. She walks upright and poised and radiates a natural elegance, as people from well-to-do families often exhibit. With a strong rather low voice, sometimes a little hoarse, she begins to speak. No, this is no regular speaking; her words seem to tumble out of her mouth so fast, as if trying to catch up with her speeding thoughts. Often the whole group breaks out in loud laughter about a humorous remark. At other times they hang rapturously on her lips as she emphasizes some truth. With enthusiasm and a bit of acting talent she holds the crowd under her spell, as she relates personal experiences of her trip to war-ravaged Europe and later about a letter that the Apostle Paul sent to the church in Rome. It rings a bell. Wasn't the word that God spoke to me in my little cold room in Bavaria also from Romans? Interestedly I listen to her explain the Bible, which she expounds with authority and humor. I look around me and see several young people bent over their own Bibles, underlining certain words or passages. Surely there is no boredom in this room!

Teacher closes the lesson with a prayer. I have never heard anybody pray like that. It is as if she addresses God personally like a friend and speaks to him, as if he would be right next to her instead of someplace far away in heaven. Her words touch something in my heart.

After the program the young people stand in small groups, talking and sipping lemonade and munching cookies. Emmy Lou introduces me proudly as a newcomer from Germany, which seems to interest most of them. I feel like an exotic animal. They gather around and I have to answer many questions. But my personal story I keep under cover. Yet one thing I know as I say good-bye to Emmy Lou, I am going to come back again!

23

⌘

The pine forests in the San Bernardino Mountains smell just as good as I formerly enjoyed the scent of freshly mowed hay fields in Bavaria. I walk by myself through the woods on the camp area of Forest Home. Three weeks after my first visit, Emmy Lou persuaded me to attend a conference in the mountains.

"What are you going to do there?" I wanted to know.

"It is just like a vacation in the mountains with a couple hundred young people and with Teacher and other good speakers. We will have a great time together!"

"But I have to work!"

"You could come for the first weekend and be back at work Monday." Emmy Lou's enthusiasm had carried the day.

When I tell Mother of my plans, she pushes some money into my hand and wishes me a good trip. The church bus takes me up and I enjoy the weekend so much that I leave early Monday morning for work with a heavy heart. My desire is to return, to listen more to Teacher and to enjoy the fellowship. I beg my boss to let me off early, and he gives me time off, being it is the Labor Day weekend. On Thursday afternoon two students take me along in their car. "One mile nearer heaven" says the banner across the road leading to the entrance of the camp. I go searching for Emmy Lou. In a rustic cabin, which four girls share, I find her and she embraces me. It is not only the new friendship that had drawn me back, but also the many unsettled and repressed issues in my life.

The last one was the experience with Henry. During the last three months we had spent many hours together and our friendship

140

had grown. I was not really in love with him, yet I enjoyed our outings together and to have a boyfriend after all of these years gave me a good feeling. On a Sunday evening, after spending a day at Lake Arrowhead in the mountains, I asked him to drop me off at the College Department, where I wanted to take part in an evening meeting.

"You want me to take you to church? You better give some thought to what you are doing," Henry said threateningly as he stopped. "If you insist on going in there tonight, it will be the last time we will see each other!"

"But Henry, after all we've been….."

"I mean what I said! You better think twice!"

I stare at him. How can he be so intolerant and narrow-minded? He himself is no practicing Jew, just attends dances at the temple, but he wants to forbid me to go into a church? Doesn't our relationship mean anything to him? I open the door to get out.

"It is your decision!" The determination and anger in his voice makes me hesitate. Shall I get back in again? I am torn by the fear of losing him and the ending of our relationship and wanting to be at the meeting. But then I remain standing on the sidewalk. Perhaps he will change his mind. Thoughts race through my head in the few seconds that I debate with myself. No, never! No one is ever going to force me to do things against my will! I am a free human being, who can make my own decisions and act according to my own convictions. I am not ready to give up that new gift of freedom to anybody! Too long it had remained a sought after and longed for ideal, and now since I possess it, I will not trade it for any person, who thinks he has the right to dictate to me against my own desire.

"O.K. Then it's good-bye! You wanted it that way."

Without another word Henry pulls the door shut from inside and takes off, leaving me standing there. I follow the car with my eyes, defiant and sad at the same time. It hurts to be left standing like that after everything that has bound us to each other the last few months. So he is a Jew and I am a Christian. My parents are too. Yet they love each other and tolerate each other's faith. Why must there always be such conflict and emotional obstinacy among religions? Why couldn't we have talked about the issue and reach a consensus? Did not both of our religions teach that you should love your neighbor? Was this love? I get no answer and sadly walk over to attend the evening service. One thing is certain; I will never see Henry again.

"Lift up your eyes to the mountains. From whence cometh your help?" Mendelssohn's song, which I sang in the choir at our Lessler Secondary School, comes to mind as I sit outside for the evening meeting on bleachers among the crowd of young people. I watch how the fingers of the setting sun climb up the mountain side, transforming the gray to gold and reaching up to the sharp craggy peaks with its last red hues. Long lost melodies appear in my head and silently I sing the soprano part and the words take on new meaning. "Your help comes", the high voices of the sopranos had sung following the lead of the altos, "from the Lord, who made heaven and earth." Where do the sudden tears come from? How can music touch the hidden memories so gently, which otherwise are closed up and locked, as soon as words brush against the hurting part? Like feelers of a snail are drawn in at first contact with the curious fingers of a child, so the delicate fabric of wounded memories will not unfold to probing questions.

The meeting has ended and the crowd disperses. I take a stroll away from the sound of conversation and laughter. Tonight I need solitude. Good friends often help when one feels depressed. They lift you up with a sixth sense of empathy, knowing just how you feel. But empathy is not what I need tonight. I am at a point of crisis and no one can help me to go through it. I have to walk this way alone. No, not alone, but with God. He has spoken to my heart through the words of Teacher and I know that I can no longer evade his questions. What would happen if I give my buried memories free reign tonight?

Like a pack of excited hunting dogs they cower at my feet, howling and impatiently barking, waiting for the releasing whistle to jump up and run for the game, sniffing noses to the ground. Would they obey me when I whistle them back? Or would they continue on their own ways, getting away from my control and bringing back a bloody bounty, dropping it at my feet, which I dread?

Darkness arrives fast in Southern California and with it an infinite sky of millions of stars opens up. One can never really see the night sky in or near a city, but here in the mountains the darkness seems to draw the eyes into an unlimited vast expanse of unknown and unexplored wonders of the universe.

I sit down on a rock still sharing the warmth of the sun. The outlines of pine trees show up against the dark sky. I hear laughter and guitar playing from a distance. Like a pale nebulous stream the Milky Way flows over my head. The nights of the Pleiades are past, in which hundreds of falling stars can be seen, but I still look for a stray one. What would I wish upon a star? The romantic longing for the transcendent, the eternal, reaching out to some mysterious distant answer to all my wishes and desires are resonating in my heart. I know I have reached a turning point in my life. Things I had buried for a long time suddenly come to life. I am afraid to touch the hurting wounds, yet I also want healing and cleansing.

There are too many unfinished things in my life, too many loose ends, too little direction or purpose. Listening to the speakers, I am convicted that I must stop running and face issues I would rather evade. The time of drifting and aimless living must come to an end. But if I face these things, I fear that they will have consequences for my life. Am I ready and willing for that?

I get up from my rock and move cautiously through the darkness in the direction from where the voices and the music came. A group of young people have gathered around a tall lantern surrounded by fluttering insects. Their laughter breaks through the stillness of the night. They are engaged in the old, ever new game of flirting, that searching for the one who will quiet the longings of the heart. It is a good feeling to be in their midst and share their laughter. For tonight, at least, the dogs were obedient. They listened to my whistle and returned.

24

"You have come up to this mountain," the full voice of Teacher fills the large auditorium, "and God wants to talk to you this morning. We want to give him a chance to speak to us, to finish unfinished business or get direction in a decision he wants you to make. So everybody just quietly and without talking to his neighbor, take your Bibles along and find a place where you can be alone with him. We will meet here again in an hour."

Shuffling feet are the only sound as everybody disburses. Where should I go? After a short hike I end up in an almost dry riverbed. A small mountain creek is jumping from rock to rock, causing little waterfalls. This must be Teacher's miracle of which Emmy Lou had spoken. Teacher was looking for a conference center all over California. When she finally came to Forest Home, which was on sale, she knew she had found the right place. But the owners wanted to sell it at a high price that was unaffordable. She had to pass on it, although it was the ideal place for her purposes. Yet she did not give up, not Teacher! She kept on praying and next spring, after a disastrous and destructive flood, which ruined the whole area, she got her dream for half price!

And what she has created out of it! I admire this woman with her vision and wisdom and her positive ability to challenge young people to give and do their best. Where she detects prospective leadership abilities, she zeroes in and helps that person to develop talents and gifts he never thought he had. But she also challenges them to keep things in perspective. When a young college student, whom she mentored, wanted to enter the ministry, he was offered a contract to play pro-football instead. She answered his questions of what he should do, play football first and later go in the ministry, with an admonition. He should read a short Bible verse and cross out one of two words. The verse was: 'Not so, Lord!' The young man came back. "I have crossed out the "Not so!" he said and became a well known minister.

Observing her dealings with people and how she approached me, I noticed another secret of her outstanding qualities. Not only was she a brilliant teacher with a sharp intellect and great sense of humor, which won the hearts of even the most skeptical listeners, but she was also a people oriented person. If you talked to her about anything, she concentrated one hundred percent on you. To her you were the most important person and she made you feel that way. She remembered names and details you casually mentioned, and many months later, would refer to that name, as if she knew him or her personally. An amazing gift!

God led me to the right mentor. As I sit down by the brook and think over my life, it is like the experience that Jacob of the Old Testament had, when he wrestled a long night with an angel, recounting his crooked, deceitful life (Jacob means 'deceiver.') He said, ' I will not let you go unless you bless me'. That is my desire also, and after a rending and painful acknowledgment of my need for God's help in dealing with the experiences of the past and my hatred and desire for revenge, I am able to accept the forgiveness offered by God through Jesus' death on the cross. And then the blessing comes. I resolved my dishonest hiding of my past and was challenged to deal with my limitation to forgive those who had wronged and hurt me. Only Jesus could call from the agony of the cross, 'Father, forgive them, for they know not what they do.' Only his spirit in me can enable me to do the same to my enemies. By repenting of harboring hate and the desire to return evil for evil, and by asking for forgiveness and applying it and receiving the new life, for which Christ gave his life, I received a new direction and purpose, found peace of heart and mind, and, most important of all, was filled with the unconditional, unselfish Agape-love from God.

As I ponder the future, one thing becomes very clear in my mind. God had spared my life for a purpose. I did not any more deserve to live, than so many untold others, who had been murdered and deprived of the joy of living. I am not better than any of the dead. What could I do with this spared life? Making plans like normally young people make at this time of their life, seems to be out of the question. I want to keep the memories alive of those, who had been so cruelly taken at the threshold of their adulthood. But I also need to turn the leadership of my life over to God, who had saved me from total destruction. I have no right to plans that leave him out. The logical conclusion to these trains of thought is the decision to serve God wherever he wants to use me.

God is a God of miracles! No mental effort, no human resolutions, no iron will power could do what he has done for me. He took hate and an unforgiving spirit out of my heart and replaced it with his love. I have only obeyed what Teacher told us: Let go – and let God! My heart is filled with joy as I am on my way to tell her of my decision and the change of heart he has accomplished. But I would also like a word of affirmation from the Bible. As I open it, my eyes fall on this verse: "No one who puts his hand to the plow and looks back, is fit for the Kingdom of God." Luke 9:62. These are my marching orders. He has chosen me as one of his laborers. With my eyes on the goal I will plow the fields to prepare them for a good and plentiful harvest.

"Look at this big world map on the wall," Teacher points behind her. "I want to challenge you to write your name over any place on this map that is close to your heart and that you want to bring before God in prayer." Without hesitation I march up to the map and write my name over the city of Berlin, my native city. From this day, the 1st of September 1947 it is MY city in a completely new way.

25

⚬❧⚭

This is the last day of my vacation. I wake up with a happy dream.

"I am going to get a new job today!" I tell Aunt Martha, waiting for me at the breakfast table.

"It's about time," her voice sounds reproachful, "you should have started looking long ago." Two weeks ago my boss surprised my colleague and myself with the bad news.

"The business is not doing well, and so I am forced to terminate the two last hired employees," he said. Aunt Martha was distraught at the news that hardly upset me. But to her I am still the substitute daughter and it is difficult for her to give up this wishful thinking, although some of my ideas seem strange to her.

"What are you doing up at six in the morning?" she asks me a few days ago. "I always see light in your room."

"I study." Her face lights up. Studying means a lot to her.

"Oh? You want to continue your education at night school perhaps? What are you reading?"

"I study a book that will make me wise."

"What is that?"

"The Old and the New Testament." She remains quiet, but I can see disappointment on her face. It is difficult for her, the secular Jewess, to share the joy and listen to my tales when I get home from some great meeting and am full of what I have heard. Once it was too much for her and she stops me cold.

"I cannot stand this any longer! I don't want the word 'church' mentioned in my house again!"

It is an order I respect. I am reminded of Henry, who never called again. But when she attacks me, while riding in the car with her daughter and husband, that she would be ashamed to be a Christian, after all the atrocities the Christians have done to the Jews, I cannot be quiet. I try to explain that those perpetrators could never have been real Christians, for Jesus challenges us to love even our enemies and to do good to them that persecute us.

"Because they have never heard the truth of God's great love for them," I try to explain, "that is the reason why they did these terrible things. How can a loving human being harm or torture or even kill another?" She still clings to her version. Fritz, the driver, asks pensively,

"Do you believe in a personal God?"

"Yes, with all my heart."

"I cannot believe that," he says and then falls silent.

I try not to broach the subject again, but attempt to make the change in my life visible not by words but by my attitude and reaction and change in life style. Yet some months later, Aunt Martha asks a question which is evidence to me that she has been listening to our pastor's weekly Sunday evening broadcast, while I attend the youth meetings.

When I told her two weeks ago that I had lost my job, I said, that I would like to take a vacation first, before looking for another job. I began my first job the second week after arriving in the U.S. and had not had a time off since. Mother had found a job and Dad worked also and they did not depend on my money any longer. I just needed some rest.

Today the two weeks have come to an end. She hands me the newspaper and I begin looking through the Help Wanted ads. Two agencies advertise promising jobs that I cut out.

'I wish you good luck!" Aunt Martha calls after me.

The first employment agency with the better paying job is my destination. The lady behind the desk advises me.

"It is a good job. They pay $185 a month. How fast can you type?"

"About 45 – 50 words a minute."

"Tell them that you can type 60 words a minute. I already sent two girls there and they did not get hired. Here is the address; you can present yourself right away."

I leave the building with the address in my hand. Outside on the sidewalk I decide against that job. Why should I lie to get a job at the expense of honesty? I put the paper in my pocket and pull out the other agencies' address. It is only a few blocks away. I open the door to the office.

"Well, what are you doing here?" My former colleague, who had been let off together with me, sits in the waiting area. "Are you also looking for a job?" she asks and smiles.

I tell her what had happened at the first agency and why I did not want to go to the address I had been given. She wants to see the job description. I pull out the piece of paper and she begins to read.

"But that sounds like a good job!" she exclaims, "why don't you just try out for it?"

"Do you think I should? But I will not lie!" Maybe she is right. I thank her and without registering I turn around again and leave.

I take the bus to the address on the paper. It is a large wholesale appliance business, distributing refrigerators, washing machines, toasters, mixers and radios. I am led to the big office of one of the owners. He gets up to greet me and I hand him the agencies' papers.

"You speak with a slight accent," the older gentleman says in a friendly tone of voice, "could it be German?"

"Yes, I have arrived from Germany just a year ago," I answer.

"Oh, how interesting!" he sits down in a leather chair behind his desk. "Well, tell me about your life and the conditions over there." I describe a few impressions and experiences. He listens and asks more questions. We get into a lively conversation that I almost forget why I came. Then he leans back in his chair and asks,

"When can you start working?"

"I am ready immediately!"

"Good. Have some lunch first, and then I will see to it that somebody will introduce you to your new place of work." He shakes my hand again and I leave the room. With a happy heart I walk outside.

No lies, no compromises, – instead a warm and personal reception! Before lunch I call Aunt Martha.

"I have a new job and I will start right after lunch. Didn't I tell you this morning, Today is the day that God would give me a job? I will be home at six thirty. See you then!"

As with all new jobs, the first days are hectic. I have ten different salesmen whose orders I have to type and whose names and faces I am trying to settle in my mind. Beside them many other employees introduce themselves, for they all must pass my desk coming and going.

"Guten Tag! Wie geht's?" I look up in surprise.

"Danke, gut. But where did you learn to speak German?" The greeting comes from a salesman in a different department.

"I learned it as a child in my family. I admit it was only a dialect, but later in college I took real German. Auf Wiedersehen!" On his way to his office he briefly stops and waves at me.

A few days later my telephone rings.

"Hallo! Einen schoenen guten Tag!" Oh, it's the German again.

"May I invite you to go out for dinner with me tonight?" the voice at the other end asks, "I know a nice restaurant by the ocean."

"I don't know," I answer businesslike. I don't want my superior to hear that I receive a personal call.

"Why don't you simply say, 'Yes'? I could pick you up at seven."

"Well, I don't...." I hesitate.

"What is your address?"

I try to sound official as I pass on the address of my parents.

"Good! I will meet you there at seven o'clock!"

After work I walk over to the apartment of my parents. They should see the man with whom I have a date. The bell rings and I run to the door to meet him on the stairs.

"Hi! Before we go in may I ask you for your name? I could not remember it and I want to introduce you to my parents."

He chuckles and replies,

My name is Sam. Sam Entz." I lead him to the living room.

"Mother, Dad, I want you to meet Sam Entz."

"Guten Tag! Wie geht es Ihnen?"

Mother's face is beaming.

"How wonderful, that you can speak German," she exclaims and shakes his hand vigorously. Dad gets up and they shake hands also. I know he has been accepted. They like this tall, bespectacled man with blue eyes and the figure of an athlete and hearty handshake, who even speaks their language. His round face bordered by ash-blond hair, combed to hide a bald spot, gives Mother the impression, that this man is about ten years older than her daughter. Her husband is also ten years her senior. Yes, she feels, taken by his open and warm manner, that she can trust him with her only child. She follows us to the door and watches from the window as we get into a brand new Chrysler convertible and drive off.

As my favorite place, the Pacific Ocean, comes into sight, we drive along the highway and find a parking spot by a restaurant, built close to the cliffs. We walk across the highway to the beach to the bottom of a small lighthouse. We sit on its steps, watching the reddish golden sun slowly disappear in the waves on the horizon, casting a red hue over the water.

During the delicious dinner, we talk about our families and our backgrounds. It is an easy conversation, as if we had known each other for some time. I discover that Sam is the youngest of seven children of a Mennonite farmer in South Dakota.

"My father is a lay preacher in their church," he mentions and my ears perk up. So he grew up in a Christian family, but I also suspect by his relating the story of his family that he is not a Christian. I want to know more about the Mennonites and he explains that they have their roots in the Netherlands and Germany, where in the 16th century Menno Simon started this pacifist group, who would not take up weapons and believed in baptism as a sign of a personal faith decision to follow Christ. Even today in America, many of them still speak German. Sam speaks a strange dialect, called 'Hutterish,' named after Jacob Hutter from Austria, who was burnt at the stake during reformation times because of his Ana-Baptist views. Through centuries of persecution, the Hutterite group had stayed together, having all things in common. Katherine the Great, the Russian empress, had given them land to settle on the Crimea and granted exemption from army service. But after some time they were persecuted again. Many of them ended up in Siberia, but others arrived in 1871 in America, starting their colonies in different areas. Sam's father had left a colony in South Dakota when he was sixteen and did not get along with his stepfather. He married the daughter of the Mennonite family that had taken him in. Together they had seven children. I assume that his parents and other siblings are praying for Sam to become a Christian.

At the end of the evening we get into this maroon dream car with leather seats and white sidewall tires and a tan top. Relaxing on the luxurious seats, I lean back satisfied by the good meal and conversation. What a nice evening this has been! I thoroughly enjoyed myself getting to know Sam and now riding in this new smelling car with automatic transmission. What a far cry from the rough riding jeeps or the old pre-war Opel! We are driving back on Wilshire Boulevard and I look at the passing scenery. Los Angeles is such a spread out city and it is still growing. The orange groves are slowly disappearing and new subdivisions are springing up everywhere. The year-round sunshine and the laid back life style and the lure of Hollywood is drawing more and more people to the West Coast..

What is that? I feel my left hand being held and instinctively pull it back. Why such an intimate gesture when we hardly know each other? A few hours ago I did not even know his name! I move slightly over to the right. This is not how I am used to be treated! Everything in its time! I am not ready for hand-holding. In my traditional upbringing the girl gives the signals when she is ready and willing. A suitor who pushes himself on a defensive girl would never have a chance. He puts his hand back on the steering wheel and continues driving in insulted silence. Well, if you don't want to talk to me, I will be quiet too! What a childish reaction! I will never again go out with a man like that! How can you be so stubborn and stop talking altogether? In front of Aunt Martha's apartment hotel, to which I give him short directions, I get out of the car before he can open the door for me.

"Thank you for the dinner," I say with icy voice.

"Not worth mentioning," he murmurs and shuts the door behind me with more power than necessary.

"Good night," I say and walk quickly into the building. What a stubborn guy! Why did he have to spoil the nice evening?

Several weeks have gone by. Each time he has to pass my desk, we greet each other politely without exchanging any more words. He never stops to talk. It is a Saturday. I had to work till noon and I am the last one from our department to leave. Suddenly I hear steps behind me and a voice says,

"Hello!" It is Sam. "Isn't it a great day outside?"

"Yes, it is really nice weather."

"I think I will take my boat out this afternoon for a spin." My ears perk up.

"You have a boat?"

"Yes, it's a four-seat speed boat and it can skim really fast over the water. It's a lot of fun." Pictures of long forgotten times dance before my eyes. Blue skies, wind blowing through my hair, sails fluttering, drops of water spraying my face – oh, how I had loved to be on the water!

"I often went sailing in Berlin," I say wistfully, "but it was a long time ago". He catches the suppressed sadness in my voice and offers,

"Maybe you would enjoy coming along for the ride this afternoon?"

"Oh yes, would I!" I would go out with Frankenstein just to be on a boat again!

This time around we get along better. After a long ride with the top down, we arrive at Lake Elsinore, where we let the mahogany boat on its trailer down into the water. To ride a bumpy speed-boat hitting the waves full throttle is different than smooth sailing, cutting through the water at slower speed. It is more like driving a car. However, I love car racing also. I enjoy the bumps and the spray hitting and drenching us at times. Often I have to laugh out loud over some funny remark that Sam makes with a deadpan face. He really has a sense of humor, which I like. After awhile we exchange seats and I learn to steer the speedboat. It is a lot of fun! I am happy and relaxed and share my joy of being in my watery element again with him.

On the way home in the car, I tell him about the life changing experience I had in the mountains of Forest Home. He listens intently and asks thoughtful questions. I find a small booklet of the Gospel of John in my purse, which I leave for him to read. It is the most natural thing in the world to part that evening with a goodnight-kiss.

On our third date he allows me to drive the beautiful new car. It must be a sacrifice for him to let me sit behind the wheel. For me a dream has come true! How often had I wished to drive a fine car and now it is reality! The top down, we drive out of the city to an Italian restaurant. The warm wind catches my long hair, while houses, fields and orchards fly by. What luxury compared to the jeeps and the aged Opel, in which I made my driver's license! I love the easy automatic transmission. No more pushing down the clutch and giving gas between shifting gears. We arrive at the nice restaurant and I am as happy as can be.

After a good Italian meal, Sam takes the wheel, but before we leave, he turns to me and looks into my eyes.

"I don't know how to put it in words," he stumbles around a bit, "but I read the booklet you gave me. Something happened inside of me, that I cannot explain," he lowers his eyes and I can see that they are moist. I listen quietly. Surely God has touched him.

"Would you like to come to church with me on Sunday?" I ask.

""Yes, I would. I have not been in a church for a long time, that is, I have gone to one but just for the dances, to meet a girl."

Dances in a church? Everything seems possible in America!

"I have been searching for a long time," he continues, putting his arm around my shoulder, "and I am certain I found the woman I have waited for." He bends over to kiss me. "I love you very much, and I would like to marry you!"

Just like that! I am thunderstruck! Did he forget that this is only our third date?

"I know that this comes very suddenly," he has seen my shocked face, "but I am so sure. I really had not planned to say it, but it just came over me."

I sit there not able to think clearly. How can he be so sure? I also enjoy being together with him, but marry? We are just starting a relationship. We have to give it time to grow. Yet this is no teenage

Romeo but a grown and experienced man who makes this offer, probably after much thinking.

But there is a great obstacle: I would never marry a man who does not share my faith. Through my parents' interfaith marriage, I have seen that if one goes in a different direction faith wise than the other, even though they may love each other, it brings tensions that could be avoided. I want a husband who shares my values, my beliefs and my priorities.

Unperturbed Sam continues,

"At work I had to reserve my vacation. It starts on the 21st of June. We could get married on Saturday, the nineteenth of June and then drive to South Dakota for you to meet my family and have our honeymoon in those two weeks."

"Now please, stop! How can you make these plans and I have not said one word!"

"All you have to say is, Yes!"

"You are impossible! No wonder that you are the best salesman in your department! You could sell refrigerators to the Eskimos!"

"I have done that already! During my college days in South Dakota, in the terribly cold winters, I went around to the farmers to sell them refrigerators."

"But you can't do this with me! I cannot stand to be pressured by anybody. Anyway, this is much too serious. You don't just talk about this lightly."

He looks at me piercingly.

"I do not speak lightly. I have given this a lot of thought. I am almost ten years older than you, and I make no rash decisions. But I have found what I have been looking for and I love you!"

I hear his earnest words, but in my heart are still too many reservations.

26

Two months follow where I am constantly torn between two things. There is resistance and desire, persuasion and obedience fighting in me. I feel more and more pressure building up. After seeing a movie with Gregory Peck at Grauman's Chinese Theater in Hollywood, we sit in the car, still moved by the performance. Sam puts his arm around me and immediately a strong feeling takes hold of me. This is what I have been seeking, what I have missed most of my growing up years, this feeling of being completely secure and safe, enfolded by loving arms. This man, with his positive and fearless attitude towards life, his self-assurance and humor can give this to me, his warm hands in mine, protecting and shielding me from threats and dangers and an unknown future.

Still I often feel like sitting in my kayak, alone on a wide river, carried along by a swiftly flowing current. At any moment my fragile little boat can hit a hidden rock and sink, leaving me to struggle for survival in the cold water. I have no idea what is really going on in Sam's heart. Is he going to church and to the youth group with me just to please me, or does he really want to? I have no indication. Had not Teacher read from Paul's second letter to the Corinthians, "Do no be yoked together with an unbeliever?" The pressure seems to tear me apart. After an evening in which he tried to force me to make a decision to either continue or end our relationship and I could not decide, I throw myself before my bed and cry to God.

"Please, Lord, help me to make the right decision. I need a sign from you. If you give me green light, I will say yes. If you give me a red light, I will say no. And I mean it! It is up to you to direct me in this far reaching decision, and I will be obedient, no matter what."

Finally the pressure and restlessness come to an end and I have inner peace. I have turned over the decision to more capable hands than mine.

Aunt Martha is expecting a visit from a niece from New York. I give her my bedroom and move in with my parents for a few days and sleep on their couch. Before leaving for work we sit around the breakfast table. Suddenly I remember something. I get up to fetch my Bible.

"This morning, just before waking up, a voice said to me, "Read Isaiah 44" and I want to hear what it says."

Dad looks at me skeptically and lifts his brows. What is happening to his daughter? She is acting strangely lately. I open the book and begin to read out loud.

"But now hear, O Jacob my servant, Israel whom I have chosen! Thus says the Lord who made you, who formed you from the womb and will help you:

Fear not, O Jacob my servant, Jeshurun whom I have chosen.

For I will pour water on the thirsty land, and streams on the dry ground; I will pour my Spirit upon your descendants, and my blessing on your offspring.

They shall spring up like grass amid waters, like willows by flowing streams;

This one will say, 'I am the Lord's,

Another will call himself by the name of Jacob,

And another will write on his hand,

'The Lord's' and surname himself by the name of Israel."

I cannot continue reading. Overflowing joy makes my voice quiver. This is God's answer to my sincere prayer for guidance! What promises! Water on him that is thirsty! Sam is thirsty! God will pour his spirit on our descendants. The children he will give to us will be blessed! I can hardly contain myself. All day long I praise God for this personal answer. There is absolutely no doubt left now! God has given his approval.

At the dinner table with my parents, the phone rings. Sam is calling from a telephone booth. His voice sounds forlorn.

"What are you doing tonight?"

"I am very happy tonight, I feel great!"

"What happened?"

"God has given his blessing to our marriage!"

"Does that mean yes?" asks a fearful voice.

"Yes! Yes!" I shout into the receiver. I hear a scream from the other end.

"I will be over in a few minutes!"

His face radiates as he enters the room, but then he turns serious.

"Would you mind leaving us alone for a bit?" he asks Mother and me. We withdraw to the kitchen and close the door. I hold Mother's hands.

"He is going to ask Dad's permission to marry me," I explain. "He wants to do it the right way like in the old country."

After awhile we are being called to the living room. Dad gives me a kiss and says, "May the two of you be happy together!" Mother embraces us with tears. Sam takes out a small box from his suit pocket.

"I have carried this with me for a long time and have hoped for the day to put it on your finger. Now the day has come!"

It is a small sparkling diamond ring. I cannot take my eyes off my finger. It is really true! I am engaged!

Just as Sam had suggested on our third date, we get married on June 19, 1948 and drive a brand new Buick convertible to the Mid-West to meet his family in South Dakota. The large clan welcomes me with open arms. Especially Sam's mother is glad to have a daughter-in-law, who speaks German and has even learned to write the old German script in school. Although his mother was born and educated in America, she had never learned to speak the language of the land well. There were German churches and schools and the Mennonites were a closely-knit group that shunned many of the modern world's ideas and so-called accomplishments. She is thrilled that she will be able to write us letters, which I will answer. The experience to be part of a large family is new to me, yet it makes me happy. I feel close to these hard working, honest, and loving Christian people. Sam's brother, Jake, who farms next to the old parents and raises 50 head of cattle, and his family become my friends. Jake's wife, Katherine, impresses me with her efficiency and even-tempered friendliness. Their three children cling to me and I like playing with them and getting to know them. We pray at meal times and Sam's elderly father reads and expounds a portion of the Bible. I can tell he has studied this book most of his life. Then we sing in four-part harmony and the old hymns, sung by heart, tie us even closer together. Only Sam sits at the table, as if he is a visiting stranger. When we finally leave, I feel that I have not only gained a husband, but have been blessed additionally with a loving Christian family.

On our way through Nevada, where gambling is legalized, I make a sad discovery. My husband likes to gamble. It takes an effort to drag him away from the gaming table, although he has won enough already to pay for our lodging and food. I cannot enjoy the meal or the nice hotel.

Back home I move into his furnished apartment and we begin our new life together. I have quit my job, for Sam does not want me to work. I enjoy the leisure time to discover the neighborhood or take the bus to the beach. At home I try out new recipes for my husband, or make small purchases to make our love nest homier. Sometimes he returns from work early and we take spontaneous rides, even across the border to Mexico, or we try out a new restaurant. It is a happy time and we do not miss our friends. We only want each other, just to be together and share everything.

At the breakfast table, before Sam leaves for work, I read a portion of the Bible and a short explanation and pray for God's blessings on our day. Sam listens, but one morning he is too much in a hurry and leaves me sitting there with my Bible open but unread. This happens more often and I have to admit to myself, that my husband shows less and less interest in hearing God's word. I begin to question God. Has He made a mistake or I? What about the promise he gave me? It was so clear to me but now I am beginning to doubt.

It is August 2nd, Sam's birthday, when a telegram interrupts the festivities. The son of his oldest brother, David, an only child, had been hit on his motorcycle by a drunk driver and had died from his injuries, just 18 years old. It is a deep shock for Sam. His usually extroverted nature changes to sullen pensiveness and sudden outbursts of anger.

Three weeks later I ask him to take myself and my best friend up to Forest Home for a College Briefing Conference, yet he unwillingly refuses. But I do not give up, for I realize that I need this time to get encouragement from God. On the 28th of August he drives us there, but his mood is anything but friendly. As I get out of the car and take a deep breath of the fresh mountain air, I exclaim,

"Isn't it wonderful up here?" Sam turns his back on me and says brusquely,

"Do me a favor, please, leave me alone!" After supper he wants to leave to drive back to town. But I beg him to stay at least for the first meeting of the conference. Sullenly he follows me into the large meeting hall.

Dr. David Cowie is the speaker of the evening. He does something unusual. He begins the conference week with an invitation to faith in Christ and ends with the words of Jesus, "Come unto me all ye that labor and are heavy laden, and I will give you rest." Then he adds,

"While we all close our eyes for a time, I want to ask those, who would want to let Jesus Christ come into their life to be their personal Savior and Lord, to briefly lift their hand." I hear a rustling noise next to me and out of the corner of my eye I see how Sam lifts up his hand. How can this be? I can hardly believe what I see!

The voice of the preacher speaks into the silence.

"Now would all, who have put up their hands please come forward, while the others quietly leave the room." Without looking at me Sam gets up and makes his way to the front, while I walk toward the exit. Outside I stand dazed under the night sky with its millions of sparkling stars. I cannot think anything but this one thought: "Thank you, Lord! Thank you! I praise you and give you thanks!" Over and over I repeat these words in my heart. It is a moment I will never forget!

When Sam joins me after a brief after-meeting, we fly into each other's arms.

"I just had to do it tonight," he explains, "since the day my nephew died on my birthday I knew that God was speaking to me and that I would have to make a personal decision. I could not run away from God any longer."

He does not think about leaving. An arrangement is made that he can stay for the night in a cabin where we are all alone. We lie in each other's arms. It is like a second wedding night, but with a new dimension of love added, which had been missing before. We had been one in body, emotion, intellect and will. But the highest dimension, the spiritual one, had been missing, and we received it as God's best gift that night. I realized that I had been given a taste of a marriage that was only between two people that loved each other, and a marriage, where God was the third party, who added a close-ness, which humanly we could have never achieved by ourselves. I am grateful for this experience. Now we are truly one. There is nothing able to separate us now – at least that is what I think that night.

27

⚜

Early the next morning Sam leaves to drive back to work. He promises to return for Labor Day weekend. All week long my heart is filled with joy. Friday evening I walk up and down the road to be ready to greet him when he arrives. Finally I see the light green cabriolet and run to where he parks the car. As he gets out we embrace again. Then he bends to pick up a package from the backseat.

"This is for you!" he hands me the large gray cardboard box. I open it excitedly. Inside is a beautiful sweater and matching skirt. "I love it!" I shout and give him a kiss. I am overwhelmed. Never before has my husband bought me clothes without my being there and trying them on. This he had picked all by himself. What a love gift!

"Could we go someplace where we could talk alone?" he asks somewhat sheepishly, and I notice that something is on his mind.

As we walk though the woods, he is searching for words.

"I – I want to ask you a question," he finally begins.

"Go ahead," I encourage him. I have no idea what is bothering him.

"What would you say if I would take all of our savings and get a bank loan to settle some old debts, so to speak, as restitution for the sins of my past?" he looks at me anxiously. I stop and look into his eyes. Without hesitation I answer.

"Whatever God has put on your heart, do it! If he has convicted you to put your house in order, you must be obedient and I will support you totally. I don't want to know what you need the money for, that concerns only you and God." By his relieved look I can measure how much this has occupied his mind. Then he confesses what has happened since he returned from the mountaintop.

The sins of his past stood threateningly before him. So he fled into a gambling casino in Gardena, an area of Los Angeles where gambling was legalized. He had confessed to me that he was addicted to gambling. Winning or losing – nothing brought him joy. How many times had he wanted to quit, but the next night he was again at the gaming tables. When he returned home from the mountain that night it was the same pattern again. He lost, but the next night he was there once more, and lost as before. Then and there he decided that he wanted to quit this kind of life with the help of God. He had to stop fleeing from his past by making a new beginning. First he needed to make restitution where he could and then start out new. And this is the beginning.

A few weeks later I realize gratefully that I have a new husband. He has thrown away his playing cards and the compulsion to gamble has disappeared. He gets up early in the morning before anybody is awake and sits in the living room studying his Bible and praying. His joy is contagious. In his gregarious and enthusiastic way he tells the people he contacts that God has totally changed his life. His customers are also included. Some complain to his boss and he is called into the office and told not to mix business with religion. But Sam does not take this to heart and keeps speaking out wherever he has or opens up an opportunity. He applies for baptism in our church and becomes a member. The promise God gave me in Isaiah 44 has become true. God poured water on him that was thirsty and streams on the dry ground.

Our first daughter is born on June 28,1949. We name her Joy Ann, remembering Teachers' definition of Joy. J for Jesus first, O for others second, Y for yourself last. Joy is ten days old when we are awakened by a knock on the door. Outside is a sheriff in uniform. He hands us an eviction notice.

"These are apartments for adults only. You have a baby and cannot continue to live here." What a nice way to welcome a new citizen! A few days later Sam returns early from work. His face gives away the bad news before he can tell me. He has been fired from work. I take a deep breath. What timing! No place to live and no work! And a new baby!

"One of my customers complained to the boss about my speaking to him about God," he says dejectedly.

"Don't be upset," I try to comfort him by faking a smile, "God will help us to find something new."

We sit together in our little living room and the reality of the situation hits me. No work, no place to live and the responsibility of a little baby that taxes my inexperience to the limit. Suddenly my favorite Bible verse comes to mind. 'For we know that all things work together for good to them that love God.' Has not God given me this verse in the darkest times of my life? Hasn't he shown me in retrospect that these difficult times did work together for my own good, for they taught me early in life not to depend on people or myself for help but to trust God to help me? Now I realize that in this situation we need his help. We pour our hearts out to him and ask for his help and guidance. Then Sam starts looking for work and a new place to live.

One evening he comes home excitedly.

"The manager of the car agency where I bought our Buick convertible, is giving me a chance at selling cars. It's not inside the agency, I will have to find my own customers outside and it is purely on commission for the first three months." I am less enthused. What kind of work is that? But he brushes off my worries.

"Cars are my hobby. Why not make your hobby your work?"

During the next years it becomes apparent that God set us on the right course. From Buick, where he became a regular salesman, he changes to Ford and later to a Cadillac agency in the heart of Hollywood, a few blocks from our church. Soon he is the top salesman, who sells more cars at the end of the year, though he never works on Sundays when the agency is open. He gives his turn to some other salesman but in the end he is ahead of them all. We live in a little yellow house in West Los Angeles, fifteen minutes from the beach, with a large garden and a beautiful view and our family grows. On September 17, 1951 our son Richard Jacob, named after both grandfathers, joins us. Shortly before that date and eight months pregnant I become a naturalized American citizen. Now I really belong! This is a special moment in my life, when I am handed my citizenship paper and with it the protection of the American government. Many months I had studied American history and Government, and finally could say with pride: This is MY country, land that I love!

Sam leads the local CBMC (Christian Business Men Committee) in Hollywood and I begin teaching a Sunday school class for second graders in our church. My parents bought a house almost behind our garden and become our faithful baby sitters, when we meet with our friends from church in the evenings. We are happy and satisfied with our lives and are grateful for God's blessings.

"I would really like to see where you grew up," my husband says one night and surprises me with a ticket on the ocean liner 'Queen Elizabeth'. We drive to South Dakota by car and leave the children with Sam's sister Mary. Then we continue on to New York and board the beautiful ocean liner. What a difference between our crowded troop transport ship that brought me across the ocean six years ago and this luxury liner! We visit several European countries by car and Sam is curious to see everything and meet people and places that mean something to me. But as we get closer to my hometown Berlin, I cannot help but get apprehensive. How will the confrontation with the places of my youth be? Will it tear open old wounds? Will the decision I made in Forest Home remain valid when I see the old places and perhaps the people that haunt my memories sometimes? Would forgiveness turn out to be something I had only imagined at a distance?

Although I experience that the old hatred no longer is there and no thoughts of revenge occupy my mind, I am accompanied continuously by pain and sadness that I cannot suppress. Too many pictures turn up suddenly; too many sad memories are connected to streets, buildings or locations. Many times I am reminded of Erika and Gerhard and their promising young lives cut short because of a maniac, willing to destroy a whole country and murder millions of people for his own ego's sake. The old pain revives again and overshadows our visits. It is almost too much for me, this confrontation with my past. Yet after we return and take stock of our trip, we feel the challenge, that Berlin is an influential place that needs help and commitment.

A few months after our return from our six weeks' European trip, our pastor, Dr. Louis Evans, reads a letter from the pulpit by German Bishop Dibelius, requesting two volunteers from our church to come to the city of Berlin for one year to help build up a new kind of youth ministry. He explains that our church would send the volunteers and the German church would take care of their housing expenses over there. We look at each other and without words know in our hearts that this is meant for us. Sam asks his boss for a sabbatical leave of one year, and our church lets Bishop Dibelius know that two volunteers are on their way. A church member has a VW bus in a garage in Southampton, England, that he will let us use for the year. For our house the church has a renter for a year and soon we are on our way to a new adventure.

Again we cross the ocean in a luxury liner. We pick up the VW in England, fly across to Le Havre and drive to Hamburg to visit my cousin. As we arrive with the fully loaded VW bus and tell her that we are on our way to Berlin, she looks at us incredulously.

"You want to drive there with this car from here?" she asks.

"Yes!

Why not?"

"As you know Berlin is a divided city with American, British, French and Russian sector. In order to get there you must pass through the Russian zone on the Autobahn. And they allow only diplomats and Army vehicles to drive through. You will have to fly in."

We look at each other. Fly in – with four people and a ton of luggage for a whole year? And we will need a car. But she is certain. We want to know for sure and drive to the American Consulate.

"No, you cannot drive to Berlin from here," is the answer we get there also. We tell the friendly lady our story, that Bishop Dibelius is expecting us and that we need the car for the youth work. She listens patiently and then sends us away with the words,

"I will see what I can do for you. But I cannot promise you anything. Please come back on Tuesday." Monday is an American holiday and the consulate is closed. A long and anxious weekend lies ahead. We clutch at the straw that possibly she might be able to do something for us. But is this realistic? We see no possibility and worry. The hours and days creep by. Never has a weekend seemed so long.

On Tuesday morning I read in Psalms, and suddenly a verse catches my attention: "With my God I can leap over walls." With new confidence we knock at the door to the lady's office. She receives us with a friendly smile and says,

"I want to help you get to Berlin with your car, but you must promise not to tell anybody about it." We promise.

"Well, then. We will supply you with papers like the Diplomatic Corps. These people are the only ones who have access from Hamburg to West-Berlin by land. All others have to fly." We look at each other with a smile. Diplomats? Is that supposed to be something special? We are children of the king! Our Father in Heaven is King over everything!

Finally we are given the special papers but the words with it dampen our spirits.

"I cannot promise you that they will let you pass at the Russian control point. But I wish you good luck!" We thank the friendly lady and take leave in the direction of the Autobahn. Our first stop is the American checkpoint. While a GI studies our papers, an officer with a pointer briefs us on a map on the wall. He tells us step by step the procedure we are to follow. We feel like we are about to enter enemy territory, which in a way is true. Suddenly the GI comes with our papers in hand to the officer. He has discovered a typing error. My middle initial is wrong. Now all of the papers in English and Russian have to be changed. As we are waiting we get more nervous.

Finally they hand the papers back to us and we are on our way. Slowly we make our way to the first Russian checkpoint. Our hearts are beating wildly. We tell the children to keep quiet. Sam parks the car and takes the papers and disappears in a wooden barrack. "Let's pray for Daddy that they will let us drive through," I tell the children, who look anxiously at the door that their Daddy entered. It seems like an eternity before the door opens again and Sam walks towards us. I can see in his face that he got the necessary stamps. Cautiously, as slowly as possible, he drives to the next checkpoint under the eyes of guards with guns on watchtowers along the Autobahn. Here he only has to hand a paper to a soldier, who peers into the car suspiciously and then waves us on. Again we creep along at ten kilometers an hour. Finally we are in the section where we can drive 100 km an hour. But the asphalt is so bumpy that we can never reach that speed and we are being shaken from section to section on a road that has not been repaired for more than 40 years. Shaken and relieved at the same time we finally cross the last Russian checkpoint with a scream of joyous relief. "Freedom, freedom!" we shout in unison as we enter our new and for me old home, Berlin. With our God we have leapt over the wall!

We find living quarters in Dahlem, close to the U.S. Military Headquarters. With two German families we build up an experimental youth work, located in a building called "Die Boje" (life buoy). Our goal is to invite young people from the street, offer them an interesting program in order to integrate them, as a second step, into a local church congregation. The concept is good. We are open six days a week and soon our rooms are filled with young people. They come from West-and-East Berlin and quickly take to the Boje as their home. Yet they refuse to be integrated in other churches. We use the opportunities we have by ending each day with a short message from the Bible and prayer. When Billy Graham arrives in Berlin to hold a meeting in the Olympic Stadium, Sam hauls two loads full of twelve teenagers each, stuffed into the VW bus to hear him. We show good science films made by Christians, which I translate sentence by sentence into German. Then I speak the words into a cassette recorder and we play the cassette simultaneously with the film. A labor of love and endless patience!

I learn to play chess, which I enjoy and become quite efficient in playing ping-pong. In general we earn practical experience of working with teenagers, trying to share our faith with them. My Godmothers are happy to have us in Berlin. When we consider the possibility of driving to the Holy Land from Berlin with the VW bus, big Aunt Martha offers to take care of our two children for six weeks. 'Who knows,' we reason, 'if we will ever be as close to the land of the Bible again.' So we make preparations after our year is over for this trip in the spring of 1955. I sew little curtains for privacy; we take out the back seats to make room for boxes of food, several canisters filled with gasoline, a spare tire, camping stove, and on top two air mattresses on which we sleep. We stop by the side of the road to cook our meals, mostly pasta, and drive slowly, due to the twenty-five-horse power engine which sometimes chugs up the mountains with the last bit of power available. Our route leads us through Germany, Austria, Yugoslavia, Greece, Turkey, Syria, Lebanon, with a side trip to Egypt, back to Lebanon and Jordan. At the end we enter Israel with a detached visa through Mandelbaum Gate in the divided city of Jerusalem. We are the only tourists standing in front of the Wailing Wall on the Palestinian side of Jerusalem. With a guidebook and a Bible in hand we explore the Biblical sites of the Old and New Testaments. After waiting for three days in Jerusalem, we get a permit to enter Israel.

We had many wonderful but also risky experiences on our trip. But I still have one heart's desire, to meet my cousin Irene again, that drew my face in childhood. I only know that she is married and lives in Israel. But how can you find a person whose married name you don't know nor his address? Impossible! But we have a God who specializes in the impossible!

Of all places I have to get sick in Israel and cannot leave the hotel room for a couple of days. One day before we leave per ship, I feel well enough to travel. All day long we visit Biblical sites and return to the hotel at night, tired but happy and filled with wonderful impressions. It was a day to remember. But my prayer for finding Irene has not been answered.

The next morning we are driving down from Mt. Carmel to the harbor to ship our car. Suddenly I call out,

"Please stop!" Out of the corner of my eye I have seen a gallery displaying paintings. I walk inside and ask the lady,

"I am searching for my cousin. She is a painter. Her first name is Irene, and she comes from Berlin. Do you happen to know some one who fits this description?" I ask hesitatingly.

"Certainly," she answers, "Irene Awram. She comes from Berlin and is a painter and her husband a sculptor and they live in Safed." I cannot believe my ears and thank her profusely. I jump back into the car.

"We went through Safed yesterday," I tell my surprised husband, "that is where my cousin lives. Do you think we have time to drive there again before we have to ship the car?" Sam thinks a minute.

"It is about 80 km from here. If we hurry we could be back by two p.m. when we have to load the car aboard. Well, let us try." The VW does its best to get us there quickly. Every minute counts. Where could we find them?

"Stop here", I have seen a sign that looks official. It is not the police but the Post Office. I run inside and ask the man behind the window.

"Do you know where the Awram family lives?" He gets up and comes out and I follow him. He points across the street and says, "There. Just walk down the steps, that's where they live."

Within a minute we have found them. As I walk downstairs after ringing a bell at the top, the door is being opened and I call downstairs,

"Guten Tag, Irene!" and without a moments' hesitation comes the surprised answer,

"Is that really you, Yola, where do you come from?"

For one hour we sit together filling in the more than twenty years we had not seen each other and marvel at the guidance of God, for whom the proverbial needle in a haystack is no challenge, but who enjoys surprising his children by answering their prayers. We get to the ship on time and for the next days we enjoy the dark blue waters and the sea air as we make our way through the Eastern Mediterranean till we reach Bari, Italy. Arriving in Rome we realize that we have only $10 in our wallet. But our faithful parents have sent a rent check to the American Express and we reach Berlin after six weeks and spending $120 for everything. This adventurous experience has given us a deep appreciation of the Bible. Instead of reading words and names of places, we can now see them in our mind's eye. We have gained an understanding of Jesus' earthly ministry by following some of his footsteps. The young state of Israel is bursting with vitality and we are glad to have seen it in its beginnings.

27

Exactly one year later to the day when we moved back into our house, our third child is born. We name her Sharon (a Biblical place) Rebecca. For us this baby is a special gift of God and I enjoy cuddling her in my arms after five years between children. While the two older ones are in Kindergarten and elementary school, I spend as much time as possible with her and experience the miracle of a new life much more consciously than with the first two. I relish just being a mother and housewife after that one hectic and busy year in Berlin. Sam sells Cadillacs again in Hollywood and meets with the CBMC every Thursday morning. He has raised our donations to the church to 30% of our income. We support a student from India and I am teaching second graders again in Sunday school. One of my second grade boys, who always is dressed in a suit and tie, is little Ronnie Howard, who was making his first appearance in Hollywood productions as an actor and later became a well-known producer. Most of our friends are from the Mariners Sunday School class, young couples like ourselves, and we have an active social life and feel fulfilled and satisfied.

In the early summer of 1959 we drive up to a family confer-ence at Forest Home. Sheri is now almost three years old. In this place, where I dedicated my life to serve Jesus Christ and where Sam received new life in Christ, we are closer to God than any place else. We can hear his voice speaking to us through the excellent teachers and musicians and are challenged to new adventures in faith. There is a strong desire in my heart to serve God more fully. Without sharing it I discover that my husband has similar desires.

We promise God in prayer to be available for him if he wants to use us in full-time Christian service.

Some time ago Sam had invited a speaker from the CBMC to our house. His name was Dwight Wadsworth and he had been a captain in the U.S.Army in Germany. After the war he had returned there with his family and had started a youth work in the city of Wuppertal. He worked together with a British missionary movement aimed at young people, called 'Torchbearers', which a British major, Ian Thomas, had started. Over dinner at our house, we had told Dwight Wadsworth of our desire to be used by the Lord again in full-time ministry, and he wrote down our address at the time.

Three weeks after this family conference, during which I intensified my personal Bible studies from 9-12 each morning, we receive a letter from Germany. Dwight Wadsworth asks us if we would be available to take over his youth work in Wuppertal, because he had to build up a new conference center for the Torchbearers, called Klostermuehle. What an answer to our prayers! Highly motivated we show the letter to our pastors, hoping to get financial support as for the year in Berlin. After waiting for a long time we hear the negative decision. There were no extra funds available in the church budget to send us to Germany. What a disappointment! We had written Dwight about our willingness to come, but now we had to withdraw our offer. Why was there no money for such an important ministry?

Many nights we discuss the issue. We had asked God to use us, and when we are ready to go, there is no one to send us. Here in California we have everything we need to live a comfortable life. As a star salesman Sam earns more than the others. We have to drive a new Cadillac every year. We have a nice home and the Christian school for the children is just down the street. We are involved in Christian work – so why not forget about our desires and get more involved here? Yet the nagging question, which keeps reappearing after we have discussed and rationalized our decisions, is the unsettled issue of discipleship. For weeks we wrestle with this thought but cannot find inner peace.

Instead of an answer I get a new challenge. I am asked to teach a group of young women from the church. The many years that I have taught second graders, I had longed to teach people my age, and finally the opportunity has come! The topic I have to teach is "Discipleship"! Surely God has a sense of humor! As I prepare my teaching material, the Lord turns to me with a question.

"How come you want to teach others how to be faithful disciples of Jesus? What kind of disciple are you, anyway? Here you want to tell others that Jesus called people to follow him and what do you read in my Word?"

"They left everything and followed him."

"Certainly! And what about you? Haven't I called you? But you cling to the so-called securities of life and are not willing to give them up, but ignore my call with your preconceived notions of what is feasible and what is not. Why don't you just trust me?"

Is it only a question of trusting? Don't we have a responsibility to our family? Perhaps these early disciples were men without families to support. And times were different and much simpler than ours. Do you ask us to put the security of our children at stake and our financial security? That would be irresponsible! Sam earns a good living here, and over there we have no income and nobody to support us. And what about the schools? The children don't know any German. How can they follow in school? Can't we serve you here?

All of these arguments sound very rational and realistic, but in our case they are unbelief and disobedience. By talking endlessly about the consequences we come to this conclusion. Do we love comfort and security more than God? Does it really mean to give up these things in order to follow him? Can God expect such radical changes in our lives from us? Why must it be Germany and not Hollywood? When we finally feel that our rationalizing has convinced us to do the right thing, we still have that feeling of not following the will of God for our lives. This feeling cannot be repressed, it does not leave us. These questions occupy our minds, but we fail to reach a decision.

In my daily Bible reading I come across a verse, which I underline in red. When Sam comes home from work that night, he tells me,

"I have read a verse today which really spoke to me." He opens his Bible and reads the very same verse that I have underlined in my Bible. "Here writes the Apostle Paul a thank you to the church fellowship in Philippi, who supported him on his missionary journeys. Philippians 4, 19: But my God shall supply all your needs according to his riches in Christ Jesus." I jump up to get my Bible. The bookmark is still on that page and I show Sam the underlined verse.

"I got the same verse today," I marvel. We look at each other and we know that God wants to help us reach a decision with this word. He commits himself to supply our needs. We take this promise as our blank check to be cashed at the bank of heaven in times of need. Sam prays, "Heavenly Father, we thank you for this promise that you have given to us personally. We trust your word and believe that you mean what you say. Thank you for giving us the inner assurance that you will go before us wherever we will go. We want to do your will and we will follow you wherever you lead us. Amen". As we look up, all of our reservations and worries about the future are gone. God has taken over the responsibility for our family!

Now begins the miracle of the provision and goodness of God. From the moment of our decision till the actual departure only one and a half weeks are needed! During this short time Sam quits his work, we rent our house, sell two cars and buy an old used Chevy from the neighbor for $150, pack for five people and set out from one coast to the other. The old car, though loaded down to the maximum, brings us without any trouble from Los Angeles to New York Harbor. There waits a returned missionary, who gives us $150 and we turn the keys over to him and with our many bags and suitcases embark on another beautiful ocean liner for another voyage across the Atlantic Ocean.

On our way across country we had stopped in Rochester, Minnesota, where our dear and revered Teacher, Henrietta Mears, was recovering from an operation at the Mayo Clinic. We stood on both sides of her bed and though weak in body, she stormed the gates of heaven, holding our hands and praying down God's blessings for the new adventure we were embarking on. It was a moment too sacred for words, but one that in our memories has a place of honor. This great saint of God, who had done so much for our spiritual development, gave us this last gift of blessing as she opened her heart to us in love and committed us to the special care of our heavenly Father.

28

~~⸙⸙~~

This is my sixth Atlantic crossing and it is a memorable one. Through a pastor on the ship, who offers evening services, we meet twelve missionary families who are on their way to different countries in Europe and Africa. For ten days we eat together, play shuffleboard and meet each evening for sharing and prayer. It is like a wonderful missionary conference and when we arrive in Rotterdam, we have made many friends and it is difficult to part. Sam has organized a car for us and we ride the train to Duesseldorf to pick it up. Wuppertal, our new home, is not far from that city and upon our arrival, there are many people expecting and welcoming us. That first night we have to stay in a hotel.

The next morning we are met by some of the leaders of the youth group.

"We are sorry, but we have not yet found a place for you to live, for we did not know if you were going to come. So Dwights' place has been rented," we are informed. It is a shattering revelation. How can we afford to live in this hotel with five people? One family offers to give Sam a bed, but they do not have room for all of us. We decide that he should stay and look for a place to live while the children and I would go to Berlin, where we have friends who would take us in for the time being. Again we drive via Helmstedt through the Soviet zone to Berlin where we have a happy reunion with our former coworkers in the Boje. Sam drives back to Wuppertal and a medical doctor friend invites us to stay in his row house in Kladow, while his wife is expecting their first baby at her parents place in

Switzerland. The doctor is gone all day and the children and I enjoy the luxury of living in a nice area close to the river Havel.

One week after another passes and we repeat the same telephone conversation.

"Did you find any thing?" And always the same answer.

"No, I am still looking. I am walking around all day long, but there seems to be no place to live." I cannot believe what is happening. Surely when God calls us he must have a place for us to live, even in a bombed out industrial city like Wuppertal.

School is starting and with a heavy heart I take the two oldest children to the German elementary school. They do not speak or understand German and I feel like a bad mother leaving them there. Yet it has to be now or never. I am relieved to hear that the teacher speaks English. At least she can be the bridge for the two in a strange country where they cannot communicate with other children. But I need not have worried. When I wait for them at the end of the school day, my children come out surrounded by a group of others who want to be close to the exotic 'Americans'. Before long they learn their first German sentences and play outside with the neighborhood children in the afternoons.

One morning the patient doctor hints that his wife would like to return with their new baby when we have found something. I know we have overstayed our hosts' hospitality and I cannot understand that Sam cannot find anything in almost seven weeks. Mother arrives from America and I see this as a chance for me to leave the children in her care and join my husband in his search for a place to live. The idea to be a burden on others is unbearable to me. There must be a place somewhere! When we are united again my usually positive husband seems depressed. He, who would never take 'No' for an answer, has come to the end of himself. Seven weeks of ringing door bells and asking people everywhere have brought him to the breaking point.

I will not give up. Certainly God must have a place for us somewhere. I decide to go to the official Department of Housing. When I tell the clerk that we are looking for a place to live, he tells me to write my name on a list.

"What are our chances?" I ask.

"There are more than 30 000 people on the list before you." Finally I realize that it is a hopeless case. After staying overnight with the family who took Sam in and hearing a nearby church clock strike each 15 minutes all night long, I have had it too. In the morning we say goodbye to the family and sit in our car.

"Which way now?" I ask Sam who sits behind the wheel motionless. It is a rhetorical question. North? South? East? West? We have no idea! The story of Abraham comes to mind. When God called him to leave his country and his family and follow him, he left obediently according to God's call, not knowing at all where God would lead him. Now we feel like Abraham not knowing where he went. We pour our hearts out to the Lord in prayer and then start the car, driving in the direction it happens to stand, which was west. Isn't it irrational to drive so aimlessly? But what would be the rational thing to do? We have never been in a situation like this before!

We stop in every town we pass through, buying newspapers and asking people. But the same answer at each stop convinces us that all doors are closed. Even in the American Embassy in Bad Godesberg we get no encouragement, but at least a sympathetic ear. Yes, there is this deficit in living quarters due to the bombing and destruction of most cities. We would just have to try our luck some other place. Shoulder shrugging.

It is getting dark when we reach the city of Koblenz by the confluence of the Rhine and Moselle rivers. We are tired and discouraged.

"I only want a bed where I can sleep without a church clock," I moan.

"Shall we stay overnight in the same hotel where we stopped on our first trip through Europe in 1953?" Sam asks. I nod and we find our way to Hotel Rittersturz. We take in our suitcase and Sam checks us in. He is concerned because the prices have increased and he is holding tight to our dwindling finances.

"Don't you have a room towards the back or one without a bath?" he asks. In a haughty and offending voice the clerk says loudly, "If this is too expensive for you, why don't you try a hotel in town?" How can anybody be so rude?

"That's exactly what we will do," Sam answers annoyed and takes the suitcase and leaves. I run behind him back into the car. "Who does he think he is?" he fumes. Silently we drive down the hill. Where will we find a place tonight?

Suddenly we find ourselves on a bridge crossing the Rhine. I see a traffic sign.

"If you want to go on the Autobahn," I say, "you must change to the right lane." Sam continues straight ahead.

"Now right or you will miss the turn-off!" I call out. He continues. He has seen a sign 'Hotel' straight up the hill. They have a nice room with a view of the river and the city that we can afford and we settle down.

"Let's go downstairs," Sam says, "and call Berlin. Today our boy has his eighth birthday." I can tell he misses his son. We walk down into the lobby. There is a telephone on the desk. The owner dials for us and Mother answers.

"Hello, Mother. We are calling from the city of Koblenz."

"What are you doing there?"

"We are just staying here overnight and tomorrow we will drive someplace."

"What do you mean? You are no longer in Wuppertal? Have you found a place yet?"

"No, but we are still looking."

"But do you have anything in mind? What are we going to do? We must get out of here so the doctors' family can be together again. And Rich was so sad today on his birthday that his parents were not there. And last night Joy was sick. What are we going to do?"

"We don't know either, Mother. I wish we knew." I put the receiver down. We stand there desolate and in despair. We have reached rock bottom.

"What seems to be the matter?" the hotel owner asks with pity in her voice, seeing us standing there.

"I could not help but overhear parts of your conversation." Our faces mirror our hopelessness and discouragement.

"For seven weeks we have been looking for a place to live, but we cannot find anything," I answer.

"What kind of a place are you looking for?" the owner asks. What a question!

"We only need a roof over our heads and a place where our three children can sleep."

"I think I know of a place," the woman answers. "Last week it was still available. In fact, it is right next-door. The owner of the house wants to visit her daughter in South Africa for six months and she wants to rent the place fully furnished for that time. Wait a moment and I will go and ask if it is still available."

The caring lady walks toward the exit and a glimmer of hope begins to glow in our hurting hearts. She returns with the news that the quarters are still available and that the owner will expect us at nine a.m. tomorrow morning. We hardly can believe this sudden turn of events. We thank her exuberantly and walk up to our room to thank God in advance for this opportunity. We fall asleep comforted and unworried. Yet in the morning light the doubts begin to rise. What if the rent should be too high, for it is a nice villa with a view to the Rhine and over the city of Koblenz. A large garden surrounds the house. As we enter the gate our hearts are beating fast. An elderly lady, the widow of a well-known medical professor opens the door and shows us through the rooms. The furnishings are superior and in one of the bedrooms there is even a child's bed for our three-year old Sheri. We worry about the rent. But then she mentions exactly the price, which we had envisioned. Best of all, we can move in immediately!

"My son and family live upstairs," she explains, "I hope you will enjoy this place and in six months I will return. Have a wonderful time!" We thank her and the same morning we are on our way back to Berlin. From one moment to the next our hopeless situation has turned into a fairy tale with a happy end. We retrace the steps that lead us to this place. The man at the first hotel had to turn us away by his bad attitude. Sam had to see the sign 'Hotel' while I was trying to direct him on the bridge; we had to make a phone call in the lobby where the owner could overhear the conversation, and the rent had to be just within the budget we had agreed on.

From one moment to the next God supplied all of our needs, even to the child's bed! Six months of luxury living, that would give us enough time to still find a place in the city of Wuppertal, where everybody was informed to tell us immediately if they knew of an available place.

The patient and hospitable doctor waves after our car as we set out to our new home. Mother follows by train. We have rented a room for her in the dependance of the hotel right below us. Koblenz and the beautiful surroundings are waiting to be discovered. Yet we feel more like tourists making an unplanned stop on their trip. After six months we will take leave of this place again. Our children attend the local German school, but it is our three-year old Sheri who soon can speak German fluently by learning it from her little playmate who lives upstairs. Sundays we visit a local church and meet a few people. One family invites us to their home after the service. They have three daughters the same age as our children and soon we become friends and spend our weekends together.

Mother has returned to the United States and we drive each weekend the one and a half hour drive to Wuppertal to lead the youth meeting, while a baby sitter watches our children. Late at night we return to Koblenz, braving every kind of weather. All of the Wuppertal friends are on the lookout for a place to live. We have six months to find one. But strangely, every time we have a lead, the door is closed right before our noses. Always somebody else gets the apartment. The months are passing and I begin to worry. How can it be that the return of the owner is coming closer, and we still have no place to live? Surely God could open up an apartment for us, but the day arrives when we have to move out and don't know where to go. Will this be a repeat performance?

In this desperate situation Sam buys a twelve foot trailer and pulls it to our place. We pack as much as we can into it and the rest of our baggage we deposit with the one family that we became friends with. All five of us will have to sleep in this crowded little trailer. Again the question is, where shall we go? The children have Easter vacation. We head South and come as far as a camping place by Lake Zurich in Switzerland. But then our son gets the mumps and during the night his fever is so high that he hallucinates. We fear for his health and turn around to the place where we just came from. We arrive at the door of our friends and they take in the three children, while we sleep in the trailer in front of their house, parked on the street.

"This vagabond life has to stop," Sam decides upon awakening in the trailer. He drives to the church, which we had attended and speaks to the social worker there. She gives him an address of a place where they rent rooms. We drive through a part of town, which we had never visited. The houses are at least over two hundred years old, as seen by the numbers on their front, and look decrepit. Narrow streets lead to an old building, which had been bombed and halfway repaired by the owners. We are lead into a stuffy room with ancient furniture and four sleeping accommodations. There is no running water but a pitcher and bowl on a chest of drawers; next to it a pail for used water. The toilet and water crane are across the courtyard. This is where five people should live and wash themselves?

"Can we put our trailer into the court yard?" Sam asks. The owner nods.

"Then we will take the room," Sam says, and my heart sinks.

"But I can rent it only till June 2nd," she adds, "I promised somebody else the room from that time on." Dazed I follow Sam to our car. We will move into this musty smelling hole? But I have no other alternative.

We pick up the trailer and park it in the courtyard. Then we leave to get some food. When we return we find a camping bed and a sleeping bag in front of our door. I walk over to the owners place to thank her. But she says,

"A woman from the neighborhood brought these things. She will return tomorrow morning." Who could know us in this neighborhood and offer these things that we really needed? We cannot solve this riddle. The next morning as we sit in the trailer there is a knock on the door. A woman my age stands there with a friendly smile.

"Good morning! My name is Frau Reinhard. We live right around the corner. My husband met you once briefly. When we heard that Americans are moving in, we thought it could be your family and that you might be able to use these extra things."

"Thank you for your thoughtfulness. We really needed this extra bed as we had only four sleeping places." Before she leaves again we invite her and her husband to visit us that same evening after work. They arrive and it does not take long for us to get acquainted and we discover that both of them believe in Christ. As we share our stories we mention that we are in Koblenz only temporarily and explain our frustrating search for a place to live in Wuppertal and how we always end up before closed doors. Valentin, our new friend, smiles and says,

"Perhaps we are responsible for the closed doors."

"What do you mean by that?" I question him. He answers with a chuckle.

"We have been praying for a long time that God would send somebody to this city to care for young people and build up a lively youth work. Wuppertal is a city that still feels the effects of a spiritual revival at the end of the nineteenth century. It has many churches and Christian organizations and the young people in your group come mainly from Christian families. Here the situation is completely different. There has never been a revival and we live in a Diaspora situation."

Later we pray together and there is a strange feeling in my heart. Is God trying to speak to us, wanting to change our direction? Didn't we come to Germany to reach out to young people with the message of forgiveness and reconciliation through Jesus Christ? But he had called us definitely to Wuppertal. But every door had been closed. Yet were not the circumstances strange, which had brought us to this particular place? All of these "accidental" leadings, our departure from Koblenz, then the illness that brought us back, this awful musty smelling room, which just happens to be right around the corner from these praying friends. Maybe God had different plans than we thought!

I wonder how God tries to convey his will to his children. When he speaks to them through his word, there is always the possibility of misunderstanding or trying to make it conform to our desires. How often I had heard the phrase, "The Lord told me…" or "God showed me to do this or that…" which precludes any serious questioning, for it means you are doubting God. Yet how many times have these "Words from the Lord" turned out to be just wishful thinking or impractical illusions. Aren't we all hard of hearing when it comes to discerning the quiet voice of God? Our hectic life styles, which allow no time for contemplation and meditation on the word of God, do not permit us the privilege of hearing in solitude what God wants to tell us. Our desire for the 'instant' answer is another hindrance.

Sometimes God speaks through circumstances, such as we are experiencing right now, and we begin to wonder if he is trying to reach us this way. Other times he speaks through Christians, like our brother Valentin. However, even the best Christian saint can be misled concerning God's will for others. If we had listened to some of our Christian friends, we would have never come to Germany in the first place. Some people go only by their feelings. Yet they are the most fickle and not to be trusted in regard to making far-reaching decisions. There remains then the living Word of God, that can speak into our confused minds to give them direction and courage to follow his leading. It takes sometimes a repeated reminder of a particular scripture verse. Yet Jesus promised that he would help us by sending us a personal counselor, the Holy Spirit. His task is to keep us restless, if we are not doing the will of God. Yet when there comes the 'peace that passes all understanding 'we know without doubt that we are doing what God has planned for us.

After Easter vacation our children return to their German schools and we begin to look for a permanent place. Our living situation begins to wear on me. At least one of the children seems to be sick all the time. With five of us sharing this one room, we often are disturbed at night. When one has an upset stomach and throws up, it takes a long time to clean up the mess, working with this pitcher of water and a pail, and often we have to cross the cold courtyard to reach a toilet at night.

One morning Sam returns to the trailer from buying some food in our old neighborhood. He brings good news.

"I think we found an apartment! They talked about it in the store, that a lawyer was being transferred and would sublet his apartment completely furnished. I called right away and made an appointment for us to meet him and look at the place." What exciting news! As we drive up the hill we realize that our villa for six months was just at the foot of the same hill. It is a nice neighborhood and the house is a modern two family building. We walk through the first floor. There are four rooms, a kitchen and a bath. The kitchen opens to the backyard and in front a large balcony stretches from living room to bedroom, from which one has an unobstructed view of the Rhine River. The furniture is modern and near new. A castle compared to our dungeon! The lawyer is polite and listens to our story. Then he says, "You can have the apartment." Even the rent fits into our budget.

We are beside ourselves with joy! Finally we will have a place to live and one that is large enough to invite young people and start our dream. When we get together with our friends that night in the trailer, we spin plans for the future. We will continue to lead our youth group in Wuppertal, drive there every Saturday, but also try to invite young people right here to our new place. All four of us thank God for the new apartment that night, before going to sleep again in the musty, crowded room, where Sheri just suffers from the itchy chickenpox.

The next morning the shrill voice of the landlady shouts across the courtyard.

"Herr Entz, there is a phone call for you!" When Sam returns I can read on his distraught face that he got bad news.

"The lawyer called and told me, that while he was showing us the apartment, his wife had already promised it to a relative. He had to withdraw his offer. That means we cannot have the place." How could this be? That is not possible! We have thanked God for it already! He does not hold a piece of chocolate in front of your nose and then pulls it away again. Why then this setback?

In my mind I recall our time in Germany. From the beginning we have been involved in many kinds of activities. We tried everything to find a place to live and grew increasingly impatient and frustrated with the impossibility of our situation. We have followed every lead, put ads in newspapers, seen real estate agents and grasped at every straw. Now we see no way out of our difficulties and problems. After trying every possibility we are further from a solution than ever before. We are caught in a dead-end out of which there is no escape. A thought creeps into my mind, slinks its way through to consciousness and brazenly stands up to proclaim,

"Yes, there is one other possibility. Why not admit you have made a mistake and pack your things and return to your home in

America? After nine months of searching, you still have not found a place to live. Everybody would understand it. The youth group in Wuppertal has developed strong leadership in the meantime. They would continue without you."

At our nightly meeting with our new friends I voice these thoughts.

"We can understand your disappointment," Valentin tries to comfort us, "but God possibly wants to teach you not only to trust in him but also to wait for him. Often you find this phrase in the Bible, "wait for the Lord". Be patient and hold on and give God one more chance." We look at each other. We are at a breaking point. Sam answers for both of us after a while.

"All right, we will put our trust solely in God from now on. We will no longer try to find a place, or put an ad in the paper nor ask a real estate agent. In fact we exclude all human help, which has not done us any good anyway, and wait only to see what God will do. We will take this word literally and just wait for him." I nod in agreement.

But the days pass and I find our new inactivity difficult and strenuous and stretching our nerves to the utmost. From childhood on I have heard and learned exactly the opposite. A German proverb expresses it, "God helps those who help themselves." How can we just sit there and do nothing? How can we expect that things are going to be dropped into our laps when we don't lift a finger? Don't we limit God's possibilities by withdrawing from people, whom God uses often to help? Day after day we discuss these thoughts and fight an inner battle. It lasts for almost two weeks. We chew on this hard word 'Wait' till our teeth hurt! To wait for God is the most difficult thing I have ever done!

Then again the voice of the landlady screams across the courtyard,

"Herr Entz, you are wanted on the phone!" This time Sam returns with a beaming face.

"Guess who called? The lawyer! The deal with their relatives did not work out and we can have the place after all! He will send us the rental agreement!" We dance through the narrow space between the walls of the trailer bouncing from side to side! It has paid off to wait for God!

Ten days pass before we get the rental agreement in the mail. I open the letter and turn pale.

"What was the monthly rent you agreed on?" I ask startled. Sam tells me the amount.

"He wants almost twice as much now!" I can hardly believe what I read. I gasp for air and then I get really angry – with the lawyer and with God! Twice we had thanked him for this apartment, and now it is financially out of our reach. What kind of game is being played with us? Is God not satisfied with us that we trusted and waited for him? After my emotions have calmed down I realize that this is no accidental or capricious happening. No doubt God is testing us.

We sit down and write a letter to the lawyer. We explain why we have come to Germany and how desperately we need the apartment, which is now beyond our financial reach. With the mailing of this letter a sense of peace and quietness of mind returns. It is no longer in our hands, we have turned it completely over into the hands of God. Had he not promised that he would cash our checks of need? It is up to him now to make good on his promise. When friends ask us what we are going to do when we have to vacate the room on June 2nd, we can answer without worry and somewhat light hearted,

"God knows about it. It is in his hands."

A week later we hold an answer to our letter in our hands. The lawyer apologizes for the raised rent! His explanation is that he thought that the U.S.Military would pay for our rent and he thought he could profit by them! We only need to pay the original rent and we can move into the place on June 2nd! This time our grateful prayers come from humble hearts, for we know that we have learned some valuable lessons and have finally passed the test!

A long time ago friends from our Hollywood church had asked us if they could stop by for a visit on their way home from Africa where they were medical missionaries. We had written them that we would be delighted to see them and that they could stay with us. On June 1st we received a letter telling us about their arrival by Rhine boat the next day. On June 2nd we say a relieved good- bye to our dump and pull the trailer out of the courtyard and up the hill to our new home. We store the most necessary items in cupboards and drawers, make the beds and fill the refrigerator. Then we hurry down to the pier to welcome our friends and daughter as they land. The first night in our new place our dear guests sleep in our new beds! Not one minute too late, God has supplied all of our needs!

29

⌘

A year has passed and again we are on our way back to the United States. Much has happened in the meantime where we could see the leading of God in our lives. Our youth work has grown. We have met a German pastor who teaches in a school where he can invite young people. Together we have met in our living room till it could no longer accommodate all of the youth that crowded into our apartment. We moved to a meeting hall downtown and more young people attend our weekly "Wednesday Group" and weekend conferences and summer vacation trips.

At the first six months' Bible School at the Klostermuehle, I have met one of the visiting teachers, a German pastor who specializes in informing and warning people of the dangers of the occult. He asks me to translate a book of his into English, 'Between Christ and Satan'. Dr. Kurt Koch is an expert on this subject, who travels widely and speaks on this topic, writes many books and counsels many oppressed people.

It takes me nine months to finish the translation, beside all of my other activities. My eyes are opened about the danger and underlying connections to psychological and physical as well as spiritual maladies growing out of occult activities. The carelessness and curiosity, through which people become victims of occult bondage, are appalling.

This understanding leads me to check up on my life and to ask for forgiveness where I have broken God's laws, in which he warns his people of going to fortune tellers or to spiritistic sessions, or seeking guidance in such 'harmless' things as horoscopes. Many defend themselves by saying that they don't believe these things anyway, but the fact is that they are being influenced, even on a subconscious level, by these forces, that God definitely forbade to get in contact with.

After the book is printed, Dr. Koch asks us to use our connections in America to organize a series of speaking engagements in the English-speaking world. A young American missionary couple we met at the Klostermuehle offer to continue our youth work and move into our apartment while we are away. Again we set out to cross the ocean in another ocean liner.

On our first Sunday in Los Angeles, Sam suddenly becomes sick during the worship service. It takes all of my strength to get him into the car and drive him to the emergency service at the UCLA Medical Center. The examining doctor diagnoses a beginning sepsis from an injury on a toe. Such small cause for a life-threatening situation! While he continues his examination he asks Sam, when he had polio.

"Polio?" Sam asks amazed, "I never had it!"

"But you must have, for your stomach muscles are paralyzed. You had the most dangerous kind of polio, which usually ends in death or the Iron Lung. Did you get vaccinated?"

I remember that while taking our children to be vaccinated, Sam also got two of the three shots.

"That is the reason you are still alive," the doctor tells us. I recall that about half a year ago Sam got sick and our neighborhood doctor diagnosed it as a case of the flue. At the outbreak of the illness, before I called the doctor, I had given him a hot bath, which I later thought was the absolute worst thing to do, as I tried to get him out of the tub and into his bed with all the strength I could muster.

"That was the best thing you could have done at the onset of polio," the doctor assured me now. We are grateful for the guidance and the protection of God, during a time while I wondered why my strong husband could not regain his health and felt weak for many months.

Now we are living in our house again, the children attend a Christian school down the street and Sam has returned to his old place of work, where they are glad to have their star salesman back.

But Sam's usual enjoyment of his ability to sell more than others does not return. He goes to work rather listlessly, while I am busy preparing for the arrival of Dr. Koch, for whom Sam has organized a six weeks' tour. I translate all of his talks into English and since he is not yet fluent in the language I am present when after his talks people ask for personal counseling or a question and answer session follows the talk. Through this practical hands-on training I learn much about the reality of the powers of darkness, which I personally had experienced during the translation of the book. Only by consciously applying the protection of the blood of Christ had I been able to ward off the satanic attacks.

Oppressed people can be freed only by this way. I witnessed many such occasions while translating for Dr.Koch in counseling with people. After six weeks many new doors have opened for him and the rest of his life he is traveling throughout the whole world with the message of liberation from the powers of darkness through the cross and the blood of Christ.

We make plans again to return to Germany. But this time it is to be a final good bye to all loophole security. Like the monk Colombo, who came from Scotland to bring the Gospel to the heathen Germanic tribes and upon arriving on the continent burned his boat, we decide to sell our house. Nothing should tie us to the past. Besides we need the money to live on. Again, for the eighth time, we cross the ocean. An unusual thought hits me while I peer into my purse. There is a key ring inside but no key on it. For once in my life I am completely free!

We plan to start a new work among students in Heidelberg. Dr. Koch has a friend there who will help us find a place to live. On our way there, we have to change trains in Koblenz. Koblenz? We can't just continue on without saying hello to our friends. We will take the next train to Heidelberg. As we arrive at our former apartment to greet the family that has taken over our youth work, we are greeted by a stranger at the door. He explains that the couple had a call to take over the leadership of the Klostermuehle, while Dwight and Velma Wadsworth, the house parents, are on a years' furlough in the States. From October first our youth work will be without a leader. We visit our faithful friends, the Reinhard family, and after the joy of reunion they ask us, why we don't return to Koblenz again instead of starting something new. There is no special reason now. But we thought that the youth work was in capable hands, and now there is a new situation. Yet we have made this commitment in Heidelberg. We meet Dr. Koch's friend there, look at an apartment, but decide in the end to return to Koblenz. On October 1st, 1962 we move into our old apartment for the second time, this time not on a sub lease. The lawyer has taken out his furniture and we furnish the place with our own things, beginning with fixtures and lamp bulbs and ending with cabinets and cupboards and the kitchen sink. Completely bare is the condition of German rentals.

The next years bring a fast growth of our youth work. We are independent missionaries now, no longer under the auspices of the Torchbearers. Every Wednesday night about a hundred young people meet in a large hall in a newly built church-owned center in the heart of town. Beside this meeting, attended also by many service men stationed in the garrison city of Koblenz, there are home Bible studies, and we offer retreats and vacation trips to different countries. Our home feels often like Grand Central Station- with many guests, young and old, coming and going. Sam tries to keep us above water financially by buying and selling cars. Some friends send us support money through an organization, CONCERN Inc., which our friend from Sunday school, Dr. Richard C. Halverson, then chaplain of the Senate, has started. We cannot use the Social Medicine system in Germany because the premiums would be too high for all five of us, so we live without medical insurance. But God keeps us healthy and free from expensive medical bills.

The children return to German schools and have their friends. Joy got her dog, which was the bribe to get her to agree to return to the foreign land. But slowly we continue to eat up our house. One day Sam returns with the news that a new law will make it unprofitable for him to buy and sell cars. But how then should we live? It is time once more to cash in our promise check! Had not God promised us that He would supply all of our needs? We are learning to trust Him with our finances. A thrifty life-style is nothing new to us. A large part of our and the children's clothes come from the second-hand shop at the American Military Installation. If I want to have a new dress, I must sew it for myself. I learn to make inexpensive tasty meals to feed lots of guests. Yet in the long run our precarious financial condition becomes a burden.

One day the telephone rings.

"This is Paris calling. Here is the Billy Graham office. Is Mr. Entz there? Your name was given to us by an acquaintance. Would you consider becoming a film evangelist for our organization? You would travel throughout Germany with our movies and show them at all U.S.Military installations." We can hardly believe our good fortune! Now Sam has a regular job, one that fits his personality to the tee! His special evangelistic gifts can be fully used in this work. Enthusiastic as his nature is, he throws himself into his new job in his office in Frankfurt, 110km from home. Over the years he puts together a program of about 20 movies, produced by the Billy Graham affiliate 'World Wide Pictures', with which he travels throughout Southern Germany, working together with the chaplains at each installation and holding meetings with an evangelistic call at the end to invite Jesus Christ into the life.

The youth work in Koblenz is growing and continuing to expand. With great joy I just returned from a year-end conference at which several young people opened their lives to receive Christ. I plan new Bible studies for the young believers. That morning I open a letter from our friends in California who have taken in our seventeen-year old son to help him get into the American high school system and prepare him for college admission. Our oldest daughter is living with relatives in Central California, also making the transition from the German system to the American. As I read the letter my heart starts pounding. Our friends ask us to return to the States and make a home for our children. Our son, who is extremely sensitive and has developed a complex because of a deformed ear, feels like an outsider in his high school and suffers from depression. Our friends, both full-time working professionals, need help.

I show the letter to Sam. What are we to do? We can't just throw everything to the winds and take off! But our son needs us. For Sam with his many far reaching commitments it is out of the question. And I? Who is going to continue to lead the many activities and groups? Sam is the first who is able to act. He picks up the phone and calls our charter club where we are members.

"When is the next charter flight to California?" he asks.

"What? Nothing till Easter? Nothing before that time? What? Tonight? And that is the only flight?" He looks at me questioningly. I have no choice.

"Can you make it?" he asks. I nod. Standing by the stove, stirring the noon meal, my thoughts race in all directions. When the door bell rings and Sheri returns from school, she greets me with the announcement,

"Marion and I are going sledding this afternoon."

"No', I answer, "you are going to America with me!"

The next few hours are filled with hectic activities. Packing, making phone calls, saying good-bye and preparing for my absence, till Sam waits in the car to drive us to the Frankfurt Airport on slippery roads. After last minute instructions we embrace and kiss for the last time. We don't know what the future holds. Bravely we try to hide the uncertainty and smile as we wave good-bye for a last time. Then we are parted. For how long? No one knows. The next morning we get out of the plane in Los Angeles. Numb and apprehensive I walk towards my waiting parents, who embrace us with great joy, while my heart aches.

We find a house in the San Fernando Valley and the three children and I move in. After awhile Sam joins us. He has given up his job and sold all of our belongings, which I had left behind at our hasty fare-well. He works again at his old place of work in Hollywood. I also work half days as social worker for the Board of Deacons at our church in Hollywood. The children attend local schools. My parents are happy to have us finally live close to them. Yet my father is worried about his wife. He sees the first signs of approaching Alzheimer in her and he worries about the future. I also begin to worry about my jovial and positive husband, who is slowly changing into a depressed and dissatisfied person. Even driving and selling the newest and most fashionable Cadillacs does not give him joy. He dreads to go to work, something I have never seen in him. Finally I can bear it no longer and suggest, that he should call his boss in Paris and ask if he could continue his work in Germany. He brightens up as he hears a positive answer. We decide that he should return and he gets permission to visit us twice a year, during summer vacation and over Christmas. We expect to be parted for one whole year, till the older children's transition to college. With a new lease on life he flies back and I remain alone with three children, two of them teenagers.

Soon I feel like a hamster in a treadmill. My days become a routine of going to work in the morning, driving to my parent's house to do their housework, since my father is increasingly not feeling well and my mother can no longer manage her household. During the height of the traffic I creep along over crowded freeways and begin at home with the housework of cooking and being father and mother to the children. My depressive son is going through a difficult time. He would need his father at this time especially, but he is far away and only available by letters. It is hard for me as a woman to face up to an 18 year old under the influence of his peers who I do not approve. It makes this a troublesome time for us all. I miss my husband from whom I had never been parted any length of time. In the group of our old friends I often feel like a stranger without Sam. When an announcement was made in our Sunday school for a Valentine's party for couples, I had to run out to hide my tears.

I accuse God for taking my husband from me when I need him most. I rebel against his leading me away from my beloved youth work. I ache for companionship and love, when all I get is trouble and difficulties. Sometimes I think that God has rejected me and spurns my prayers. I feel lonely and unable to pray many times. There is no one to whom I could pour my heart out. Who would understand that I, a missionary from the First Presbyterian Church of Hollywood, had to go to the police station to bail my son out for possession of marijuana? My inner rebellion grows to the point that I no longer pray nor read the Bible. That in turn brings more self-accusations. You will never again be able tell anybody that God helps you and supports you in difficult times! Just look at yourself how miserably you have failed! He will never use you again!

Mechanically I go through the days and do my work, counting the hours till Sam will be with me again. But when he finally arrives and we are together as a family again, I dread his leaving me alone once more. The one year that we had planned to be separated, has gone by and since my father's health is deteriorating and my mother is unable to cope, I as the only child feel obligated to take care of my aged parents in their time of need. Yet my own situation grows increasingly worse. I feel shattered into a thousand pieces, laying on the ground, with no end in sight and without real hope for a change. Another year passes and as his condition worsens my father asks worriedly,

"What will become of Mother when I am no longer here?"

"Please don't worry," I answer, "I promise you that I will take care of her". Gratefully and relieved he takes my hand in his. This worry is the cause of his sickness, and I hope that he will get better again. It is difficult to see how a beloved person, who all of her life has been a dynamic business woman and a philosophical seeker after truth, becomes more and more disabled and separated from all memory of who she is and those around her.

Ten years ago we had the joy of seeing my mother, who had been an ardent follower of the Anthroposophical Society and their branch, the Christengemeinschaft, become a new person through Jesus Christ. When we formerly talked about issues of faith and the Bible, we always ended in disharmony. Her critical and rejecting spirit concerning the Bible and specially the miracles that Jesus did, made it difficult for me to communicate with my mother, whom I loved and felt very close to. But since she had written to us in Germany, that a friend had taken her along to Forest Home (!) and there she had heard Major Thomas, founder of the Torchbearers, preach, she was born-again, we could hardly believe the change. Never again did we have any more disagreements or discussions about miracles or other topics, which she had vehemently rejected. She began to read the Bible with an ardent desire to know every-thing about the Son of God. The miracles of Jesus, which she denied before, she accepted as part of his God-nature. Her favorite book next to the Bible was no longer one of Rudolf Steiner's' deceptive messages of the occult, but Oswald Chambers daily devotional, My Utmost for His Highest, which she read daily and underlined and surrounded with comments.

Through the contact with Dr. Kurt Koch, who had opened my eyes to the danger of the occult, I had realized that my Anthroposophical baptism, which my mother arranged for me at twelve years of age, was not biblical. Therefore I was baptized by a friend, a Mennonite pastor, in the little river Wied near Koblenz, and now have the assurance of having experienced a valid Christian baptism.

The bitter knowledge, that the personality my mother had once been was slowly being taken away from her, is hard for my father, who has no personal faith in a personal God. His illness is getting worse and my duties at their house increase, as I nurse my father after he came home from the hospital.

One day a sudden thought strikes me like lightning while reading 2nd Corinthians 1:3. Could it be that all of these difficulties that you have to undergo, are really not a sign that God has rejected you, but that he is allowing you to grow under suffering to become a more mature person? You may be able in the future to understand and empathize with those, who go through the same kind of suffering, as you have been experiencing. God can use your brokenness and feeling of useless isolation and loneliness to make something whole and good out of it. Through this one thought the rebellion is gone and new hope awakens and for the first time in years I feel loved by God again.

30

I am working in the deacon's office at church when the telephone rings. An unknown voice, a neighbor of my parents, tries to inform me gently that my father has died suddenly this morning. As I enter the house of my parents, my father is sitting upright on the couch, covered with a sheet. He was reading his newspaper when the stroke hit him. My confused mother had run to the neighbors, who had called for help. In spite of the grief of losing my beloved Dad, I am grateful that he was spared a long time of disability or suffering. Sam is here on vacation and is a big support to me. My father's wish is to be cremated and his urn is to be buried in the Jewish cemetery in Culver City. My beloved Daddy, who made my childhood loving and carefree and protected and who never tried to interfere with our going back to Germany, though it meant separation from his only daughter and grandchildren, will never hold me in his arms again and stroke my hair. Will I meet him again in heaven? I do not know, and that makes this parting so difficult. Though he was not a believing Jew, he also did not accept Christ, though he often acted more Christian than some of those who call themselves Christians. I trust that God, who sees into the hearts, is a righteous judge.

In November 1970, almost three years after arriving, having rented my parents' house and packed once more, I set out with my mother to cross the ocean again. The older children are in college and the youngest, Sheri, has gone along with Sam to Germany and is in a boarding school for English speaking missionary children. After being in American schools we do not want her to have the stress of changing into another language and school system once more.

As we arrive in Koblenz, where Sam has rented a room during our absence, we decide to visit or former landlords. They greet us friendly and tell us that they did not rent our apartment since our leaving three years ago, because they did not want strangers in their house.

"If you would like, you could move in again", they offer. Would we?! We have been looking for a suitable place and now this great opportunity appears to make an entrance into Guinness Book of World Records, to move into the same apartment three times! Happily we move back into our old apartment, though with a whole new set of furniture, since Sam lives in a furnished place and he had sold all of our former furniture. Mother gets one of the children's rooms and after a time Sheri joins us again. She was unhappy at the boarding school and is glad to be home. She travels every day to the American school in Bonn-Bad Godesberg, one and a half hours by train and bus. I drive her to the train station at ten after seven in the morning and pick her up each evening at ten after five. But in spite of the long rides she loves the school with children from all nations, who live in the different Embassies in Bonn and she is happy to be with her family again.

My youth work has been carried on by my successor and I stay away. Never again do I want to do things on my own initiative. This is one of the lessons I have learned in these three years. If God has a work for me to do, he will have to take the first step. He knows that I am ready and eager to do his will. For a whole year I stay home, caring for Mother and the rest of the family.

One day my successor comes for a visit. He has something on his heart. He tells me of the condition of the youth group, which is no longer growing to make up for the loss of those that had moved. He asks me if I would like to join the work again. I ponder the offer. In America I have experienced a new kind of youth work in our church, which was a hit with our young people. I tell him about the coffee house ministry, which the Jesus People movement started. He has heard of a similar work in Berlin, a so-called tea house ministry. We pray about these opportunities and a short time later we are on our way to Berlin to get a first-hand impression of this new kind of work.

We are inspired and I give a report at the meeting of our weekly prayer group, which meets each Monday since our arrival in 1959. I describe the possibilities of inviting young people from the streets and in schools and to create a place where one can talk without interruptions and answer questions young people are struggling with. But after my presentation several questions remain unanswered. Who is going to finance this risky adventure? And who are going to be the people to feel the call to work with young people, Christian or not? I do not have the answer and so I suggest we ask the Lord for a sign to show us his will in this matter. The others agree and in our prayers we ask God to make it clear to us by giving us green light.

A week later we receive a letter from Sam's sister Rebecca. She is single and works at present as chambermaid in a hotel. On a slip of paper she writes: "God put it on my heart to send you this check. I know you have prayed for it, so I went to the bank and got a credit. Use the money for whatever you need." Included is a check for $500! She did not know anything about our plans or our prayers! In fact she had mailed the letter before we even prayed. God has faster ways of communication than we have. This is the green light from God we have prayed for!

The youth leader and I set out to search for suitable quarters. We want to be downtown where the discotheques and bars draw young people on weekends. Within two days we find a whole first floor of an older building, which we rent and renovate together. Most of the furnishings are donated and slowly the many large rustic rooms look inviting. What we are doing spreads like wild fire through the youth scene and when we are finally ready to open, it is Carnival Saturday, we can hardly make our way upstairs through the crowd of expectantly waiting young people. Once inside about a hundred curious youngsters mill through the many rooms. Our faithful helper, Grandma Schlosser, counts 76 pots of tea she made before the evening is over way after midnight. Exhausted but happy we fall into bed. The Teestube 'One Way' is a big success.

Soon I find out that this is a completely different kind of work than I have been used to in a Christian setting. We are a hand full of Christians trying to cope with about a hundred young people coming and going all evening. There is no other place in town where young people can meet and get free tea. Our guests are as varied as life itself. They come from all levels of society. There are many high school and college students or young apprentices, and soldiers. Yet there are also gang leaders with their noisy followers, political groups reaching from extreme right Neo-Nazis to extreme left Communists. In between we discover prostitutes, pimps, alcoholics, drug addicts and criminals. Once in a while, a pastor or religion teacher or theology professor mingles with the crowd. Their intentions are not always what they seem. They want to find out who is the magnet that draws their young people here week after week. They are the most difficult visitors, trying to find reasons to support their prejudiced point of view of this 'American sect'. In a local paper lies about me are spread and even Christian evangelical groups prohibit their young people from visiting us. But they keep on coming anyway.

Yet over time hardly one in five well-meaning helpers can withstand the pressure of this constant confrontation. They are not trained to cope with such opposite and aggressive worldviews, and the methods of young people to aggravate and constantly challenge and confront in order to see your reaction. Only after one has stood this test of being provoked almost to the point of losing your temper, yet keeping it under control, a step forward in trust is being made. Yet it takes all our inner strength when we have to patrol the rooms like police watching for forbidden drug dealing or alcohol consumption or stepping between an NPD Nazi and a Communist who are ready to fight. Our goal is to bring Jesus to these people who do not believe in God and for whom the Bible is a fairy tale book. We end each Sunday evening with a short evangelistic message. But even a well-known German evangelist, whom we invite, cannot make himself heard against the sarcastic remarks and outright ridicule, with which his words are met. Only very few can speak the language to reach these young people.

Often, after another one of my helpers informs me that he is not coming back, I feel my strength and enthusiasm waning and many times I am tempted to give up. But then some unexpected encouragement gives me the necessary power to once more open the doors after a short prayer, "Lord Jesus, please go in before me." Slowly bridges of trust to certain ones are being built. Different groups claim special tables where only members of their group may sit. My favorites are the young Communists who have high idealistic goals. Often I sit in their round till way after midnight, listening and discussing and praying for opportunities to tell them of Jesus' goals, who is the only one to create the "new man" for their utopian world.

After two and a half years of hard struggles and diminishing strength, there is a core of young people who have become Christians and are now changing the atmosphere. They sit in the front room, playing guitars and singing Christian songs. The guests feel their influence and some curious ones even visit our Wednesday night Bible Study.

In retrospect I realize why I had to go through those three difficult years in America. Without this experience of brokenness, I would have never been able to cope with all the problems that young people shared with me. I would have never understood them in their loneliness and feeling of being lost or their relational hurts. Never could I have gained their trust or devotion, never have felt real empathy with their struggles, never could I have carried on in spite of disappointments and wearing and tearing experiences to continue to open the doors again and again with new courage. It becomes clear to me that God has prepared me for this work, even while I was rebelling against his leading.

31

～⚭〜

My mother's Alzheimer condition demands more and more of my time and care. It becomes a growing burden for me under which my shoulders chafe. Two strokes and two bouts of pneumonia have robbed her of her means of communication. She cannot understand words or make herself understood. That is the reason I never took her to a hospital but nursed her to health at home. Dementia makes it difficult to leave her alone even for a short time. Beside the work at the Teestube, which takes most of my energy, there is this disease, robbing my beloved mother of her humanity and burdening me increasingly with no relief in sight. When it threatens to undo me, God himself intervenes.

It is Saturday. I was unable to get somebody to be with Mother for this evening and my husband had meetings of his own. This does not happen very often, yet I have to open the Teestube. Before I leave, I turn on the TV, which she is not able to follow, but it gives the allusion of not being alone. Then I sit her in her armchair, put some cookies on a plate next to her and leave. Upon my return some hours later I am greeted by absolute chaos. Everything that could be moved has been carried around and deposited elsewhere. Flowers from a vase lie carelessly strewn on the rug. Torn newspapers cover the floor, throw rugs are rolled up and neatly laid out on our beds, and sofa pillows grace the kitchen table. But the worst part is that I cannot find mother's dentures. I run from room to room, looking in every corner, lifting every pillow, yet they are not to be found. My frustration and my blood pressure increase while I am trying to bring some order to this mess, till I can no longer contain myself, and it comes to an explosion in the kitchen.

Suddenly my eyes are caught by a small card, which I placed on the refrigerator. "Lord, give me patience – but please hurry!"" is the humorous text. This is the hour of truth for me! Here I have asked God for patience – and he is answering me by putting me in his school of patience. He wants to give it to me, but my impatient, impulsive nature works completely against Him. Suddenly everything becomes clear to me. I realize that the situation with my mother will not get better but worse. In order not to collapse under the burden, I will have to change my reaction. I decide certain new ways of dealing with the inevitable. If I have to leave her alone again, I will tell myself before I put the key in the lock, 'You know what is awaiting you inside. You clean up as much as you can. If you do not find something, don't look for it.' It will show up again, like the dentures, which I found a couple of days later while dusting and lifting up a vase that made a clattering sound.

From this moment on my attitude is changed. Instead of aggravation there is more quietness, instead of impatience there is more stability. Mother, who would look at me with anxious eyes, that made me feel badly about my lack of control, now thanked me by nestling her head on my shoulder or stroking my hand. That is her way of still being able to show love. Everything else has been destroyed in her brain, but the emotions of love, which have dominated her life, were still there and she could show them.

This new beginning is being tested and tried on many occasions. Three times we have to ask the police for help in finding her after she managed to get out. The fear and anxiety till she is found again take their toll on our nerves. But the everyday care is no longer a burden to me, but becomes the priority around which my life is centered. I even have to give up my beloved youth work as the year's progress. After fourteen years of taking care of her, our doctor informs me that this time she is not going to survive the third bout of pneumonia. I plead with the Lord to leave her with me a little while longer, yet after one week she dies at home with almost eighty-seven years of age. I can be with her to her last breath, but afterwards I fall into a deep hole.

Her death is a terrible loss to me. Fourteen years I have cared for her like for my own child. While children develop and grow, she has regressed to the state of infancy. But her mother's love was there till the end. Nobody will ever love me selflessly like she did. I thank God for giving me a mother like that, who is my shining example and whose love molded my life and influenced it so deeply.

A wise saying sums it up:

"When you were born, everybody rejoiced and was happy! Only you cried.

Live such a life that at your death everybody cries, and only you rejoice!

32

It is 1984, our children are married and the first two grandchildren, though far away, are the joy of our lives. Sam has been working for seventeen years as a Billy Graham film evangelist. Though he is 69 years old, he does not want to hear the word 'retire'. There is still too much vitality and energy inside him to want to live a life of ease and rest. With over 200 meetings a year he covers many areas of Germany. After 25 years I am still enjoying my youth work. Many times I had the joy of realizing that at that age one still can influence decisions in the lives of young people, which will have long lasting effects. Working with the young keeps one young too. Constant confrontation with other worldviews has sharpened my mind and given me joy in conversing with those who have other points of view. Many young people have found a living relationship with Jesus Christ, which now serves as foundation for their lives. Many others, over twenty couples, have found their mates at the Teestube, and at their weddings I feel like a very successful manager of a marriage institute.

Yet during all of the years in Germany there is an inner battle I have to fight. Sudden emotions of defensiveness and revulsion take a hold of me whenever I hear or read anti-Semitic remarks. Once it was the passing remark by a pastor, whose sermons we enjoyed.

"I would never marry a Jewess" he said in my presence and it stabbed me to the heart. Then there was the rise of Neo-Naziism going uncensored with their anti-Jewish jokes and their denial of the Holocaust. Often I am asked to tell my life story in front of an audience. But as soon as the word 'Jew' is mentioned, I can see in about one third of the older audience embarrassment or open hostility in the eyes of my listeners. This hurts me personally, the daughter of a Jewish father. Yet among the young people I feel no rejection or resentfulness. I can open my heart and mind about the Nazi past without restraint.

I do not believe one can hold a whole generation responsible for the misdeeds of a few, but as a whole I have felt that there is a burden of unforgiven and unrepented guilt keeping the whole country under siege of secularism and Godlessness. The old generation tries to defend their position in regard to Hitler and do not want to face up to their part in supporting him and his henchmen. The young generation does not feel responsible for the sins of their fathers (and mothers!) and hide behind the phrase of former chancellor Helmut Kohl, who spoke of the 'fortune of a late birth', as if that excluded one from taking on the burden of history.

Yet I met one family in Koblenz, who belong to the younger generation, which showed genuine empathy and felt a personal responsibility to right the wrongs as best as they could. I will never forget the tears in Oskar Lorentz's eyes upon hearing my life story, nor will I forget his wife, Monikas', friendly invitation to spend the 9th of November with them, when I yearly remember the so-called 'Crystal Night' when the synagogues were burnt down and the store windows smashed. Their deeds of love mean more to me than many words of others, which are lacking in genuine warmth and heart feelings.

When it comes to forgiveness I never forget Forest Home, where God freed me from my unforgiving heart and made it possible for me to forgive those who have hurt me. Yet once in a while those old feelings seem to take possession of me again through my negative attitude. When I am aware of it, I pray that God may give me love for the person concerned.

I am visiting Berlin again. Our friends, Hildegard and Valentin Reinhard are there also seeing their daughter and grandchild. Together we go for a walk, pushing the stroller with their grand-daughter. In Kreuzberg district there are not many public parks, so we head for a cemetery with tall old trees, an oasis in this section of rows of grey tenement houses. Hildegard carries a small plastic bag with a wet cleaning pad.

"We saw a grave," she explains, "which has an old weather beaten metal plaque with a nice Bible verse on it. We want to polish it so one can read it again." We push the stroller through rows of graves. They stop at a tall white marble monument. She takes out the pad and begins to scrub the dull metal plate. Soon the metal begins to shine, but an ugly brown stain runs down the white marble monument.

"Do something! Wipe it off, quickly!" Valentin shouts excitedly. But there is nothing to wipe with. I run to a garbage box, find a plastic bag, fill it with water, run to the monument, splash the water on it and douse the stain. I repeat this several times till the marble looks white again. Then I read the name of the deceased. Alfred Stoecker. It sounds vaguely familiar.

"Wasn't he the preacher at the large Dome Cathedral?" I ask, but Valentin just shrugs his shoulders. He does not know.

After a while I leave to visit the famous State Library. I am looking for some more information, as I am going to lead a youth conference, where I will speak on Nehemia, who rebuilt the broken down walls of Jerusalem after the Babylonian exile. Perhaps I can find some archaeological discoveries or other materials. As I enter the building I see large signs leading to an exhibit on part of the ground floor. The theme of the exhibit interests me. "History of Jews in Prussia." Curious I follow the signs to movable walls depicting the plight of the Jews from the Middle Ages till the present. I see enlarged pictures of medieval Jews, who were then already discriminated by pointed hats and persecuted by not allowing them to earn a living by excluding them from learning any trade. There is an explanation for each picture. I am the only person looking at this exhibit.

The next wall is titled "Men who prepared modern times for Anti-Semitism". I see a picture of Heinrich von Treitschke, a historian. I have never heard his name. But this one down there I know well! It is a picture of Julius Streicher, the infamous publisher of 'Der Stuermer' the hate filled propaganda paper against the Jews, spewing out threats from each showcase, overshadowing my life with fear. Right in front of me a third face looks me straight in the eye. The name hits me like an electric shock. "Alfred Stoecker".

I am beside myself with rage. Accusations roll off my lips without restraint.

"You!" I shout at the picture, "You are responsible for all the terrible things that happened! You prepared the people to kill, even my best friend Erika and her parents, who died in the gas chambers! And I – just an hour ago, I had to clean your grave! It is unbelievable!" I cannot think clearly being so agitated by this provocation. Of all the hundred thousands of graves in Berlin, I had to clean this man's grave! My heart races, my mind is in shambles so that I cannot see another picture. I turn and leave the exhibition. Even while trying to pour over books upstairs, I cannot concentrate. Too deep has the shock been and too unsettling the thought of my part, however unwilling, in it.

Thomas, one of our young men from the Teestube, a student of Catholic theology, picks me up the next day to drive me to the conference. Still under the impact of what happened to me, I tell him my version of the unbelievable incident. We have talked often and sometimes into the early hours of the morning, about sin and forgiveness and the position of the Jews in history. He had even given me books to read on the subject.

Now I end my emotion-filled tale with the words,

"See, Thomas, how the devil tripped me up!" Silence. Then a quiet comment,

"Perhaps God wanted to test you whether you really had forgiven."

I sit there like somebody just hit me with a baseball bat. In my minds' eye I see myself standing there, hurling these hate-filled words at the picture of Stoecker. The evidence is against me. What I called full forgiveness is just a superficial veneer. Underneath are mountains of unforgiven memories.

In the evening we sit in a circle with the young people and read the prayer of Nehemia. As I hear the words I can no longer contain myself. "I pray before thee now, day and night, for the children of Israel thy servants, and confess the sins of the children of Israel, which we have sinned against thee; both I and my father's house have sinned." Tears of repentance start flowing and the young people look at me with concern. Only Thomas moves closer and holds my hand. It takes time to collect myself.

At the end of the weekend, several young people have come to faith in Christ and I return with joy. God has blessed and I feel forgiven. A few weeks later Sam tells me of finding a new bookstore, which sells antique books. Collecting old Christian books is a hobby of mine. He takes me there at my next visit to Frankfurt, where he has his office. I look through rows of precious antique books. Suddenly my eyes see the name Alfred Stoecker. I page through it and then quickly put the book back. Why pay money for the life of this man? I look at many other books, but in the end I take Alfred Stoecker home with me. That night I begin to read his life story, which started out so well. He did many good things working for the kingdom of God. But then he got side tracked into the wrong kind of politics, and the rest of his story ends lamentably. After reading his story, all feelings of rejection and condemnation are gone. All I can feel for him is compassion. A person who started out well but ended up badly. God has worked deeply in my heart and the forgiveness, which only he can impart, has sunk to the bottom of the heart.

Once, a young journalist, interviewing me, posed this question, "When you talk about forgiveness, is it a one time thing or an ongoing process?" I had to give it some thought and then answered,

"I think it is both. First you decide you want to forgive. It is a question of your will, because you know that God requires you to forgive others. How else could you pray the Lord's Prayer, 'and forgive us our debts as we forgive our debtors?' But often our emotions cannot keep up with this step of the will and it takes time to reach the depth of the heart."

I see it like a picture of fresh, clean raindrops falling from the sky; that is God's forgiveness that wants to cleanse and refresh us. But then the rain comes in contact with dusty leaves or dirty roads and it gets contaminated. Who would want to drink out of a puddle on the road? But then the dirty water sinks into the ground, and going from strata to strata it is cleansed again, till it reaches the ground water level and is pumped up as pure clean drinking water. So forgiveness takes time to go through the different strata of emotions, which have been hurt, but in the end when forgiveness has reached the ground level, hurts are healed and I can truly say, 'I have forgiven'.

The Biblical story of Joseph spoke to me in this regard in a new and different way. He had been so wronged by his brothers, who would have left him to die, unless some Egyptians had come by. Instead they seized the opportunity to make money by selling him into slavery. When they later came to Egypt to buy food because of a famine, Joseph immediately recognized them but kept himself aloof from them. Only after they have brought his blood brother Benjamin does he disclose his real identity. The Bible describes it this way in Genesis 45: "Then Joseph could not refrain himself...and he wept aloud...and said unto his brethren...be not grieved, nor angry with yourselves, that ye sold me hither: for God did send me before you to preserve life.' And he fell upon his brother Benjamin's neck, and wept; and Benjamin wept upon his neck. Moreover he kissed all his brothers, and wept upon them: and after that his brothers talked with him.' What a touching story of forgiveness, followed by actions that gave his family a new home in the best part of the land. There is no question that Joseph had forgiven their wrongs

But then the story goes on in Genesis 50. Seventeen years later his old father, Jacob is dying and he says some strange words to Joseph, which his brothers repeat after his death. "When Joseph's brothers saw that their father was dead, they said, Joseph will peradventure hate us, and will certainly requite us all the evil which we did unto him. And they sent a messenger unto Joseph, saying, Thy father did command before he died, saying, So shall you say to Joseph, 'Forgive, I pray thee now, the trespass of thy brothers, and their sin; for they did unto thee evil: and now, we pray thee, forgive the trespass of the servants of the God of thy father.' And Joseph wept..."

Why did Joseph weep? Was it a sudden recognition that his forgiveness had not gone deep enough to reach the level of the heart? Did his brothers sense that there were remnants of unforgiveness beneath the surface? Did it lead him to repentance as he was confronted with his sin of superficial forgiveness? I can identify with the feeling of Joseph and what caused him to weep. And afterwards 'he comforted them and spoke kindly unto them' for now he had truly forgiven.

This experience leads shortly afterwards to a life changing crisis. Although I have worked for many years and built up what men would call a 'successful ministry,' I feel a lack of power in my personal life. Where was the promise that Jesus gave to his disciples, 'that ye shall receive power after the Holy Spirit is come upon you' in my life? Why do I have this desire for more of God? A small book, 'They found the Secret', with testimonies of people who had the same desire and who had received this power that changed their lives, made me storm heaven's gates, as Jacob of the Old Testament had done in that particular night, when he wrestled with an angel and said, 'I will not let thee go unless you bless me.' God honors this request and it becomes the hour of truth for me. My illusionary picture of myself is being shattered piece by piece as God holds up a mirror and I see clearly how he sees me. The confrontation with my pride, my often loveless attitude, my obstinacy, my selfishness and other things which do not please God, lead to a complete confession and surrender and under tears I ask him to make me new and fill me with his spirit. This confrontation and cleansing is a very painful battle and takes several hours, but in the end I feel the peace that passes all understanding and have the inner assurance that I have been cleansed and filled and experience the wonderful freedom of the children of God. From this moment on I have an intimate connection to God that makes his word more alive and speaks to me in a way that I had never experienced before. The joy that fills me cannot be contained. Also I receive a different kind of love for my fellow men, finding its expression in a love for prayer. I feel like a new person and gratefully acknowledge the power of God to fill my longing for 'more of him'.

33

✎☙❧✎

In November of 1984 Sam and I are again invited to a conference in Mesa, Arizona, of the Billy Graham Evangelistic Association for their worldwide workers. From the moment of our arrival till the end of the week, we feel like cherished members of a great and loving family. We listen to exciting reports of what God is doing in many parts of the world. Among the 350 people present are many of World-Wide Pictures, that branch that produces the Billy Graham movies, which Sam has been showing to thousands of people during the last eighteen years. Together we rejoice in the protection of God and His blessings with which he has blessed Billy Graham and his organization for so many wonderful years. We share visions for the future and renew old acquaintances. This conference is so different from others, for here are people, who feel free to be themselves, open, sharing, accepted and loved, without the star-worship or the artificial 'holy' nimbus often surrounding well-known evangelicals. No hero worship here, instead what impresses me most is the genuine humility which makes a man great, that emanates from Billy Graham himself and is echoed by his co-workers. 'To God be the glory, great things he has done,' seems to be the motto of the whole group.

We feel like we are on a second honeymoon trip, after thirty-six years of marriage. Each day we are surprised by little tokens of love, which mean a lot because they are unexpected. For instance we each get a portfolio with our names engraved on it, or we are taken on a day trip to the red mountains of Arizona to see a former cliff-dwelling village of the Indians, or we celebrate a fabulous outdoor Western barbeque. All of this makes us feel loved and cherished. And Sam and I look back over the last eighteen years and are thankful, how God has enriched our lives through the ministry of this work, which he has blessed so abundantly.

It is the beginning of November, yet the temperature in Mesa is still high. When we arrive at the hotel, we first go for a dip in the pool. I observe my husband with increasing concern. He comes from a physically strong family, and his tolerance for pain is high. In the spring of that year he complained about pains in the area of the stomach.

"It must be my gall bladder", was his explanation. When he was finally willing to see a specialist, the doctor told him that it was not his gall bladder and that he wanted to make further tests. But Sam, who never was one to run to doctors but tried to cure himself, started a juice-only cure and sure enough he would wake up and say,

"I feel so much better today!" He even began to jog and ride his bike again. His strong athletic stature (he was an all-State football player in South Dakota) and his positive attitude had helped him many times to overcome health crisis. But after a few days at the conference, with good food, he turns unusually quiet and I suspect that he has pains again. We take part in the different activities, but I notice that he does not laugh as much and lays down for a rest rather than take an afternoon excursion.

"Promise me," I demand expecting resistance "that you will see a doctor when we get to the children in California." But he only nods his head. After the wonderful days in Mesa, we return to Los Angeles and Sam undergoes a series of tests, which last from the middle of November till December. Finally we are seated opposite three physicians and in their eyes I can see that what they will say will be serious. In the midst of my fear I feel like a bubble of glass is surrounding me, shielding me from the impact of the words that my ears hear, yet my heart does not want to believe. Words like 'removal of the pancreas' filter through to my mind, but everything seems unreal around me.

"We will have to make more tests" is all I can remember when we leave the hospital, still under shock.

A few days later we sit in the practice of the surgeon to find out about the results of the test. On the way there both of us are silent. What is there to say when facing a death sentence? I accompany my husband into the examining room.

"Well, Mr. Entz" the surgeon begins, "your last test has not shown any cancer cells."

"Thank God!" we exclaim in unison.

"But, "he continues, "in spite of this we will have to make an exploratory operation to find out about an obstruction as soon as possible." Sam agrees, but because of his work he will have to fly to Germany first.

With the joy of a new lease on life we celebrate Christmas with our children, make plans for the future and accompany Sam to the airport on December 29. In ten days he will return. In his pocket he carries a small bottle of aspirin, given to him by his son-in-law against pain. When we embrace and say good-bye, I cannot help but think of the many times we had to part. I cannot count them, there are too many.

After eleven days getting his work in order, he comes back with a return ticket to Germany on March 2nd, 1985. On January 11 I drive him to the hospital. An old friend of ours, now one of the pastors in our church, is there to greet us. After we pray together I promise Sam,

"Tomorrow when you wake up from the operation I will be there." I give him a goodnight kiss and leave. The next morning I sit in the waiting area of the hospital. The surgeon told me that he would meet me there after the operation. Relaxed I look forward to the hours of waiting. I will use the time to catch up on my correspondence with friends in Germany.

Suddenly I see a man in green garb standing in front of me. Perplexed I look up into the face of the surgeon. What? So soon? After only one hour? His expression says it all.

"I am sorry, but I have bad news." No, no! Please, don't say it! It cannot be true!

"The operation has disclosed an advanced state of pancreatic cancer. We cannot do anything more for your husband."

How can one continue to breathe and speak, when the heart stands still? How can this other self ask questions, when the waves are crashing down, threatening to pull you under, to let you drown? Whose voice is this asking, 'How long will he have to live?'

"We never know for sure", the voice of the surgeon seems far away. "I am very sorry," he says and leaves. Without thinking I get up and find a dark corner. The tears begin to flow. They drop like dark spots on my dress. Quietly they roll, salty, like the waves that threaten to drown me. 'When you go through the water...I will be with you...' Where do these words come from? Oh, my father, you want me to know that you are there, going through the sorrow with me, as you have promised. Please give me now the strength that I need. My daughter Sheri will be coming in a few moments. She is seven months pregnant. Please protect her and the unborn baby when I have to tell her.'

It is the first of numerous prayers for strength. We are given four more weeks to prepare us for the final parting. There are medicines that help dull the physical pain, but there is no medicine for the pain of the soul facing the end of a loved-one. But even knowing that the end is near, Sam continues to be a witness to nurses and doctors and the visitors that come to see him. When sorrow tries to overwhelm me, I flee to the hospital chapel, where I read the 23rd Psalm, or I make my way to the newborn station, to wonder at the miracle gift of life. Again and again we receive strength to accept what God has willed. Never do I hear a word of complaint out of my husband's mouth.

Once more the family gathers around Sam's bed and he takes personal leave of each one. We pray together under tears, yet we know at the same time that death does not have the last word. Through our resurrected Lord Jesus Christ we have a hope that goes further than the grave.

"Don't come to my grave or bring me flowers," my husband tells me, "for I will not be there, it's only my old body. I will be with my Lord in heaven!"

On February 13, 1985 one month after his operation, God calls his faithful servant and untiring worker into his heavenly home. During his last night on earth I share his room at the hospital. Though he lies in a coma I recite Bible verses and songs to him and repeat God's promises. I want to accompany him as far as I can on his road towards his eternal home. At nine o'clock in the morning he leaves his body, which still looks strong and almost unchanged. Quietly and not moving, filled with reverential awe, I sit by his side as he breathes his last. A deep sense of touching the eternal fills my heart, reflecting some unseen experience, which our limited mind cannot grasp.

Only as I leave the room to inform the nurses does the visible world become real again and I can no longer control the tears. Sitting in the room by the bed of my husband, the pain of parting hits me deeply. Never will I feel his strong arms around me again, never hear his voice on the phone, never laugh at his jokes. Sobbing I give in to my pain and sorrow. Suddenly I feel a hand on my shoulder and as I look up I see our friend, the pastor

"How did you know...?" I ask.

"I did not know. I only wanted to visit Sam." He sits down beside me and his presence alone is a comfort till the children arrive. Later he offers to hold the funeral service. I ponder what text to use and then share a special experience with our pastor.

While Sam was in Frankfurt finishing up his work, I attended a New Year's Eve service with a friend. The only words that I remembered when I got home, were a phrase from the Prophet Isaiah, 'The oil of joy for mourning'. As I do every year on New Year's Day I ask God for a special word for the year. In my Bible reading for the day I come across this passage again in Isaiah chapter 61, and the same words I heard in the sermon the night before. Again God speaks to me through this word," the oil of joy for mourning and the garment of praise for the spirit of heaviness." What does God want to tell me? I wonder and cannot understand it.

I have a little box of Bible verses, which I take out and read occasionally. I draw out the first little card and read another verse from Isaiah 26:19, 'Yet we have this assurance: Those who belong to God shall live again. Their bodies shall rise again! Those who dwell in the dust shall awake and sing for joy! For God's light of life will fall like dew upon them.' Living Bible.

This seems to match, I think on this New Years' morning, this 'oil of joy' and the 'singing for joy'. But then there is also the mentioning of death. At the breakfast table I tell my children,

"I think that God wants to prepare me for something difficult this year." But I never give my husband's illness a thought. Did not the doctor quench our fears? Once before, God had prepared me for the death of my beloved mother. During her last bout with pneumonia, our bathroom was flooded over night. As I was wiping the floor, a small white card swam towards me. I picked it up. It only bore a scripture reference, Isaiah 51,12. I laid it aside and when I had a chance I looked it up in my Bible. "I, even I am he that comforts you" God says. A few days later my mother died and I felt the comfort of God in a special way, through the funeral and the weeks of mourning like a soft touch on my shoulder, just as he had promised.

At the funeral our pastor speaks about 'my' text. Family, friends and co-workers of the Billy Graham Evangelistic Association gather on February 15 in the white church at Forest Lawn Hollywood cemetery. It is a warm, sunny day with typical California sunshine, and it feels more like a celebration of thanksgiving than a funeral. While our friend from College Department times, Ted Franzle, sings in his warm baritone voice the uplifting song, 'Because he lives, I can face tomorrow', I am reminded of other occasions, Ted sang at our wedding in 1948, then in 1959 when we had our farewell before going to Germany as a family, and now he sings his last song of parting for Sam and me. I am reminded of the little poem that was used to close the Sunday evening broadcast of our church's worship service,

Only one life, 't will soon be passed,

Only what's done for Christ will last.

After the funeral, Sam's boss makes plans to close up his office in Frankfurt. I will also have to dispose of our apartment in Koblenz. My son-in-law, Dr. Richard Blackmon, takes off work for ten days to accompany me. He helps with the sorting and packing. We begin with Sam's office, his work, which he loved so dearly. Everything reminds me of him. The telephone, where he spent so much of his time, is now orphaned. Never again will I hear his voice calling me from this phone,

"Hi, the weather is so nice today. Why don't you pick me up at the station and we could drive along the Moselle River and later have a bite to eat?" Constantly I am confronted with the reality of my loss.

After we have cleared the office we drive back to Koblenz. I am so grateful that Rick is there, to enter our apartment before me, holding me when the pain and sorrow overcomes me. He is the strong rock in the middle of my storm-tossed emotions. He sorts and packs with me, counsels and helps in many ways. But most important, he helps me with bereavement counseling. As a Christian clinical psychologist and psychotherapist he spends long hours just listening and guiding my thoughts in sorting out my new life as a widow. Every night we sit together for hours talking and praying. These ten days seem to fly by in a hurry, but when he leaves to return to California, I feel that the worst is behind me. After six weeks, when everything is stowed away in a container to be shipped to California, I conclude my 25 years in Germany and fly to my children.

Soon the reality of my newly widowed state catches up with me. Where will I live? I want to be close to my children, who just bought their first house, a small fixer-upper, which they are reno-vating in preparation for their expected baby. The insurance money will enable me to buy a small house near them. But never did I have to make these major kinds of decision without my husband, who was the financial manager of the family. A friend from church is a realtor and she gives me lists of houses. I pour over the lists and drive by he ones I picked from the list and later go through some of them with my friend. But I find nothing suitable. The house is either too run down or too expensive. Time is getting short, for the container with my furniture and household goods will arrive soon. I do not want to pay extra storage fees. The thought of not having a place to live pressures me more from day to day.

One night I wake up with a strange dream. Sam is walking through a house with me and I exclaim, "What a beautiful house! Tell me, what did you pay for it?" He names a certain amount and I wake up, still remembering it. In the morning I take out the list again and look for houses for this amount. I pick out three, and the realtor drives me to all of them. But again my hopes are dashed. There is nothing that suits my needs. Before I get out of the car, the realtor remembers.

"Just before I left the office there was a phone call from a lady, wanting to put a house on the market. I have not seen it yet, but she told me where the key was since the house is empty. It should be around the amount you want to spend." We drive to the address and looking at it from curbside immediately I think:

"This is Sam's house!" We walk once through it and I know for sure, this is it!

"I want to buy this house," I tell the realtor.

"Just like that?" she questions. I make an offer and she contacts the owner and is accepted. Laughingly she tells me that other realtors in her office wanted to take a look at the house in the afternoon.

"It is sold already," she told them as they looked at her unbelievingly.

I dread Easter approaching for it will be the first one without my husband. While in the States, Sam had made it a tradition to greet me each Easter Sunday with a white orchid corsage before we attended the worship service. After a visit to his grave, I see a sign announcing an Easter Sunrise Service at the cemetery. I decide to attend. Saturday morning I wake up in the children's house depressed. I still cannot adjust myself to be alone after 37 years of sharing life with my husband. At lunchtime I am just putting some food into the refrigerator, when Rick comes into the kitchen and puts a plastic box into my hands with the explanation,

"This has just been delivered for you." It is a beautiful white orchid! Sam has sent me an orchid, is all I can think. I burst into tears, run into my room, throw myself on the bed and give in to the sorrow and pain of separation. Only later do I hear that my daughter Joy Ann wanted to cheer me up by remembering the gift of her Dad.

On Easter Sunday morning, early before sunrise, I sit among two thousand people in the cool morning air at the cemetery. The birds are singing, yet my eyes wander to the grassy slope where just a few weeks ago I stood by an open grave. Why did I come here, feeling lost and lonely among all of these strangers? I wanted to be close to him, who could no longer sit next to me, holding my hand. The first song of the choir pulls me out of my sad reverie. Slowly my mind begins to open to the redeeming message of Easter.

"The Lord is risen! He is risen indeed!" I hear the familiar Easter story from the Bible as if for the first time. In my mind's eye, I can see Mary Magdalene weeping at the grave and hearing the angel say to her,

'Why are you looking for the living among the dead? He is not here, but he is risen!" A man gets up to sing a solo. His voice soars out over the audience, who probably have lost loved ones just as I had.

"Because he lives, I can face tomorrow..." It is MY song, which Ted has sung at the funeral and which so comforted me. I concentrate to hear every word and some of the words of hope enter my heart.

After another song by the choir, a minister, whom I don't know, gets up to preach. He begins his sermon with an explanation.

"As I was preparing myself for this service, I searched for a special word from the Bible. I came across a verse, which seemed to call out: "Preach me! Preach me!" So I listened and I will preach on this verse from the Old Testament Book of Isaiah, chapter 26, 19, "Yet we have this assurance, those who belong to God shall live again. Their bodies shall rise again! Those who dwell in the dust shall awake and sing for joy! For God's light of life will fall like dew upon them!"

Oh, Lord! This is MY verse! The one you have given to me on New Years' Day! You guided this man's thoughts so he would preach about it. How can I thank you for this personal gift to me of healing, comforting love! You, and only you, can comfort as a mother comforts her children. You know how to soothe the depth of pain. You impart hope and strength. I can hardly contain the joy that fills me. And now it becomes clear, what you meant with the promise, that you would give to all who mourn, 'Beauty for ashes; joy instead of mourning; praise instead of heaviness.' Oh Death, where is thy sting? Now I know for certain that I can face tomorrow without fear, for you will go with me, as you have promised, step by step.

34

❧❧

On May 8th is the fortieth anniversary of VE Day, commemorating World War II victory in Europe. Today the moving company brings my container. I did not have to pay for any storage. While the men carry out the furniture and I tell them where to put each piece, my pregnant daughter Sheri drives up. My house is just a mile from theirs. She watches a bit and then leaves to buy food at the supermarket. Within a short time she drives up again.

"I was at the supermarket when my bag of waters broke. I guess I will have to go to the hospital."

"But Sheri, how can I leave now?" I am in a quandary.

"These men don't know where to put things. Can you still drive home?" She nods at me reassuringly, and I am left standing there, torn between my concern for my daughter and impatient men that want to get a job finished. Providentially her husband comes home unexpectedly and drives her to the hospital. I keep in touch by phone. The arrival of the first child takes time. Exhausted by a strenuous day I lie down a bit, and then call the hospital again to hear that things are progressing. At 9 p.m. I drive there and come into the maternity ward just as my son-in-law comes out holding a bundle in his arms.

"Meet your new grandson Andrew", Rick says. I only wish Sam could have shared the joy with me.

In July 1986 Billy Graham sets up another conference in Amsterdam for Itinerant Evangelists from all over the world. I had worked as a helper in the bookstore at the previous conference in 1983 and I want to make myself available again. As I pour over travel agency ads in the Los Angeles newspaper, my eyes become riveted to a small ad announcing a round-the-world trip with stops in Canada, where the World Expo just opened, Amsterdam, India, Singapore, Indonesia, Australia, New Caledonia, New Zealand, Tahiti, Los Angeles. The price of the ticket is less than double the price to Amsterdam and will be valid for one year. Tahiti! My one and only dream place for many years! Wouldn't it be wonderful to actually visit it instead of just dreaming about it? How many times did I make the boring trip across the Atlantic? I cannot count it. Would it not be a great chance to see something new and different? I could visit many friends, who are working in these countries either in the medical or educational field. And perhaps I could find an answer to the question that lately has occupied my mind. Does God want to use me again? Perhaps on some mission field or what else he has in mind for me? I am ready and available to him.

Yet suddenly doubts crawl into the happy visions of undisturbed white beaches with palms bordering the azure blue warm waters. You must be out of your mind! How can you even think about world travel without your husband, who has always pushed ahead when things got tight and who was there to protect you when needed? You can't even barter, and who is going to help you carry your bags? And what about your age? You are sixty-one! Forget it! And worst of all you don't have the money for such a trip! But the little ad does not give up that easily. It pops up in my mind in the most unexpected places, urging me to act. Yet there are too many real obstacles in the way that cannot be denied.

I am reminded of what I have read in the Bible recently, when I stumbled across a word in Isaiah 54, where God says through the prophet to the unmarried women, 'For your creator will be your husband...' Does that mean widows too? God - my husband? What a strange thought! A nice picture, all right. But can God in reality take the place of a human being with whom I shared 37 years of my life? Who I could trust in all difficult situations to find a way out for us? I will have to read this passage again. As I open my Bible I wonder if there is anybody else but the prophet Isaiah for me. Over and over my life has been directed by his words, either in dreams or while reading my Bible. I am reminded of the promise that God would bless our marriage and our children. All has been fulfilled. Now I read the words again and they fill me with assurance:

"Fear not, you will no longer live in shame. The shame of your youth and the sorrows of your widowhood will be remembered no more, for your creator will be your "husband". The Lord of Hosts is his name; he is your Redeemer, the Holy One of Israel, the God of all the earth. For the Lord has called you back from your grief..."

It has never been difficult for me to take God at his word, which means to take literally what I read at a certain time or with a particular question in mind. Not allegorically, or twisting it to make it more to my liking, but to let the word stand on its own instead of editing it. I have experienced how God speaks to me directly through his word, and he expects me to be obedient and follow the light that he gives. Debates about the credibility of the Bible, which often end in hot arguments, seem to be like a ventilator, whirling around much hot air, produced by proud, yet limited, human minds, who put themselves above the Bible as near sighted judges, shaking their little fists at Almighty God, instead of taking their allotted place, which is humble submission under the Creator and his revelation to men.

Through Francis Shaeffer's definition of the two sides of God, the infinite-personal God, my understanding and grasp of deity has been clarified. On the infinite side we will never get close to God, for we are finite beings, unable to break through the barriers of infinity. We can only say with David in his 139th Psalm verse 6, 'Such knowledge is too wonderful for me; it is high, I cannot attain it.' Knowing our limitations would keep us from many unfruitful debates and false conclusions. In our times we have lost much of the awe that permeated the attitude of God's people of the Old Testament. They still knew that there is an unbreakable wall between the holy God and sinful man. They did not even dare to voice the name of God, but circumscribed it. Even a man like Moses was not granted his request, 'Let me see your glory'. All he could see was a glimpse of the back of God as he passed by. Yet modern post-Christian man let go of the concept of a holy, righteous and just God of infinite wisdom and power; instead he concentrated on the personal side of God, at the cost of excluding the 'fear of God' for his love. He has become a companion, even a buddy, a psychological advisor, a servant of man.

The other side of God, the personal side is experimental. God makes himself available to his creation and reveals himself to those, who will seek him with all their hearts. Jesus, as the only one, could stand before the people and proclaim, "He that has seen me, has seen the father." John 14:9. If we want to know what our personal God is like, we only need to look at Jesus. He has lived among men and was tempted as we are, yet without sin. He freely offered his life to break down the wall that excluded us from God. In him we have access into the holy of holies, into the throne room of God, the father. Through him our relationship to God is being changed from strangers, aliens, and enemies to God's beloved adopted children. The either-or mentality by which we categorize life should change to synthesis. There are questions that never will be answered in this life, but the main thing is that I live up to those things that I already understand and put them into practice.

Yet philosophy circles around the question, 'What is truth?' and finds different answers in each generation; while one stands beside them who could not only say, "I can point you to the truth" or "I show you a way to find truth", but who said of himself, "I AM the truth". It is so simple and logical to believe him, who knows the end from the beginning, rather than build one's life on a foundation of constantly changing insights of men, whose limited minds can only grasp parts of truth. Therefore I decide to take this word of Isaiah as my own personal promise with me on a trip around the world. It is enough to know that God will be my companion, and I want to test if he can also be my husband in this adventure.

35

❦

I am sitting among 10 000 Christians from 174 countries at the final meeting of the Congress for Itinerant Evangelists in Amsterdam. Meeting many people from out-of-the-way countries, like Bhutan or New Guinea, the many deep searching messages, the rousing singing or praying the Lord's Prayer together in hundreds of languages, and the shared communion service, all have served to make this week an unforgettable experience.

While serving in the bookstore, I met a man, who stood in my line at the cash register. I saw that he was a Papua from New Guinea, a country that had aroused my interest by watching movies of their culture and tribal dances. When I saw that he was carrying an arm full of books, and that his shirt was ink stained, I wondered if he had the money to pay for all the books. Halfway through tallying up the books, I asked,

"Do you know that these books have to be paid in Dutch Guilders?"

"Yes," he answered and pulled out an envelope from his shirt pocket. I continued, yet wondered if he really understood me. The amount was already the highest I had sold so far. When it came to paying, he took out of his envelope the amount and laid it before me. My curiosity got the best of me.

"What do you need all of these books for?" I asked.

"They are for my Bible Institute."

"You have a Bible Institute?" I am amazed.

"I started it three years ago, and now I have 28 students. I asked the Lord how I could reach more people for him, and he gave me this vision of training others to multiply my ministry. That is why I need these books."

"I would like to visit your Institute some day," I was impressed by his manner. He pulled out a calling card and handed it to me.

"You are very welcome," he said with a friendly smile and picked up the two shopping bags and left. I read his little card. Underneath the name of the Bible Institute was printed his own name. Below that in small letters I read: Unworthy servant of the Most High.

What a lesson in humility to a proud and presumptuous person like me, thinking about ink spots and outer appearance and judging with a superior attitude! The rest of the time I was watching to meet this man once more, but among the thousands I never saw him again.

Sadly I think that soon this will come to an end and each will return to his home country. Like the pastor from Nagaland in North India, whom I met several times. The long journey from Amsterdam to his hometown will take three days for him, first by plane, then by bus, and the rest on foot. It was a fascinating experience for me to walk with him through the streets of the big city and to see things that are common to us through his eyes. For instance, we walked by a hotel lobby and he stood still in enthralled wonder, looking up at a large crystal chandelier.

"It glitters like the starry sky!" he exclaimed. Or the road, which we crossed on green, where he suddenly runs backwards from the middle as he sees a slowing car approaching. He did not trust it to obey the red light.

I look for a place and sink into my seat. Next to me an African evangelist reads his Bible.

"What are you reading, brother?" I ask him to repress the sadness of the moment.

"I am just reading in the Psalms," he answers with a friendly smile.

"Why don't you share it with me?" I request and he begins to read verses from the 91st Psalm. I feel like God himself is speaking to me through the words this man is reading to me:

"For God has ordered his angels to protect you wherever you go. They will steady you with their hands to keep you from stumbling against the rocks on the trail. You can safely meet a lion or step on poisonous snakes, yes, even trample them beneath your feet! For the Lord says, "Because he loves me, I will rescue him; I will make him great because he trusts in my name. When he calls on me I will answer; I will be with him in trouble, and rescue him and honor him. I will satisfy him with a full life and give him my salvation."

He closes the Bible and I squeeze his hand. Together we rise and join in song from the bottom of our hearts. When the service reaches its conclusion there is much embracing and leave taking. I am being swept up in an ocean of love, such as I have never experienced in my life before. Strangers from every nation embrace each other with affection and joy, wishing each other God's speed and blessings for their travels and work. Very slowly I am pushed to the exit by the crowd. I wish this night would never end! This is the way it must be in Heaven, I think, and I know I was given a foretaste of what is waiting for us at life's end.

I sit in the first of twenty-three airplanes, which will take me around the globe in the next seven months. I have booked an economy tour through Rajasthan in North Western India. For a start to travel alone through India seemed too risky to me, yet the last week I would be on my own, going to South India to visit a missionary friend. I hold a silent conversation with the Lord.

'You know, Father, that I have decided to prove your word about being my husband to see if it is really going to be true. In order to do this, I have to get out of my secure surroundings. I am setting out now on an uncertain journey to unknown destinations. When I will face difficulties, with which my husband used to deal with in the past, it's your turn now. I depend on you now completely!' Doesn't that sound very trusting? Or does God smile benevolently at these words?

I have written to friends in Jakarta to pick me up at the airport. After the letter is in the mail, I find out to my consternation that there is only one weekly flight and it is fully booked. They put my name on the stand-by list. I am now dependent on somebody not showing up at the last minute. I cannot communicate with my friends. A travel agent will try his best to get me on the plane, but there are others before me on the list. I stand there watching in ever growing nervousness, as one after the other of the waiting passengers are called in, till at last I am the only one left. The clock is seemingly making a hundred meter dash. My pulse races just as fast. I trot up and down, waiting anxiously for a sign from the travel agent. What am I going to do if I don't get on this plane? Wait another week? And what about my friends waiting there for me in vain? My frustrated thoughts run in circles. Suddenly I remember, 'Lord, I am at my wit's end! Now it's your turn to please help me!'

Literally at the last minute the agent motions for me. I run into the airplane and the doors are immediately closed behind me. With heart pounding and in turmoil I plunge into the last seat and fasten the seat belt. As I slowly calm down, I hear in my heart the friendly reproof of God.

"Why were you getting so upset? You said you would trust me to be your husband, but then you act as if I was not in a position to help you."

"Please forgive me, Father," I reply meekly, "I am still learning to connect myself to you in these trying situations. I know that you care about me and I am grateful that you opened the way for me to be in this plane – just as my husband would have done. Thank you!"

Not only in difficult or dangerous situations the truth of his promise is being fulfilled, but I am swamped with little evidences of God's love and care and guidance. After four weeks in India I sit in the airplane going to Singapore, one of the few places I do not know anybody. Next to me sits an older Indian lady in a cream colored sari. During the flight I turn to her and point to a slip of paper on which missionary friends in Nellore have written the name of a hotel.

"Do you happen to know this hotel?" I ask her, after she told me that she lives in Singapore. She looks at the slip and then turns her face and looks into my eyes.

"Are you a Christian?" she asks. I am surprised at this unexpected question.

"Yes, I am," I answer. She is not satisfied.

"Are you a born-again Christian?" she looks at me searchingly.

"Oh yes," I nod trying to convince her.

"But how did you know?" I wonder.

"Well here under the address of the hotel is another address of a Bible Institute." Then she continues,

"I have been visiting relatives in India and I got sick and had to go to the hospital. I am just recovering, and I prayed to the Lord to send me someone who could help me with my bags."

"Certainly, I will be glad to help you," I assure her and she smiles.

At the airport in Singapore her daughter is expecting her and she introduces me. Later both of them pick me up at the hotel and take me to the plush home of the daughter with a swimming pool. I get introduced to several groups of Christians, who invite me to Bible studies in other homes or take me out for dinner. One young woman approaches me.

"I have applied to study at the Fuller School of Missions in Pasadena and I will arrive there next year," she relates.

"I will be there to pick you up and help get you settled," I promise and she is overjoyed. Another young woman, a financial advisor at a large bank, wants me to start missionary work with her in one of the indigenous tribes of India. She spends a lot of time with me and I stay overnight at her place, getting to know more of her friends. I had planned on staying only till the next flight three days later, but after one week of meeting so many interesting and hospitable people, I make plans to leave. Yet again the plane is fully booked. So I decide to use the week to see Malaysia. I book a bus round trip in which I am the only non–Asian among some thirty people.

My new friends come to my hotel to bid me farewell and I accompany them down to the lobby. As they are about to leave, a couple arrives through the revolving door and there is surprise and a happy reunion followed by much talk. The couple lives in Kuala Lumpur and they are Christians also. They have just arrived and will be in town for a few days. When I am introduced, my friend mentions that I will be in Kuala Lumpur shortly.

"Then you must give us a call and we will come and pick you up," they insist. I take the telephone number and thank them for their offer. A week later I arrive in the city with the golden dome that I saw from the airplane, flying into Singapore. I call the number, and get picked up and taken to another nice home, where a group of Christians is gathered for a Bible study. At the end all of them kneel in a circle on the hard tile floor and pray for me and my trip. I am touched by the sincerity and love of these brothers and sisters in Christ.

"Where are you going from here?" they ask me. When I answer, 'Malacca', they smile.

"One of our members moved there recently," they explain. "What is the name of the hotel you will be staying?" When I mention the name, there is happy surprise.

"That is the place where the young man works now!" Coincidence? It seems like an unseen hand is pulling the strings behind the scenes. On Sunday morning in Malacca I get a phone call.

"Would you like to attend church service with me?" a young man's voice inquires. Again I meet other Christians and we praise our wonderful Lord together. And so it continues. All I have to do is to go through prepared open doors. The journey becomes the greatest adventure of my life.

36

⤜⤛

When I return to California and my family after seven months, I have so much to tell them, that it would fill another book. But most important to me is that I am fully convinced that the question, with which I had begun my venture, had been clearly answered. The experiences of God's help and guidance will control my further path of life as a single widowed woman. Not only has he been a loyal caring Father, a trusted partner, who knows my human needs, accompanies and counsels me, and showers me with his abundant love gifts. But he also knows my need for human closeness when I miss the physical presence of my husband. When I feel the loss, he sends someone to give me a big hug, or call me with an invitation to have dinner. My friends from church provide my social needs and my grandchildren love to be cuddled. Holding a new baby in my arms is one of the greatest joys.

Yet the question, if and where God wants to use me in the future still has not been answered. Though I had several invitations along the way for missionary service in different places, I still do not have the inner conviction that this is God's way for me. Through many experiences of life, beginning with the time in Wuppertal, I have learned not to take my own ideas and feelings as a measuring rod for God's will. Only after having a clear word from the Bible, or seeing circumstances pointing in a particular direction, or meeting people, that I feel are brought across my way for a purpose, I can discern his leading. If the inner conviction continues over a longer period of time, I dare to assume that this is God's will for me in this situation and I act, having prayed before that if it is not his will, that he should close doors. In this way I have not made too many mistakes or ended up in dead-ends. Yet the mistakes taught me to have my ear tuned in on God at all times and to rely on the urgings of the Holy Spirit, who gives discernment in times of decision.

It is the year 1987. My grandson Andrew is already two and a half years old and has recently received a baby brother, Alex. My son-in-law has a new practice in Thousand Oaks away from the city of Los Angeles. We sold both of our homes to buy a large new house together. I have my own part upstairs and it helps my daughter, who is working half days as a Presbyterian minister, to have a grandma in the house when she is away. I enjoy the privacy I have, yet the opportunity to share in the lives of my family. The air is clear outside and I enjoy the flowers we plant, the surrounding hills and nature, and the inviting swimming pool. Life is at its best.

In the fall I receive a desperate call for help from Germany. In fact there are two calls by two people with whom I am closely connected since the days of my youth work. I realize that I cannot solve the problem by letter or phone. I have no rest about it till I decide to fly there to speak with them in person. I book a cheap flight for three weeks and am once again crossing the Atlantic. While stopping at my old friend, Bita Muehlendyk, to celebrate her birthday, we mourn the passing of her husband a few months earlier. Wim, a renowned ceramics artist, had been a long-time friend of our family. Before I left Germany I had ordered a round table with ceramic tiles, depicting my life story in symbolic pictures. In the center he had engraved my life motto and favorite Bible verse from Paul's letter to the Romans, 8:28.

'For we know that all things work together for good to them that love God, (who are called according to his purpose.)'

Just as the container, carrying our belongings back to the States, was being loaded, he delivered my table and it stood outside on the street. The moving men looked at it and asked,

"What do these pictures mean?" I circled around the table with them, pointing out places in my life where God protected and led me till now. And that was not the last time. In fact almost everybody coming to visit me, wanted to know about my table, and it became the opportunity to speak to many people about our Creator, who has a special plan for each of his children.

As I attend Bita's birthday celebration, she introduces me to a lady sitting next to me.

"Meet Ilse Lenhard," she says, and we shake hands.

"Now Ilse, tell Yola about the work you are doing," and graciously my neighbor begins to share an incredible story.

"We have started in Bonn "Breakfast Meetings for Women" and we have from 300 to 400 women at each meeting. These meetings began in Zurich, Switzerland and they are spreading into Germany now." I am more than impressed. Next to my youth work I also had meetings for women. If we got 50 together for a Christmas program, we thought that was quite an accomplishment. I inquire about the secret of their success and she explains the program and its goal. They try to reach modern secular women at their own level. Meetings are held in neutral large halls or ballrooms. There are no Christian trappings, which mean no public prayers or Christian music, nor pious language, which would immediately turn off the secular sceptic German women. The motto of the group is, 'To share a pious message in impious words', offering topics of interest to women and ending them with just enough of a Christian emphasis to make them interested to hear more. For those interested ones they offer small groups. These groups, start often as problem-sharing get-togethers, but soon turn into serious Bible study groups, as the women themselves seek true answers to their life problems. It is a non-denominational work, which appeals to me immediately and we get into a lively conversation.

At my second stop I visit friends in Stuttgart.

"I have to tell you about something new," my friend's face is radiant. "We attend "Breakfast Meetings for Women" and they fill the largest hall with a thousand women, and I am one of the workers." This is getting bigger all the time! At my next visit in a small village, my hostess excitedly tells me,

"We have a new thing in the next town. It is called "Breakfast Meetings for Women." I take my neighbors there, and when I am unable to go, they drive there by themselves." Isn't this eerie, how the "Breakfast Meetings for Women" seem to pursue me and dog my steps? Arriving at the train station in Koblenz, I run into one of my former youth workers. I tell her of my experiences and then spontaneously ask her,

"Would you be willing to work together with other women, so you could start such a breakfast here in Koblenz?" When she agrees immediately, I am encouraged to push on. After some phone calls I have a list of thirty names of women who are interested. I turn the list over to one of my former young people, give instructions about the next steps, and having talked to my problem people, without much success, I once more cross the Atlantic, destination my nice new home.

Time passes and I receive a letter from the young woman, to whom I gave the list of names. She writes that due to personal reasons she cannot take on the responsibility of starting a new work. I sit down and write a letter to all thirty on my list, telling them what must be done now and encouraging them, and trying to motivate them to undertake the first steps. I wait a long time, but nothing is happening. When I again enquire, I am told that nobody is willing to take on leadership. Well, I have done everything that is possible for me. If they don't start the ball rolling, I cannot help them from a distance. But it is a shame, nevertheless!

A letter arrives from Koblenz, written by my friend Elka Kann, who had given us floor coverings from her building supplies store when we furnished the Teestube. She writes of meeting a lady, who knows me, at an IVCG conference. This is an organization, whose goal it is to reach people in leadership with the Christian message. Years ago I had started a chapter in our city, feeling the need to reach businessmen and others in leading positions. The lady she had met was Ilse Lenhard, who I had met a Bita Muehlendyk's birthday party and who had been the first one to tell me about the Breakfast Meetings. They discussed the need for leadership for this fledgling group and Elka writes,

"We found out that we both knew you and we prayed that God would put it on your heart to return to Germany and to get involved in this new work". Strange, they are praying for me to hear God's direction and I am praying that God would show me my next place where I could serve him.

On December 1st 1987 I receive another letter, this time by the founder of this new movement, Barbara Jakob from Switzerland. She officially invites me to return to Germany and help build a structure to be used nationally. Is this the answer to my question? I want to be sure and turn to my Bible reading for the day. It is Psalm 30 and I read and while I am reading I know the answer and write into my diary,

"Thou hast turned for me my mourning into dancing; thou hast loosed my sackcloth and girded me with gladness, that my soul may praise thee and not be silent. O Lord my God, I will give thanks to thee for ever."

I take the letter to my children and ask what they think I should do. Their answer is prompt.

"We knew that you would not stay long!" How providential, that I can leave without having to worry about my own house. After six months of pure enjoyment I pack two suitcases, kiss my children and tear myself away from my two little boys, and in April of 1988 I set out again into a new adventure.

37

⚜

Though I know that this is God's will for me, the beginning proves to be very difficult. Once more God tests my motives and reasons for coming. And these tests come at unexpected times and one wonders if perhaps one made a mistake or has misread the will of God. Yet God knows what he is doing. He can see into our hearts. We ourselves have a difficult time often to sort through our motives. There is much of self even in the holiest of motives. We are complicated creatures, and to know ourselves is a life long affair, which only a few hardy souls pursue. It is painful to have a mirror put in front of you, which dispels illusions and delusions, making them disappear like soap bubbles. Am I really that way? Is this the character I am envisioning myself to be? Why do I act in ways that I despise in other moments? Reality and truth about yourself are hard to accept but necessary for one's own growth. Oswald Chambers, my favorite devotional writer, says in his book, 'My Utmost for His Highest,' "As long as I remain under the refuge of innocence I am living in a fool's paradise. We resent what Jesus Christ reveals. Either Jesus Christ is the supreme Authority on the human heart, or He is not worth paying any attention to." After an often-frustrating period of testing, God enlists me again in his army.

My first task is to build up a local chapter in Koblenz. Now I follow all the steps that I had asked others to do by letters. We pray for forty women to attend a first information meeting, and exactly forty women show up. We plan to have our first breakfast in November. At the meeting for coordinators in October of 1988, our new organization, called "Fruehstuecks-Treffen fuer Frauen in Deutschland e.V." bearing its own logo is officially entered as a non-profit organization. I am on the national board and am responsible for a large region, called mid-western Germany. Twenty-eight existing groups join the organization and we are off to a good start.

At our first local meeting in November, where Barbara Jakob is our speaker, we have 250 women attending in a large hall rented from the city. Fifty-eight women register for follow-up, and we begin the important work of helping them to establish a personal relationship with Jesus Christ and getting into the Bible by starting six small groups. I begin to get invitations to speak in different cities and prepare my first talks, which are so different from anything I have done before, because they are meant for a non-Christian audience, that is very secular and opposed to all-out evangelism. We have to tone down our messages but give it enough content, to make people want to hear more and entice them to sign up for the small groups. People are weary of being taken in by sectarian groups and are very careful due to their bad experience with the Nazi past. Often they come to the meetings with reservations and prejudice in their heart.

"Are you Jehovah's Witnesses?" I have been asked more than once. They are put at ease by the fact that we do not seek members and that attendance at these meetings is totally non-committal. The only members are the local coordinators

Once they have attended a meeting, though, they are so enthused that the next time they bring friends and neighbors. There is hardly any advertising. It is by word-of-mouth that the groups grow, and that is definitely the best advertisement. My workload is growing continuously and the demands are changing. Not only do we board members try to lay a strong and solid foundation, to give this rapidly growing movement structure and goals, but we also want the local groups to have autonomy and freedom to put their ideas to work. Yet there is a basic concept, which all groups are required to adhere to before they can join.

In the beginning we are eight, later six women on the board. We cannot seem to catch up with the fast expansion. Several times a year we have two-to three-day board meetings, where we literally work till the wee hours of the morning. The unity among the board members is often strained to the breaking point, for we are leaders with our own ideas and ways of handling crisis. Yet even after a hotly debated session, we somehow find a way to meet again, often in spite of our differences. Soon we discover the strength of each person, and we marvel about the wisdom of God in bringing together such different people to make out of them one whole working tool in his hands.

This new fastest growing missionary movement in Germany faces much opposition, sometimes caused by envy or misunderstanding of our goals, and often we teeter along from crisis to crisis. But these attacks from the outside, rather than weaken us, bring us closer together and make us stronger, and our relationships are no longer just working ones, but we develop strong ties of friendship. We also know how to have a good time. We celebrate together when we hear that another dozen cities have joined, or when after the work is done, we sit down to a good meal, laughing and enjoying our fellowship.

There is not much free time for me with the work on the board, being local coordinator and supervising and training some 30 women to help in our local meetings. Beside this I travel through my large territory, helping new groups to get started, by holding information meetings, training the helpers in seminars or on weekends. Then there are larger worker's conferences, or evangelistic weekends for women from small groups, and training seminars for group leaders. More and more invitations follow to speak all over Germany, especially after the fall of the Berlin wall in 1989. In 1990 our chair person, Ilse Lenhard and I, make our first trip through former East Germany, and we cannot stop marveling at this miracle of the collapse of the Communist system without shedding of blood, which held countries under its iron grip for over forty years. We hold our first information meetings there to interested women and it becomes the beginning of rapid growth, even as the vacuum of Godlessness seeks to be filled. When I receive my first invitation to speak in East Germany, I ask God what he wants me to tell these people, who are biblical illiterates, due to 40 years of atheistic propaganda and before that twelve years of Naziism. The two words, which guided my life in the West were the same that I should proclaim wherever I spoke: Forgiveness and Reconciliation.

Ten years of this busy life follow, until I decide to step down from the board. We have the first of several nationwide conferences. Now there are 183 cities and towns offering breakfasts and the numbers are constantly increasing. At a conference in Siegen in 1998 before 2000 women, I moderate my last meeting as a board member.

One day Barbara calls me and lets me know that she is starting a series of small books for women at a Christian publisher.

"Why don't you take one of your talks and enlarge it to twice its size?" she asks and it is a challenge for me. All of my life I have liked to write, but had always 'more important' things to do. Yet I knew from grade school days, when the teacher let me read my compositions in front of the class, that God had given me a gift in this direction. Now was the chance to do something about this unused gift. I sat down and wrote about letting go all through life. Its German title is "Loslassen- ein Leben lang." Letting go of plans and attitudes, of belongings, of security, of relationships, of health, and even of your life. "Let go – and let God," Henrietta Mears would tell us as we listened to her in the College Department, and somehow it had stuck with me. Then I handed the manuscript to Barbara.

This first book became my stepping-stone into published writing. The little book is now in its 9th edition, a sign that many people are struggling with the problem. The publishers asked me to write more, and since 1995 I have written fourteen books. I never realized how fortunate I was to get anything published without an agent, and without any strain or even trying on my part. I simply walked through open doors, like I had most of my life. As I get older I want to use my time more in writing than in speaking, for God has done so many wonderful things that I need to share with others, who may still be struggling to trust God with all the different aspects of their lives.

38

There have been also times in my life, when I needed correction. God's dealings with a wayward child can be severe. He first uses a speaking voice that can be clearly understood. But if by obstinacy or plain carelessness the message gets no hearing, he begins to shout. If that still does not bring the desired results, he starts shaking the disobedient child, till it finally sees the seriousness of the situation. I am such a child that he had to shake, before I learned the lesson he tried to teach me. The first seven years since returning to Germany, I rent an apartment in the center of Koblenz on the forth floor without elevator. The fifty-six steps keep me in shape, but I will have to make a change before I get too old to carry everything upstairs, even my heavy suitcases when I return from a visit with my family.

One Saturday night I come home after traveling to a distant city to speak at their breakfast in the morning. It has been a tiring trip and slowly I make my way up the 56 stairs. As I try to put my key in the lock, I notice that the door opens by itself. A first glance into the hall and the open wardrobe with sweaters scattered on the floor, shows what has happened. During my absence somebody broke into my place and ransacked it! The drawers, where my jewelry has been stored, are pulled out and empty. Only worthless necklaces and rings cover the floor between clothing. I run into the other rooms and look at the damage. Whoever it was did a thorough but fast job. A feeling of helpless rage takes over. My jewelry, the collection of a life time with gifts from my parents, my husband's gifts for special occasions –the necklace my aunt gave me for my wedding, everything is gone and with it the tangible memories of thirty-seven years of married life. I am not insured. I am devastated.

I call the Fire Department, who are the only ones to come out on weekends and they fix my door in the early hours of Sunday morning. When I report the theft to the Police the next day, they don't give me any hope of getting these things back. There are gangs from Eastern Europe in transit, which break out the valuable stones and melt the gold of the jewelry. On Monday I hear that they also broke into another apartment in the back of the building. My case is one among many. I am too upset to speak to God about this. Later I ask myself why he allowed it. Doesn't he want me to hang my heart on things? But these are special things! It does not sound like a loving father, taking away the objects that really matter to me.

Another time I rush to catch a train to Muenster, where I am to speak the next morning. I have bought a paper that I carry under my arm. I also have a bag and my purse in my left hand. In my right I hold the ticket and reservation. I have just looked up the train and seat numbers. Inside I find my reserved seat by the window. I squeeze into the narrow space, put my purse on my seat, trying to take off my coat, while in the seat next to mine a man plunks himself down. 'What an impolite person!' I think, 'not giving me room even to take off my coat.' Finally my coat hangs on a hook and I sit down. I glance at my neighbor. He wears a shabby suit and carries no bag. The train is ready to leave, when he suddenly jumps up and rushes to the exit. Just before the train starts, he gets off. 'Good riddance' I think and enjoy the extra elbowroom.

"Tickets please," the voice of the conductor sounds through the car. I take my tickets out of my coat pocket and hand them to him.

"May I see your train card please?" he asks and I turn to my open purse to take out my wallet. But there is just emptiness, where the wallet should have been. It is gone! In lightning speed I add up my loss. Quite an amount of cash, check card, train card, drivers' license, and worst of all, my American passport is gone! Could I have lost it in my rush to catch the train? Suddenly I remember the impolite seat neighbor who jumped out of the train at the last minute. The conductor promises to call back to see if anything was turned into the lost-and-found department. I arrive in Muenster without a penny and am fortunate to be picked up by the coordinator. I never recover my loss.

A few months later I visit a friend, a French medical doctor who lives in Alsace. On this Sunday morning we want to attend a worship service in one of the historic old churches in Strasbourg, some twenty-five kilometers away. Later she wants to show me the city. I am rearranging things in my car, so that she can sit next to me. Then we drive off. We get out in Strasbourg and I open the backdoor to take out my purse and Nikon camera. No purse, no camera! I remember for certain that I took them down to the car. Then it hits me! I had deposited both of them on the trunk of the car, in order to have my hands free to change things around.

Both of us had gotten inside, chatting with each other, without looking at the trunk. Somewhere between their village and Strasbourg they must have slipped off the lid. My new wallet is gone again and with it my new drivers' license and other cards. But the worst thing to me is the loss of my day planner, in which I had written all speaking dates for this and part of the next year. How could I remember all of these important commitments? Also my new passport is gone! What will they think of me, when I apply for a third passport in such a short time? I feel like a criminal already! Again I have to go home with borrowed money and worry about being stopped by the police for driving without a license.

"You poor thing," my sympathetic friends say, when I relate another one of my loss stories.

"Why do these things have to happen to you?" I ask myself the same question. This cannot be a mere coincidence. What does God want to tell me? Why didn't I ask him sooner? I think. The minute I ask the question, I suddenly know the answer. It is as clear as day!

"Why have you become so careless about your giving?" At the beginning of our marriage, when we decided to follow the Old Testament rule to give a tenth of our income to the Lord, somebody said, "The tenth is just like the rent. What is above it can be called a gift." This was our decision. Others have different views on the matter, but we adhered to it. There were times when Sam was still in the business world, that we would give thirty percent of our income. What has come of it?

I had reasoned that my small social security and pension check and the gifts I got from my church in Hollywood, did not cover my expenses, especially with the erosion of the value of the dollar, which forced me to dip into my savings each month in order to pay the bills. I felt that I was exempted from this rule. Wasn't I serving the Lord full-time? And didn't I have to pay medical bills out of my own pocket, because I could not afford the medical insurance in Germany? How could God expect me to give him the tenth in my situation? But that was what he was telling me,

"I expect you to trust me to supply your needs. Why aren't you obedient to the commitment you made earlier in life? Are you afraid to become poor, when you put me in first place financially? Haven't I taken care of all your needs all through your life?" What could I answer? It was true, I had mistrusted God. I hung my head in shame and asked him to please forgive me. Then I started the good habit of putting aside ten percent of everything I get financially. Ten percent of my monthly check goes to my church in Germany and whatever I receive by speaking or in royalties, I take off ten percent to send to a worthy cause, and I enjoy this special giving greatly.

When I mention 'my church in Germany' I have to give an explanation as to how it came into being. Due to the secularization of German society as a whole and even of the Protestant State Churches, whose pastors are educated by professors, who adhere to the historic-critical view of the Bible, not believing in its inerrancy, there has been a struggle going on between evangelical Christians and the Lutheran State Church Christians as long as I have been working in Germany. Evangelicals are a tiny minority, at the most 3%. To most Germans there are only two churches, the Catholic and the Protestant. Any group outside it is suspected of being a sect. Only recently have relations between Protestants and Evangelicals become less strained, as they are being accepted on their own values, whereas before they were snubbed.

While living in the center of town, my friend Elka and I attended a Protestant Church service, where a born-again minister, originally from Hungary, was the pastor. Yet when he was forced into an early retirement, due to illness, we were left homeless. His illness was in great part caused by the persecution he faced from his fellow ministers. His wife told me once, that three days before a ministerial meeting her husband could not eat anything. I could write more about it, but I am glad that finally things seem to change. Not knowing where to go, I attended Sunday service at the largest Protestant church in town. But often I came home so disturbed, that the rest of my Sunday was spoilt. How can one sit still, when the basics of the Gospel are withheld from the people, instead politics or humanism fills the sermon? Sometimes I felt like getting up and shouting, "Give them bread instead of stones!" but of course as a well-bred polite individual one does not interrupt a service. But I stopped attending.

The need drove us to prayer. And then God acted again. In retrospect it is wonderful to see how he initiates things when the time is ripe. I got a phone call from an Evangelical Free Church minister, who had become a Christian in our youth work while stationed in Koblenz for military service. He has his own church not too far from our city and wants to visit me with his wife. We reminisce about 'the good old times' and I mention our desire to start an evangelical church for the many young couples and others who had come out of our youth work. He suggests that we call a certain leader in charge of starting new churches. I write him a letter and he comes to visit me. Elka is there also, as we convey to him our desire for a spiritual home for the many people we know, where they can grow and invest their gifts for the Lord. We are surprised to hear that leaders of the EFC have also been praying for a church to be established in Koblenz.

"By the way," the visitor tells us, "we have a pastor already. There is a couple, he comes from Canada and she is from the United States and they had been working in Germany, but then returned to run a conference center in the States. They have written to us that they are planning to return to Germany."

When Wesley and Barbara Peters are introduced to us a few months later, we feel that God has picked the right couple for us. We have an immediate bond of unity in purpose and a blending of personality and begin to lay the groundwork of our new church. The official document of the founding has six signatures on it, but after months of Wes's visitation and inviting the many people on our lists, we hold our first service in rented rooms. It is the first of Advent and one hundred adults and fifty children are our opening congregation. During the following years, many young couples and their children are added as members and today there is a membership of over 200 and a sister church is growing some 30 km from Koblenz. Five wonderful years with Wes and Barbara follow. One day Wes informs us that the Lord has called him to start another church in the city of Trier by the Moselle River. With sadness we see them move, yet God has supplied a German minister, Siegfried Petry and his family. Under their leadership we buy a large hall and renovate and build on, as a project in which all members participate. When it is finished after a year of hard work, we have a beautiful sanctuary, seating 400, and Sunday school rooms, a large Cafeteria and kitchen, and pastor's offices.

My work includes moderating and planning worship services and leading the counseling department. Often I wonder about the way my life has been led. I never had even the privilege of a high school education. My education ended with sixteen years, thanks to Hitler. When I came to America, I had to work to support my parents. Years later I took some night courses but never got a college degree. I never attended secretarial school. We were never sent by a missionary organization. We never were trained to become youth leaders, only I had experience in teaching second graders. I never had a theological education, never was trained as a social worker. I never took rhetoric courses, never had training in psychology or in counseling, never took a course in church planning, never was taught how to conduct board meetings. In spite of it all, God put me in all of these positions. Yet I had the privilege of listening to the greatest preachers and sat under the best teachers for years in our First Presbyterian Church of Hollywood, which has been the main influence on my personal spiritual life. God trained me by putting me in situations where I would say, 'How can I do this, Lord?' And he would answer, "Swim!' Over the years, where I felt a need for further education, I bought books and read articles or attended seminars on different topics, in order to be more useful. Yet I often have appropriated the verse from James 1:5, 'If you want to know what God wants you to do, ask him, and he will gladly tell you, for he is always ready to give a bountiful supply of wisdom to all who ask him; he will not resent it.'

This does not mean at all that I am against formal education. The opposite is true. How I wish I could have had the privilege of learning like my children and grandchildren have! When I go through the Christian high school, where my daughter now is Chair of the Bible Department, I cannot help but feel a little envious for all the opportunities these young people have of creative learning and participating in sports. I just want to say, 'If God wills, even a broom stick can blossom.'

39

⁓⦿⁓

Once again I am able to celebrate Christmas with my children, due to the generous gift of a friend from the board and her husband. On New Years morning, as always, I read my Bible, seeking direction for the year ahead. Suddenly a verse from a Psalm catches my attention. I have to read it over and over again. I know this is meant for me. God says he will bless my plans. Plans? I have not made any. But God impresses on me that I should make plans for the future. Has not he always been the one to shift the switches and all I did was follow his leading? And now he wants me to make decisions? What kind of decision? Soon I get a clear answer. I have evaded making decisions for the future, for my old age. Here in California I can enjoy life in a nice large home with my children and grandchildren. Yet returning to Germany, climbing up to my rented apartment, huffing and puffing, dragging my heavy bags from one floor to the next, I wonder, 'How long will I be able to continue this?'

When I ask my children whether it would be possible to take my financial part out of the house, in order to be able to buy a condo in Germany, they agree. I should not worry about them, they can finance the house on their own, they assure me. After the last earthquake with the help of earthquake insurance, the house has been repaired again and looks like new.

I can remember that day when the earthquake hit. I was visiting my daughter and family in Nevada. My flight ticket was for a return flight on Monday. Yet my daughter begged me to stay another day. I had to pay an extra amount to change the ticket, but I obliged her.

My son-in-law and my granddaughter took me Monday on a days' trip to Lake Tahoe, while my daughter had to work. What a beautiful sight were the glass clear waters of the lake and the distant snow capped mountains! We were drawn with other tourist to old deserted ghost towns, walking on wooden sidewalks, imagining scenes from a John Wayne Western, and looking for remnants of the history of the Old West.

After a full day of enjoying the sights and experiencing the past, we were jolted into the present by the evening news, when we returned home. All day long we had not had the radio on, nor seen TV. An earthquake in Los Angeles? There had been several that I had gone through, waking you in the middle of the night, the bed shaking, making you run outside instinctively, suddenly wide awake, while the floor buckled and the rose trees in the garden swayed crazily without the wind blowing. Yet this one had been a much stronger one. As we watched with increasing worry, we saw pictures of crumbled apartment buildings and burning units at a mobile home park. And Sheri, who was eight months pregnant, being in the middle of it all! Our phone calls never got through, and finally we stopped trying to reach her.

Early the next morning the plane brought me back to L.A. Again I tried calling her, and I was relieved to hear her voice. But I was not prepared to see the havoc it had caused to the house. Sheri was still in shock. In the early morning, before dawn, the house shook and roared and the rafters creaked while she tried to get out of bed, which was difficult in her condition. Rick had run to the children's bedroom, scooped up little Andrew and had run downstairs. The noise of falling and breaking ceramics by my friend, Wim Muehlendyk, was added to the groaning of the wooden frame, swaying in all directions. When she finally got out of bed, she ran barefooted over the piles of books and broken shards downstairs and outside in her nightgown.

The next night the family slept outside in their cars. I, having been spared the shock of the night before, was brave enough to sleep in my bed, only a few times waking up from small after shocks. About ten o'clock the next morning, I was upstairs in my room and all alone at home, when suddenly the house began to tremble and shake again. The noise of the creaking rafters increased constantly, till I feared that the house would collapse, burying me under it. In panic I tried to run downstairs, the steps coming to meet me, till I reached the door and was outside, my heart pounding and my hands shaking. Only very slowly the awful feeling left, of having lost the essential security of solid ground under your feet. The uneasiness, caused by the knowledge that there is nothing solid left, that everything one thought of being secure had changed into insecurity, remained for the following days, when again and again we were jolted by after shocks. At night all four of us slept, huddled together, on the living room floor, prepared to run outside, should another earthquake hit. After a scary experience like this, it is amazing that in all earthquake prone areas, after a while life returns to normal. Houses are rebuilt, cracks filled and memories fade. Though one always carries the possibility of another one striking in the recesses of the mind, there is this astounding resilience, which is either born of foolishness or courage in the face of the unavoidable and untamable forces of nature.

When I return to Koblenz, I immediately begin to look for a condo, yet, though I try, I cannot find a suitable place. One Sunday afternoon after church, I drive up to the area, where we had lived for twelve years prior to Sam's death. I sit down on a bench, which has been placed to enjoy the 180 degree panorama overlooking the Rhine River valley, with the volcanic peaks of the Eifel in the background. How I had loved this view, changing with the clouds, sometimes reflecting the water of the Rhine in blue colors, yet often changing to dark grey, as the weather often clouds over and the light breaks through storm clouds with stabs of sunshine, spreading over the landscape like a child's drawing of the rays of the sun.

I am upset and feeling very sorry for myself. Why did I have to move out of our nice place, I complain to myself, and now I can't find a place where I would like to live. I am so unhappy. I would like to live here again, but I find nothing. I feel very lonely today. Even the beautiful view cannot cheer me up. I am bathing in self-pity. As I drive home, still in a melancholy mood, I see out of the corner of my eye an unusual sign in a window of a house. It says, "For Sale". You hardly ever see a sign in Germany that a house is for sale. You go to a realtor and he tells you about the houses on the market, or you see a display in the window of a bank with little pictures of houses for sale. But here this house announces itself, looking for a buyer. I stop the car and write down the phone number of the realtor. We meet there a few days later and he shows me the two-story house, after telling me that they were thinking of dividing the house into two condos. When I enter the living room, I am overwhelmed. It is almost straight up from my complaining bench! The view is even better than the one we used to have.

"I want this part of the house," I declare and am surprised when the realtor explains,

"We have thought of doing this, because there are two separate entrances already. But we much rather sell it as one unit. We have a man, who is interested in buying the whole house". Well, my hopes are dashed again. Back to scanning the newspapers and driving from place to place without success. Weeks are passing and I have almost given up the idea of finding my own place. Until one day I get a phone call from California. It is Sheri.

"Mom, we have just sold our house. We have bought a new one, smaller and closer to church. The people who bought our house want to move in within three weeks. You have to come right away and take out your stuff."

Wow! I stand there dazed. My head is spinning. What must I do first? I call the travel agent and she gets a cheap ticket for me flying in three days. What a luxury! Once I had to leave Germany within five hours, because there was no other flight. Now I have three days to get ready. Then I call the realtor.

"I wonder, have you sold the house I looked at?" I ask with trepidation. No, they had not. The man had backed out.

"We will divide the house into two units. You may have the upstairs one-bedroom condo."

Once again I am crossing the Atlantic with mixed emotions. There are so many uncertainties and sudden decisions which need to be made. In Thousand Oaks I order a container to take my 'stuff' once more across the ocean, for the second time. Days are flying as I sort and pack and decide what to give away. It is most difficult to separate myself from the many books I have. Yet there is a certain weight limit and some of my books must go. Finally, after ten hard-working days, the container is filled and my furniture is on the way to Germany again. Then I help Sheri with their packing and once again say good-bye to my children and grandchildren with one eye laughing and the other crying for leaving our nice house forever.

Although we have here no lasting city, as the Bible says, it is difficult to give up a home, which holds the memories of so many happy experiences. This was our first house together. We had so much fun decorating the rooms and making them into a pleasant place to live. The garden with its many flowers and the inviting swimming pool with view of the mountains, it all holds a personal connection. Who would tend our favorite roses after us? Or the nightly enjoyment I had looked forward to of squeezing into my leather chair with a three year old, his wet hair smelling baby fresh after just being bathed.

"Can we see 'Wild Animals' together, Grandma?" Or there were the exciting days of birthdays and Christmas or the nights after the earthquake, all four of us huddling together on the living room floor. Each room holds too many bonding family moments to leave without regret.

It is Monday after Easter. Because of my booking at such short notice, I did not get a non-stop flight. I will have to change planes in Dallas, Texas. With other passengers I sit waiting for my connecting flight in Dallas, when I hear an announcement over the intercom.

"We are sorry, but the plane is overbooked. For travelers who give up their seat voluntarily, we will put you up in a hotel for the night and the next day we will upgrade you from economy to business class. You can also receive a gratuitous ticket either through the United States or Europe." Nobody is expecting me on the other side, so I rush to the desk and give up my seat. In turn I am driven to a nice hotel, given enough food certificates that I cannot finish eating all of it, and the next day I find myself luxuriously reclining on leather seats with enough leg room to stretch out and sleep through the night. When I look at the airline's destinations in Europe, I find that the furthest is St. Petersburg, Russia. I tell my friends that I want to visit that city at Easter, and the ladies of my breakfast group surprise me with a cardboard plane hanging from the ceiling. When I take it down, I find it is filled with money, enough to pay for one week hotel and guide through St. Petersburg! I enjoy a special Russian Easter celebration and see the great historic city with its treasures of art – and everything is a free gift!

My first call after returning is made to the realtor. Yes, I can start renovating the place, because my container will soon be there. The busiest weeks follow. Without the help of friends I could not have done it, the moving and selling of furniture from the rented place, the renovation which turned out to be more difficult than I had imagined, for the house had been empty for two years, and there was extra work that needed to be done.

In all of the details I saw the caring hand of God, for whom nothing is too insignificant or too small. I have learned to include Him in my every day life, and may it be such a mundane thing as getting a new toilet from the building supply store. I place the new toilet in the trunk of my car and return to buy some bread in the supermarket next door. Standing in line at the bakery I find myself right behind my pastor's wife. What a happy surprise!

"Why don't you have a cup of coffee with us," Barbara invites me, "Wes is sitting in the cafeteria waiting for me." As I walk up to the table, I greet Wes,

"Hi, I have a toilet in my car now!" He laughs and knowingly asks,

"And who is going to install it?"

"I don't know," I answer truthfully.

"Well, I just happen to have my tool box in the back of my car, so we will follow you home after coffee." Wes is a great man with his hands. Within minutes I have a new toilet in my bathroom.

Another time he drives with me to the same store and has a new counter top cut to fit the kitchens' dimensions. Very early the next morning he comes to install my old kitchen cabinets before he has to leave for a meeting. Such a pastor is Wes! He does not only preach, 'love your neighbor,' but his whole life is a sermon of love and care and service to others. A sceptic could say, 'Yes, he only does this, because you are a member of his congregation'. But there are other incidents, one of which was only observed by God and me.

We are guests at a wedding being held in a medieval Gothic church. The service has just ended and everybody is headed for the narrow door leading to the open area in front of the church, where the newlyweds are receiving congratulations from a line of well-wishers. The line moves slowly and we are still inside the church. Near the entrance I see a sad looking old woman with a walker. She haltingly gets up and pushes the walker in the direction of the exit. She is not one of the invited guests, but just walked into the church, while the wedding was going on. The waiting people are engaged in conversations. Barbara and I are talking to each other. Nobody pays any attention to the old woman who tries to push her walker towards the exit.

Only Wes has seen her and makes his way from the waiting line to her and speaks to her. Her care-worn face lightens up as Wes takes hold of her walker and pushes it slowly through the line till the two of them are outside. I watch him how he says a few more words to the old lady and she nods her head and smiles gratefully. Minutes before she had felt like nobody cared, but now she felt like a valued and respected human being. Wes shakes her hand and joins the line again. This is more than a polite gesture. Here one human being has given another one kindness, active help, encouragement, and love and has brightened the day for an unknown old woman. A small incident, yet to me a lecture of a quiet act of caring for your neighbor, which counts more in God's eyes than ostentatious activities that are applauded by many.

In retrospect, it seems to me that everything in life has its purpose and its time. There are the warm times of love; the dark times of testing; the green times of growing and ripening; the golden times of harvest. God makes everything to fit a harmonious and completed whole. But God does not want to do it alone. He wants us to participate and creatively shape our life, instead of letting ourselves drift along without purpose and goal.

Two types of building supplies stores have become a living parable to me. One is the average supply store. You find it in every larger town or city. But that 'special' supply store I only discovered in Sittensen, a small town in Northern Germany. Both stores carry in principle the same assortment of building materials and tools and other home improvement articles. Both are in huge halls and have wide parking lots. But what makes this one store different from all others is what one discovers behind the store.

After speaking at a Breakfast Meeting in Sittensen, I am invited to stay for a barbeque for the volunteer workers that evening.

"We are meeting at the Building Supply Center in town," I am told and I wonder, what a strange place to hold a barbeque. In the evening we walk around the building, past heaps of cement sacks and stacks of wood, till we reach a nice looking garden portal. I feel like Lucy going through the back of the wardrobe into never-never land! We step into a beautiful park with a large man-made lake and many smaller ponds, arched over by rounded or straight bridges. There are gazebos and pavilions, inviting you to sit down and enjoy the views. A wooden cabin with little windows and porches offers shelter in case of rain. Winding paths of gravel or flagstone are bordered with colorful flowers. A little creek babbles along the way till it ends in a small waterfall. Little windmills are turning and birds are singing in the healthy trees, of which, I am told, there are 180 varieties. The ponds are filled with many edible and other fish, jumping up when the owner lovingly feeds them, before he starts the barbeque for his guests.

He has created this little paradise with his own hands. It started with a requirement by the fire department to make a reservoir of water. This man-made lake was the beginning of this beautiful park. Everything else had been created with materials from the building supply center. Seeing the many possibilities must challenge even the most untalented hobby do-it-yourself-worker to try to copy it on his own piece of land. I ask myself at this moment an existential question. As a Christian, am I trying to sell only building material, or does my example, to make something beautiful for people to enjoy, encourage them to copy it?

To create a garden and to take care of it requires money, time, effort, and work. Often drops of sweat nourish the ground on which beautiful flowers grow. Yet when plants begin to grow and bushes and trees bear their fruit, not only the gardener enjoys the result of his labors, but others can enjoy the beauty of the garden, too.

40

⌘

S ince I have reached the Biblical age, I enjoy each day as a special
gift. When I wake up in the morning, beside the usual aches and
pains of old age, I thank my God that I can get up and that He has
some surprise for me in store. And I am never disappointed. My
later life consists of a series of surprises and a never-ending supply
of gifts. Sometimes I am so overwhelmed that I say, 'Please, Lord,
it is enough!' but mostly I just enjoy what he sends my way. For
instance, when I was in Nuremberg, the city of my mother's birth,
I was not prepared for his surprises when I joined a group visiting
the only medieval cemetery in Europe. The famous painter, Albrecht
Duerer, is buried there and many other historic persons.

My cousin, who was interested in the genealogy on my mother's
side, had told me the life story of one of my ancestors, who lived at
the time of Duerer. Because I was so impressed by his strong character, he had given me a copy of an engraved picture of this Patrician
council member. This man had been the treasurer at the court of a
prince, who had embraced the new teaching of the Reformation.
When the sovereign turned to Protestantism, all of his subjects also
had to take on his new religion. Yet soon the Counter-Reformation
swept Germany, trying to bring back the straying sheep into the fold
of the Catholic Church. Rather than fight, the prince had returned to
his old faith and his subjects with him. But Christopher Gugel, my
ancestor, went rather into exile, than renounce his newfound faith.
Later he settled in Nuremberg and became part of the Patricians, the
governing body of the city, which at this time, was one of the most
important trading centers in Germany.

The guide took us to this huge cemetery, where the caskets were built above ground, covered by metal plaques, engraved with names, dates, and often Bible verses. On the spur of the moment I asked the guide,

"Do you know if there is perhaps a grave from the Patrician family Gugel here?" To my surprise he answered,

"Yes, and I will find it for you." Not too far from Duerer's grave, he waved me over. When I peered down at the metal plaque, I was overcome with emotion when I read the name. Christopher Gugel, my ancestor, whose picture I had hanging on the wall in my living room! Here I am standing at his grave, almost 500 years later, feeling so close to this man of Christian conviction as if I had known him personally. Thankful for the Christian heritage, which was displayed by figures of Adam and Eve and Christ on the Cross with two Bible verses on the head of the plaque, I thanked God, that this faith has been passed on throughout the generations, and that I had been the latest recipient. I vowed to pass it on even to my own grandchildren.

I had another surprise recently when I spoke at a Breakfast in a town, where previously I had to cancel my speech because of a sudden medical emergency. My daughter had developed breast cancer, and I flew there to take care of her and the three boys and her husband for four months. It was a very difficult time for all concerned, but she is doing fine now and we hope it will be for a long time. It had not been the first case of cancer in our family. My other son-in-law, Douglas Soleida, had Hodgkins Lymphoma while stationed in Germany as a journalist. He is healed today and we are grateful to God for having spared him.

Now before this Breakfast I sat together in a circle with the volunteers, praying for God's blessings on the morning. There were some 250 women in the hall next to us, which is the average, yet I spoke to as many as 500 at other Breakfasts. After the prayer, the lady sitting next to me took my arm and said,

"I have to tell you something before we go out there. I have waited two years to tell you and now is the time." I was curious to hear what she had to tell me.

"Two years ago," she started, "upon his retirement my husband and I fulfilled us a life-long dream. We traveled with a small motor home through the United States and Canada for eight months. We started in the West in the winter, going towards Spring Eastwards. We found ourselves in January in Flagstaff, Arizona on a deserted camping place. It was freezing cold, there was snow on the ground and we felt lonely and decided to drive to town. We found a mall, where we could warm up. As we walked through a department store, speaking in German to each other, a woman approached us saying 'hello' in German. She was so friendly and we talked awhile. She told us of places to see and we had a nice talk with her. We no longer felt lonely because she could speak our language. Before we parted she stated, that her mother lived in Germany.

"Perhaps you know her?" she asked, and I thought, 'Big chance, with 83 million people, I would know her mother.' But politely I asked for her name.

"Yola Entz," she answered, and I almost collapsed.

"Sure," I cried, "I know her! She was supposed to speak at our Breakfast where I am one of the volunteer workers, but she had to cancel because of her daughter being sick."

"That is my sister in California," she said and we both marveled at the guidance of God, who would bring us together in the big, wide USA. And now, after two years, I finally have a chance to pass on greetings to you from your daughter Joy!" What a small world – when God pulls the strings!

Most of the surprises come unexpectedly; otherwise they would not be surprises. But once I told my small group that on my vacation I expected a surprise from God – and I would tell them about it upon my return. But then I was flabbergasted, when my name was called before boarding the plane for another flight to California. At the desk, the smiling airline employee that had checked me in told me, that I was upgraded to business class. I could hardly believe my good fortune. She explained,

"You were so friendly when I checked you in, so I thought I give you special treatment."

"May I come behind the counter and hug you?" I asked. She nodded, and that's what I did. And I had my surprise story for the small group!

Life over eighty seems to get fuller with each year. Though health has become an issue lately, I am still meeting new people all the time as I travel to speaking engagements in one of the 228 places that offer Breakfasts now, put on by 6000 volunteer workers. It makes boredom an unknown word. Exciting adventures wait at every meeting, getting to know so many places in the German speaking world, each with its own history and beautiful landscape.

The work of counseling people, either by phone or in person seems to increase. Perhaps there is something to the phrase, 'wisdom of the aged'. A long life has taught me many lessons and I can pass on some of the secrets I learned along the way. Opportunities open up to help people see their problems from a different viewpoint, or to encourage them to do, what in their heart of hearts they know they must do. With age also a certain amiable detachment increases, that keeps you from taking things too seriously, or getting upset over issues that seem of less importance now. Finding oneself getting closer to the exit, things take on new dimensions and the priorities change.

But that does not mean that I don't remain involved in the issues of the day. Writing a new book or articles for magazines, or being interviewed on Christian TV or radio, or speaking in talk shows, all helps to keep the grey matter alert. E-mails, laptop or computer are my daily companions, and I sometimes wonder how I ever lived without them. Through these means one keeps at the pulse of time, be it on the youth scene, which is still my favorite group, or politically involved, mentoring some young politician. Having younger friends call or visit gives me added pleasure and the work in my church is a specially fulfilling function. All in all, aches and pains aside, for me old age is not what it is made out to be!

Yet one thing has remained the same all through my life. I am still attending school! The extremely patient and goal oriented teacher, called Holy Spirit, is still trying his best to change my lazy human nature, in spite of all the lost opportunities, the wrong attitudes, the thick-headed resistance, my slow learning ability. Yet so far he has not given up on me, which makes me hopeful to graduate some day.

To give you an example of a slow learner, I recall one New Year's morning in 1997, when I read in my Bible, searching for a motto for the year, "Take my yoke upon you and learn from me, for I am gentle and humble-hearted; and your souls will find relief." I keep this word in my mind, as I board a train to a meeting. The Rhine valley, which I love so much, is sunny this morning. The water glistens and the steep vineyards behind the little villages along the edge of the river, with their old half-timbered houses with grey slate roofs, mirror themselves in the water. Once in a while one of the old castles appears, perched on some craggy peak, some of them in ruins, calling to mind another time when they were the only secure places in a seemingly never ending chain of wars. Our city of Koblenz, in its over two thousand years of history, had been destroyed and rebuilt many times, as the conquerors changed.

In spite of the holiday, the loaded barges slowly make their way upstream. Looking out the window of the speeding train, I once again recall what God's word for me for the New Year had said. What does it mean to be 'gentle' anyhow? Be like a gentleman? Polite, friendly, composed, courteous? Some people are blessed with personalities like that. They seek harmony, don't argue for the sake of peace, raise no objections, and don't get visibly upset. They are just gentle by nature. This is not true of me. I am more the type that likes differences of opinion, does not shy away from conflict, is spontaneous, and stands up, sometimes emotionally, for what I deem important. What does this 'gentle' then mean for me?

I gaze out the window again, watching a container ship, fully loaded, which we are just passing. I can hardly believe what I see! The ship's name in black and white large letters, is, "GENTLE"! How can a ship on the most German of rivers carry an English name? And one with a meaning about which I am just now meditating? This is more than a coincidence! Like Mary, I keep these things in my heart and often think about them.

Today is the first day of spring. After a long, dreary, and cold winter, this gives us a reason to celebrate. My friend of many years and I sit in a restaurant with a view to the Rhine. We enjoy our companionship and the food, as I take in the changing scenery on the river. Suddenly I see a containership passing.

"Hey! There is my ship again! My "GENTLE!" My friend cannot understand my excitement, and I tell her the story of New Year's morning and the strange first meeting. At home I take out my Bible once more, in which I had written the date next to the verse, "Learn of me…" Why does God remind me again of this verse?

A few months later, I take a walk with another friend along the Rhine. We are in deep conversation, when suddenly I can only jump up and down and cannot get any words out but,

"My ship again! My ship! My "GENTLE!""

"What do you mean your ship? Did you take a boat ride on it?" My friend cannot understand my excitement. Again I try to explain. A few days later I read in the local paper, that there are twenty-eight-thousand barges traveling on the Rhine, from Rotterdam to Basel. The probability of seeing one ship three times in such a short period is less than a slim chance. Again I ponder the strange coincidence. What does God want me to learn?

It is fall and again I am traveling through the Rhine valley by train. I am sitting on the side of the river by the window, reading an interesting book. Passing through the Lorelei tunnel, it gets too dark to read. At the end of the tunnel I want to continue my reading. At the moment when it gets light again, I see in passing out of the corner of my eye, a ship. It is my "GENTLE!" It is just a fleeting moment at the right angle. Would it have been 50 meters further up the river, I could not have seen the name. Finally a light begins to dawn. My thoughts go back to the last board meeting from which I am returning just now. We had debated a controversial issue and I had taken a stand. I had emphatically represented my view of the question and had become more forceful than would have been necessary. In retrospect I am reminded of other situations in which I responded equally emotional. Why did it take me so long to learn, what God wanted to teach me? 'Learn of me for I am gentle…' How many times did he have to remind me to be more self-controlled before I understood the lesson! Contrite and ashamed I beg forgiveness and ask him to bridle my temperament, and to continue to send "GENTLE" across my way when I need reminding.

Many years have since passed. Often I have carefully looked sideways when I saw a big container ship. But I have never seen GENTLE again. This does not mean that I am an example of gentleness. I still get carried away sometimes. But God is working at present on some other area with me. It is something new and I will not divulge the secret. But if we ever meet, you can ask me, "When was the last time you have seen GENTLE?"

41

As in all life stories there are times of unencumbered happiness, though not as many as one would wish, and other times of unrelieved darkness, which seem too many and often seem too long to bear. Yet in retrospect the memory accomplishes a wonderful feat. The dark times seem to have receded and the happy occasions jump to the front and take on a special rosy glow, as if time with its benevolent fingers tries to erase shadows and enhances the colorful palette. Yet when we go through these times of darkness, we either feel comforted and uplifted by the presence of our faithful God, who promises never, never, no never to leave us, or we suffer through the abyss of loneliness and desperation in hopeless silence. These are the times, when our faith is being sorely tried and often found wanting. Perhaps this is one of the reasons why some older people, who have once been outstanding examples of the Christian faith, fall quietly by the wayside or recede into a mediocre, almost nominal Christian life, for their once shining light example has diminished to a smoking wick. Yet even though the glow has gone, we have the assurance that our Lord will not quench the smoking flax.

When I thought I had completed my story, God surprised me with unexpected events. In order to close my story, I need to add a few significant pictures. So here are some recent snapshots.

Finally the winter is over and I try to stack the heavy winter tires in my garage, as I do every year. But this time I hurt something in my lower back. For a few weeks I hope that it will heal itself, but it gets worse and the pain finally brings me into my German doctors' office. I do not go to see her often, because I am not medically insured in Germany, only in America, and I have to pay for each visit out of my own pocket. She examines me and suspects a slipped disk, which it turns out to be. At the same time she makes an ultrasound exam. As she looks through my abdomen and continues to circle at a certain place, I begin to worry. What has caught her attention? She sends me immediately to an urologist next door, who takes x-rays and makes an appointment for a CT-scan the next day. When I ask him, he answers in medical language, incomprehensible to me. "What does that mean?" I question him. He looks at me with a serious expression. "It means a tumor on the kidneys."

The next day two doctors explain some strange looking pictures to me and show me a nebular white substance over one kidney. "It may be Non-Hodgkins Lymphoma, a blood cancer." With this diagnosis I cancel all of my appointments and fly across the Atlantic again. There the diagnosis is confirmed and I am told, that though Hodgkins lymphoma could be healed, like in my son-in-law's case, this type of cancer could only be contained. For two years I had to return for treatments, involving infusions and chemotherapy, being surrounded by people in different stages of fighting their cancers, young and old. For a person that had received the great gift of good health most of my life, and who suffers more by watching others suffer than from my own pain, it was a difficult time. Yet from the beginning there was peace of mind. One way or the other, I accept God's will for my life. Naturally one clings to life and loved ones and friends, that have been the great joy of my life, but one also knows for certain, that there will be an end, sooner or later, and that after our time on this earth, there will be waiting for us the most wonderful experience of meeting our Lord face to face and being able to thank him personally for all the love and good things, with which he adorned and blessed our lives.

At the end of the two years I sat in my oncologists office, not knowing what to expect. In these moments of anxious waiting, while the possibilities of bad news loom like over-powering monsters in the air, threatening to swallow you up, the heart beats faster and your fingernails press into the flesh. You try to read the doctors face as he pours over the final report of the last test. Does he look concerned, or is it only my imagination? Then he turns to me and says,

"Let's dance!" Never have I heard a more joyful word, and in response my heart skipped a beat. "It says here," he continued, "there is now no evidence of lymphoma. You can return to Germany and continue your work." My death sentence has been revoked, I have a new lease on life! God spared me once more! According to the doctors' word, I floated, no I danced into the beautiful California sunshine, rejoicing in God's goodness to allow me to live somewhat longer and continue to serve him. What a privilege to once more return to my ministry, which has become more impressive to my hearers, because of my age. Most women my age in Germany are expected to be helped across the street and sit in their easy chair knitting or watching soaps on TV. The least you are expected to do is retire at a certain age and take life easy. "What? You are still driving?" I am asked often. "Yes, and I have entered the Nuerburg Car Race next week!" I answer laughingly. I never felt that need to retire, instead I am glad, that God gives me health to continue what has been my life calling, sharing the Good News of the liberated and exchanged life through Jesus Christ with the thousands of people God allows me to reach for him. How many people are struggling with their life questions and problems, to which only a personal relationship to the Living Lord is the answer! As long as I have breath, I want to be a witness to Gods' unfailing love and his power to transform a selfish, rebellious human heart into one capable of loving him. Out of that love grows love for our fellow men and the ability to forgive those that have hurt or wronged us, like Jesus forgives us our many sins, with which we hurt him.

Through my daughter I had several opportunities to relate my life story to Middle-and High School students and was touched at the end to be hugged by lines of kids, or even muscular football guys, thanking me for sharing with them. This is one of the most satisfying experiences for me, that I can still relate to young people, who have been the love of my life, and to pass on to this new generation the torch of truth. Beside all of these blessings, God still had a special surprise in store for me.

It is a grey October morning in 2008 and I am looking through the morning mail. Beside the usual amount of advertising and bills, there is one envelope, which looks strangely out of place. It bears an official looking seal from a German Government Agency. I open it, not knowing what to expect. Inside a letter on impressive Government stationary informs me, that Germany's president, Horst Koehler, wants to honor me with the high order of Bundesverdienstkreuz am Bande for fifty years of volunteer public service. There would be a ceremony on November 26, 2008 at a local Government agency, where I would be honored. Unbelief and surprise mingle, as I sit stunned for a time, trying to control my thoughts. How come I? And how did he find out about me? I have only known one other person in all my years in Germany, who was given this honor, my dear friend, Wim Muehlendyk, the ceramic artist, whose life work and public service was so honored.

When I called my daughter in California to let her in on the news, her response overwhelmed me. "Count on us being there for the ceremony," she said immediately. What a wonderful surprise! Later that week she called to tell me, that they had made flight reservations for all five of them, parents and three grandsons, twenty-three, twenty-one and fourteen years old. Since it was Thanksgiving week, they would only lose a few days of work. The prospect of having my family with me meant more to me than all the honors in the world.

All of those years being separated by an ocean and a continent and nine hours of time difference, I had missed out on attending birthday parties, anniversaries, graduations, holidays, vacations, and just ordinary family times to share each others' lives. Many a time did I sit at home on Thanksgiving Day, having just any old meal, thinking of the family gathered for this special holiday and enjoying their time together, while I was far away in a country that did not celebrate that day. Even the phone calls did not make up for this lack of personally being there, and sharing in the joy of connection and communion, that special brand of love that holds families together. But this was our decision and the thing to be sacrificed, for the honor of being a representative, an ambassador for Christ, whom he had chosen to enlist in his work force. A small sacrifice in view of the great honor!

I called back to confirm my acceptance. When I asked, who had suggested my name, I was told that an elder of our church had started proceedings one and a half years ago, and that several of my friends had been involved in writing about me, though none of them had let out the secret, not knowing if I would be accepted. Upon hearing the final outcome, they were visibly pleased. I was told, that it had taken so long, because my background had to be thoroughly investigated, first in Germany and then in the United States. Even the FBI and the California police department and highway patrol had to give me a clean slate before the honor came my way. All of this happened, while I was totally unaware of it. Isn't it wonderful to have nothing to hide, no dark closets, of which one is afraid that they will be found out one day? God dealt with my sins and forgave them through the blood of the sacrifice of Jesus Christ on the cross, and gave me the intention and the power to live by his and man's laws. Nevertheless, we will remain sinners, even to the end, but forgiven sinners.

I was surprised when I heard the laudatio. It clearly brought up the terrible injustices of the Nazi regime and several times mentioned my Christian faith and work among the young people of Germany and later on the women's work, for which I was being honored. I was asked to give an acceptance speech after the bestowal of the order and the laudatio. This gave me an opportunity to pass on the honor to him, to whom it belongs, who is the only one worthy of praise and the author and finisher of every good work. As I stood there before the German flag and had the red enameled cross on a tricolored band pinned to my lapel and listened to the laudatio telling of my life, different emotions rushed through me. There was gratitude, that my grandchildren could witness this moment. Then there was a feeling of justice finally being done, as the words included an apology for the terrible Nazi years of pain and fighting for survival. Finally there remained a feeling that the circle of my life had closed with this ceremony. I had forgiven long ago, yet here my former enemy also asked for my forgiveness in a way.

At the party after the reception, which we celebrated in a nice hotel right by the Rhine river, I m-c-ed a program for the eighty-five invited guests. There were several people from each of the different chapters of my life of service that I interviewed. It started with my twenty-five years as a youth leader, gathering young people in our living room till it got too crowded, then moving downtown, where leadership of the "Wednesday Group" as it was called, occupied many years of my life. This was followed by thirteen thrilling years of coffee house ministry, only we served tea. During that time, starting a chapter of the Christian Business Men's' Committee, was my next project. It is called IVCG in Germany, and we offer four dinner meetings a year for people in leadership. Then in 1988 I started the local group of the Women's' Breakfast Meetings, and worked on the national board for ten years. Several of my board sisters attended, sharing anecdotes of our years together. Then followed our minister, whose church my friend Elka and I founded fourteen years ago. It has grown to 200 members and a sister church. We have a large building, seating four hundred people. As I listened to his words and prayer, he spoke on my life verse Romans 8:28, I was grateful, realizing that all blessings come from God. At this day in my life he allowed me to draw a resume' of my activities, done in the name and for the glory of Jesus Christ.

When I arrived at home that night, loaded down with gifts and cards, and continued to celebrate with family and some very special friends, I felt rich beyond words, smothered by so much tangible love. The next morning was Thanksgiving Day and the six of us took a train to Berlin, requested by my daughter, who wanted her sons to see the places connected to my story. I had reserved a furnished apartment in the center of the city, and we set out to discover the sights. This city had been my home for the first seventeen years of my life. A devastating war had erased most of the buildings with personal meaning, like the house where I was born or our store, next to the red city hall, that was still standing. But I found places that helped resurrect the years for the sake of my grandchildren. I wanted them to feel part of the time that had been written about in history books. I shared with them the morning after 'Crystal Night', when the synagogues burnt and the persecution started openly. I recited the thought that had burnt itself deep into my memory on the bus that morning, 'I will never forget this day! I will tell my grandchildren about it.' Now we were standing, where once the synagogue stood in which I worshiped as a child, and told my grandsons about it.

But they were most impressed when I acted out in the rebuilt house where we had lived, how I balanced on a broken down stair case and reached on tiptoes through a small hole in the wall and pulled out three photo albums and my diary as a special gift from my heavenly father. While acting it out, it seemed that time stood still and I was reliving that special moment of joy. Then we walked together to the subway station, where I had said my last good-bye to my best friend Erika, before they were shipped to Theresienstadt concentration camp and from there to the gas chambers of Auschwitz.

One can tell stories and paint pictures, but nothing compares to seeing things in person. As we walked through my familiar neighborhood, thousands of memories welled up. I could have told a lot of stories, but they were important only to my mind. I noticed that the passing of the years and the ability to forgive had changed my attitude to confront painful scenes. Whereas at one time, seeing certain places had given me almost unbearable pain, so that I begged my husband on several visits after the war, "Please, let us get out of this city, for I cannot stand to be here any longer,' I now could stand and point them out to my family in a normal voice. With the distance of the years and the feeling of completeness and the mellowness of old age, it even gave me some satisfaction, that this new generation should feel something of the horror of a world gone mad and be prepared to watch out for the erosion of personal freedoms in their time, which the people of my generation never had the chance to experience.

In America I had found freedom and with it dignity of the individual. I wanted them to cherish that special gift against the backdrop of what can happen if evil gains control. The future will be in their hands. Though their time is different, the issues remain the same. All people need God to live a fulfilled and blessed life, no matter what the circumstances. This is my greatest desire, that my story will encourage and help some person to put their trust in God and begin a daily walk with his maker, which is and will be a never-ending great adventure. To that I can testify!

One more recent highlight of my life was preaching at my own church, the First Presbyterian Church of Hollywood. It was Missionary Sunday, and I was given the great privilege to address three different congregations at three services. First is the contemplative service in the chapel, where our children were baptized and where our youngest daughter, who became a Presbyterian minister, was married. On the steps of this chapel a photo of us as a young family was taken, before we set out on our first assignment to Berlin in 1954. This picture under the inscription, 'Dedicated to the service of Christ' was beamed into the second, the traditional service. Hymns are sung and there is a beautiful choir and the artistry of a gifted organist, who closes each service with a special great piece of organ music, which makes the walls reverberate.

When I arrived for the last, the family service with praise band and extended praise songs, I saw three of the left front rows filled with family members, which put wings on my words and made my heart skip. I owe my spiritual life to this church and its great preachers, like Dr. Louis H. Evans, Dr. Richard C. Halverson, former Chaplain of the Senate, Dr. Lloyd Ogilvie, former Chaplain of the Senate and Henrietta Mears, whose Sunday School built the membership up to 6000 when I joined the church in 1947. Friends from my Sunday school class, the Voyagers, have supported me with their prayers, their financial gifts and personal concern and love for all of these years. Here I was challenged to a life of faithful service, upheld by the prayers of God's people, and learned to trust God's guidance and experienced his supply for every need. My favorite hymn's refrain sums it all up, and my prayer is, that someone reading these lines will be encouraged to put their hand in the hand of God and sing along:

He leadeth me, he leadeth me, by his own hand he leadeth me,
His faithful follower I will be, for by his hand he leadeth me.